For my grandchildren, their children
And the children of their children....

INTRODUCTION

Alfonso Reyes wrote "The immediate past is in some way the enemy."

For Peter Katz and his European generation the "immediate past" has had the continuing immediacy of the enemy, from the experiences of that war that the Third Reich launched against the Jews.

An indescribable trauma where Vienna was never the same and nor was Peter Katz.

The odyssey from Austria to Belgium to France then back to Belgium and finally to Mexico forcefully created a wall of silence since otherwise the horrible wounds would open up and not allow him to live.

Katz breaks his silence by writing his memoirs, in a revolutionary and individual step he allows himself to look back on his past in order to free what has been hidden for half a century.
The act of telling his children and grandchildren about his life in Europe represents a catharsis for Katz and a healing for his children who as descendants to the Holocaust had had to bear so much and had been part of that "wall of silence."

The truth is painful but ultimately finally liberating.

The specificity of his work does not reside only in his dark trail through Nazi Europe, but also in the stories of his childhood and adolescence that in his maturity, he feels and lives all that previous young people have felt: the beauty, the experiences with the opposite sex and the rebelliousness. So this work by Peter Katz is not only just another book about the Holocaust. It is a work that tells in its most expansive way the story of a Jewish young man during the never-ending darkness of 1938 through 1945.

Peter Katz lived in that violated and assassinated Europe but transmits to his children and grandchildren that sensed but not verbalized information. And it is why his writing opens up possibilities for an encounter not only with himself but also with others.
For many years after the Second World War the world has remembered the Holocaust as a symbolic stereotype, a terrible composition of gas chambers and sealed cars that lived in Germany's conscience.

Katz' work appears parallel to the fact that although evil resided in Auschwitz or Treblinka, it echoed in the financial transactions in Stockholm, Lisbon and Zurich.
His timely publication permits the reevaluation, not only in the personal and familiar, of the international hypocrisy. Germany has kept its moral obligation to date; Katz raises again those responsibilities.

In another way, Peter Katz opens a window where we, the post-war generation, can discern the beginning of the consolidation of the Mexican Jewish community which in the forties, opened its doors so that he could live that nightmare behind.

Bill Landau

Psychoanalyst- writer

PROLOGUE

Many times my children have asked me: Papi, why don't you tell us about your childhood? Why don't you tell us about the war?" Many of my friends have asked me the same question.

I probably suffer from the same syndrome that affects many other survivors where you repress what happened in those years. Of staying quiet....

Leyb Rosenthal, poet from the Ghetto of Vilna, expresses this very well in a song that he wrote in 1943.

> Don't think that the gutter spawned me,
> Don't think I have no claim...
> A mother and a father loved me too
> Both were taken from me,
> It's useless to complain,
> But like the wind I'm lonely, it is true
>
> My name is Yisrolik,
> And when no one is looking,
> From my eyes
> I wipe away a tear
> But this anguish...
> Is not for speaking
> Why remember,
> How much can one heart hear?

After many years of silence, I feel that I have the obligation to speak. That it is my duty- in memory of those who are no longer here- to write and leave a testimony for future generations.

I attempted to write about my experiences from the perspective of an eight year old boy who reaches the age of eighteen, one who in many ways had matured but in many other ways was still immature. Simply because he did not grow up normally: in a home and protected by his parents.

In reality, I feel that I was very lucky. It could have been much worse. After being separated from my loved ones, I was picked up by good and decent people. By people like Buci, a straight and good man, personification of what is good in our faith, I found a role model, a man who unquestionably followed the precepts of our Holy Books.

What happened to the Jews during the Second World War was atrocious and systematic, as per the plan devised in 1926 by the then young Hitler in his book "Mein Kampf:" where he says "Wir werden die Judenfrage loesen". We the Nazis will solve the Jewish issue. The "solution" was adopted as part of the political platform of the German Nacional Socialist Party NSDAP with which they won the elections in 1933. In 1934 the racial laws were proclaimed conforming to the legal profile of such solution

How to explain that in 1944 when the war was already lost to Germany and the Teutonic armies were withdrawing in defeat by the Red Army as well as with the American and British armies who had landed in Normandy, Adolf Eichmann traveled to Budapest to start the massive deportation of Hungarian Jews- up until then safe- to the extermination camp of Auschwitz.

Did Eichmann hate the Jews? He denied this when he was on trial in Jerusalem in 1954, after his capture from his Argentinian refuge. Eichmann, like millions of Germans, said to have only followed orders according to the Deutsche Sachlichkeit. Irrational? No, very rational. And in the face of all of this, why so much indifference? The indifference of an entire world was the worse. Sometimes, staying quiet not only grants but converts the silent into an accomplice.

How to answer the questions of today's youth? They will ask- How did they allow themselves to be killed? How do you explain that the Germans had proposed to degrade their victims, take away their dignity and resistance and above all to take away their human essence until they were reduced to being like animals *Betes Humaines* until finally kill them?

It was a gradual tormenting process; they were denied the privilege of having a name, instead they carried a tattoo on their arm, a number on their left arm. Their hair was shorn. In the camps it was almost impossible to discern whether the prisoners were male or female.

The mother who walked to the gas chambers holding her child in her arms. The child was fearful. All of a sudden a German officer would snatch that baby from her arms, throw it up in the air and shoot at it, while the terrorized mother watched. The column of women continued on their march. The mother, now childless, stands up and throws herself, like a wild beast, upon the officer. The officer takes two shots and disposes of her. These scenes would repeat every day. Those who walked towards death had lost all human traits.

Did they deal humanely with the university professor, dedicated to teaching and to research, forced to interrupt his class and taken by force to a Ghetto? Then forced to climb aboard a crowded cattle car among filthy and desperate people like him, for three long days and killed upon arrival, one more victim of the extermination gas; that man, who when apprehended stopped being a man. Walked to the gas chambers like a taunted and tormented animal.

And what to say of the prisoners, badly nourished, far from their homes, deprived of their belongings, of their possessions and of their dreams. Without a doubt they could scarcely hold themselves up, they could barely think rationally. Nevertheless, there was as we now know uprisings at the Warsaw, Vilna and Bialystok ghettos. Escapes from the Sobibor and Chelmo camps. There were also numerous partisan groups in the forests of Poland, Lithuania and Russia, especially after 1943. And we surely do not know of other uprisings or revolts.

Under these conditions there were unlikely heroes, mostly victims.

Leyb Rosenthal, the aforementioned poet, called for an uprising with these words: "If no Jew resists now, who will want to be a Jew in the future? He was surely thinking of the future generations.

My daughter Gaby, who took upon herself the arduous task of translating this book into English, asks me" "Papi, why do you write about the Warsaw uprising? That was not your war."

No, I was not in Warsaw in the spring of 1943, but it was my war. Unfortunately we Jews have a common destiny. What happens to one concerns the other. During the war in Europe we had a common enemy. The Germans had declared war on all the Jews regardless of where they were located.

And I respond: "My daughter, if something happens to the Jewish community in Buenos Aires, it affects the Jews of Mexico. If something happens to a Jewish family in Rabat, it affects the Jews in Paris.
If I had been captured by the Germans in Brussels, the same thing would have happened to me as happened to a young man being captured in Salonica. That is our common destiny."

Graciela Beja, dear friend for many years, said to me after hearing me recount an anecdote from that time; "You must write about your life experiences, many of us find them very interesting but above all you must keep them for our children."

When I read, last year, "Lilric," written by the siblings Lily Heinemann, Berthold and Werner Nathusius, a story about a German Jewish family who emigrated to Guatemala in the 1930's, I decided to go ahead and write my story. In reality it only covers the decade between 1938 and 1948. It does not pretend to exhaust our family history since as an eight year old boy, I obviously was not aware of many things and ignored others. However, this is a true telling of what happened to me, how I was enriched by the same family members who survived and are now scattered all across the globe.

I deemed it absolutely necessary to describe the political and social environment of the time, so that future generations can, or at least try to, understand the cataclysm lived in its true context and significance.

I took hold of history so that I could illustrate the reasons- if it is even possible- and situate the reader in the "Zeitgeist"- the spirit of the time. I tried to document, consult and compare texts in order to achieve a *Coretezza Storica*, and why there Bibliography at the end of the book, so that whomever is interested can consult these fountains of information as I did.

I remember the first time I returned to the city of my birth, Vienna, in March of 1958. It was cold and there was snow on the streets. I did not recognize anything on the way from the airport, Schwechat, to downtown. It was as if I found myself in any other Austrian, Hungarian on Czech city. The buildings of the old Austro-Hungarian Empire look alike. However, when the taxi reached the Innerestadt or city center, I was able to perfectly recognize buildings and streets where I had walked as in my childhood. The small hotel where I stayed, in the *Dorotheergasse*, was two blocks away from the *Seilergasse* where my father's store was located.

The first three days I felt an enormous sadness, I was a prisoner of a profound depression. My mother walked down this street, my father would take me down this street to get to Temple, here our family would gather, this is how I would get to school. Here I played with my friends, down that street is where my mother and I first went to the movies. All my memories were as alive as they had been when I had been eight years old. I knew how to get from one place to another without having to ask for directions.

I found it interesting that twenty years had gone by, I was returning as a twenty eight year old and I remembered it perfectly.

To remember was to relive that happy time in my life: my city, my home, temple…. To remember that my life had been not that different to anyone else's. I visited the second floor apartment in *Dominikaner Bastei* # 10. I took the elevator, which required I insert a Schilling in it in order to work. I remembered that from the war. I rang the doorbell. The door was as I remembered it, a heavy walnut door. A blond young woman opened the door. I told her who I was and that this had been my home in 1938. I asked whether I could come in and see. She was surprised. I felt her hostility. As her response she closed the door on me. End of conversation.

Surely I frightened her. Or did she think I was a ghost? What was a Jew doing in post war Vienna? Hadn't they all died? No one likes to see ghosts. *Logica Imperat Vienae.*

By 1958 Austria was independent. The *Staatsvertrag or* Austrian State Treaty had been signed in 1955 making it the Second Republic. Vienna had suffered damage during the bombings and then during the capture of the city by the Russians in 1945, a destruction which cost innumerable lives. The most affected part of the city was the Leopoldstat section, the old Jewish neighborhood. Of course there were no Jews left there. The Opera was also destroyed as where some other buildings in the historic center. The Cathedral of St. Stephan went up in flames.

In Vienna, I inquired about the father of Psychoanalysis's house, at the time largely unknown by many. Rather, the Viennese did not want to remember him. Only the tourists inquired about him. His apartment in *Bergasse 19*, where he resided until 1938, had been taken over by a Viennese family. It wasn't until his daughter Anna Freud, visited Vienna in 1971 that the city government offered to turn it into a museum, which today is visited by thousands of tourists every year.

From London, where Anna lived in exile, arranged to have shipped some of his furniture, diplomas, photographs and books that had belonged to her father.

As of 1943 the city was "*Judenrein*," the Viennese were finally rid of its Jews. And in spite of this, massive numbers of tourists would come. What to do with them? Well, they could see them as a source of income, through tourism.

The situation has changed, albeit slowly. There is now a Jewish Museum in Vienna, in the old Eskeles Palace in the *Dorotheergasse,* and there is now a small

Jewish community of about eight thousand souls. Very few Viennese Jews returned from exile. The majority are survivors from the Displaced Persons camps or are Hungarian Jews that were able to escape Hungary in 1956. Lately there are new Jewish arrivals from Bukhara and other Russian regions.

Today the tourist guides will mention its large and rich Jewish community in Vienna prior to the Anschluss in 1938, as well as Leopoldstadt, Matzo Island as well as the multiple Synagogues and Shtiebels.

One time I visited Vienna with some friends, Salomon Lasky from Mexico and William Blitzer of New York. The latter who commented as I showed him around "Do you know where you come from" – referring to the undoubted rich cultural and historic past of the my city of birth.

Whenever I walk around the streets of Vienna, I remember my grandfather Juer. I see him with his deep eyes, where I see calm, peace and tranquility. My grandfather with his Kippah, which he always wore, would ask "Do you know who you are? You are a Katz, a Cohen Tzedek. Behave as one, faithful to your tradition. Honor your forefathers and take care of our tradition for the generations to come.

I want to thank my friends who encouraged me to write this testimony of my life.

I thank my wife and companion her advice, her criticism, her support and understanding.

To Isaac Kelerstein, author of "Cuando el sol se avergonzaba", where he shared his life experience during the war and who encouraged me to follow suit.

To Boris Albin who helped me in writing about the Soviet period illustrated with its pertinent Russian expressions.

To my Rebe, Samuel Lerer, who helped me with Hebrew and its interpretation.

To Hans Neumann who provided me with important facts about emigration.

To my cousins Ruth Bachruch and Gertrude Weis, invaluable fountains of information regarding the Bachruch- Gruenfeld families.

To my cousins Fred Stark, Paul Curzon and Hilde Leder from whom I obtained much information and anecdotes about the Katz family.

To the patient and responsible Becky Rubinstein, my style editor.

To Ana Maria Alcantar for typing this manuscript.

From the translator

It took me a long 15 years to finally complete this project. I felt that it was important that not only my daughters could read my father's account, but also all the family that we are still fortunate to have around the world, as well as friends that have throughout the years asked me for this translation.

My goal was to maintain my father's voice present in this translation.

Thank you to my daughter, Laura, for your help in editing this book.

Thank you to my daughter, Hannah, for your support

Thank you to the Alexandra Sears, wherever you are, who helped me get this started.

Thank you to my husband, Michael, with your help with the photographs and for your unending support.

Gaby Katz- Fleischmann

Our roots lie in the mountains of ancient Judea, in the fertile valleys of Emek, in the deserts of Samaria, in the Mediterranean...

Around five thousand years ago, Yahweh, our Lord, appeared to Abraham in Ur, between the Tigris and Euphrates, which is now Iraq. Yahweh said to Abraham: "Go forth; from your country, your people and your father's household to the land I will show you. I will make you into a great nation, and I will bless you; I will make your name great, and you will be a blessing to others." (Genesis 12: 1-2). Abraham and his family set out for the Promised Land. This was the proclamation departure of Lech, Lecha.

Sometime afterwards, we learned; that a terrible famine struck Eretz Israel, land of the Israelites. And so they migrated into Egypt, where they were enslaved. Generation after generation they toiled until Moses, raised as an Egyptian prince, and his brother Aaron freed them from slavery and led them through the Sinai Desert for forty years until they were allowed into the Promised Land. In those forty years a new generation emerged, free from the shackles of slavery mentality. Moses, Moshé Rabenu, was the true forger of the Jewish Nation: he gave us the Torah, a social structure that allowed us to live among other people to this day.

We know for certain that our grandfather Juer was a Cohen Tzedek. Most likely we descend from the Cohanim, priests in the Temple of Jerusalem. Each male child will continue to be Cohen until the end of time. This has been established according to our doctrine *Dibrei Torah*, the first monotheistic religion conceived by man.

A truly religious Jew follows to the letter the commandment that one must not pronounce the Lord's name in vain. In Hebrew, one says *Adoshem* (The Name), but never *Adonai*. If one speaks Yiddish, *Der Oibershte*, "the one who is above," or *Ribonu shel Olam*, "Lord of the World." *Gotenyu* is an affectionate way of referring to him. In Spanish, one writes *D'os*.

After the destruction of the second temple of Jerusalem (70 B.C.) the Jews were forced to leave Israel to seek refuge in other parts of the Mediterranean. Some went to Asia, others to Rome, the vast empire spanning from Spain in the west to Romania in the east, from England in the north to Africa to the south. And so began the diaspora or dispersion of the Jews. *Judea Capta.*

According to some conjectures, it's possible that our ancestors arrived with the Roman legions to the Rhineland, or Alsace around the seventh century A.D.

These first communities in Central Europe, situated among little German Hamlets, were decimated, effectively dispersed in the name of Christ during the First Crusade, around 1096.

The survivors fled deep into East Germany, Silesia, Moravia, Bohemia, Pomerania, Prussia, Poland, Lithuania, the Ukraine, Crimea, Moldavia, Romania, Podolia, and Moscovite Russia, where they won protection from nobles and landowners in exchange for collecting payment of tributes from the local serfs.

Grandfather Juer Katz—our family was living in Brody at this time—married a woman from distant Odessa. It's interesting to note that there were strong bonds between the Jewish communities of Brody and Odessa, both located within the territory ruled by the Tsar of Russia. In Odessa, the most famous banker from 1860-1917 was Brodsky, originally from Brody.

It was probably a marriage arranged by a *Shadjan,* or matchmaker. Because Grandfather was a *Talmid Chochem* he spent the majority of his time in the Yeshiva or in the Temple. This was his world. They married and Grandmother Rivka kept house, was in charge of the education of their eight children, and sought sustenance for Parnassa.

In Biblical times, during the festivals of *Rosh Hashanah* and *Yom Kippur*, namely the New Year and the Day of Atonement, the High Priest or *Cohen Gadol* dressed with extreme simplicity, wearing a white cotton robe and and no adornments of any kind. He was inducted into the Holy of Holies, in the *Kadosh Hakadoshim*, and pronounced the name of G-d. He would beg pardon for the sins of the People of Israel.

The *Cohen Gadol* had to be free from sin, or otherwise be struck dead uttering for the divine name.

We think that after many long years, expulsions, and massacres, our ancestors on my mother's side, the Gruenfelds, arrived around 1600 in Prague, home to a large Jewish community. And by 1700 the Katz arrived in Brody, near Lemberg—now Lvov, in Ukraine—where several *Yeshivot* were to be found. Later, around 1800-1900 it became one of the bastions of Hasidism.

This Hasidic movement, arising in the eighteenth century, established a more human and democratic relationship—less arid—between the Jew and his creator. He could speak directly with G-d, and also reproach his actions. Call him to task and question his actions, with all due respect.

The Hasidim, in Hebrew *Chassidut*, formed a religious movement often deemed a cult. Although in Judaism, Sectarianism is not given, because *Kol Israel*

Chaverim. ("All are one in Israel").

The Hasidim arose in an era of profound depression and disorientation in the eighteenth century, after many messianic movements (Shabatai Zvi, Jakob Frank, and others), the pogroms perpetrated by Chmielnitzki (1648-1655), in which more than 110,000 Jews were massacred in Poland and Russia. It was a desperate time for Eastern European Jews. Hence the search for a light to guide them.

The Jewish liturgy had become very dry, due to the precepts of the *Vilna Gaon* (1720-1797), observed by the Mitnagdim, opponents of any deviation from the traditional religion. In such circumstances, Israel Baal Shem Tov is revealed as a *Tzadik*, a righteous person in the Shtetl of Medzivosh, in Podolia.

Baal Shem Tov was the first *Rebbe*, a *Wunderrebbe*, or maker of miracles (circa 1736). He gathered his Hassidim, and he sang and danced with them. He tried—as mentioned—to introduce joy in the lives of those who were so downtrodden. But moreover, he tried to instill their lives with meaning. The Hasid had to do a *mitzvah*, a good action every day. Have you brought joy to someone? Have you done something today to better the world? Have you helped a widow, or maybe an orphan?

He placed great importance on the spiritual and its expression through melody. He sang with *Kavvanah* devotion, eyes closed, keeping time with bodies and hands. The Hasidim were thereby sublimated, their souls elevated to great heights. Drinking wine from the cup of the Rebbe, touching his vestments, this was considered *mitzvot*. The *Rebbe* was a mystical figure.

Thus returning to the mysticism of the Spanish Kabbalah, emphasizing the life of the simplest mortals: *Basar Vadam.*

The Chassidut reintroduced mysticism into Judaism. The Viennese philosopher Martin Buber dedicated his life to studying it. He wrote various books on the subject. Menachem Mendl Shneerson was the most renowned rabbi of the modern Chabad movement.

Hasidic groups have been increasing in numbers, thanks to a religious rebirth among young Jews around the world after the Holocaust.

In Brody, the Kingdom of Galicia and Lodomeria, Juer and Rivka Katz gave birth to seven children—Poldi was not born yet. Around 1890, they immigrated to Vienna. In the Katz family, many stories are told about this journey: arriving at the train station in Vienna, they took stock and noticed that one child was missing—an enormous worry for all—until they found him asleep in one of the train wagons.

Back then, Vienna was the capital of the Austro-Hungarian Empire. With two million inhabitants, it was the most populous city in Europe after London. With many possibilities for personal and economic development, it attracted immigrants from across the empire: from Moravia and Bohemia, Hungary, Bukovina, Ruthenia, Galitzia, Transylvania, Slovenia, Istria, and Croatia.

Vienna arose in the time of Marcus Aurelius, who while commanding a Roman legion founded a settlement for his legionnaires, where the Wien River converged with the southern arm of the Danube, very close to modern day Seitenstaetengasse, formerly Judengsse—they called it Vindobona. Here also was the Griechengasse, the Greek neighborhood. It's known that around the year 1100 at the time of the Crusades, there lived Jews, Armenians, and Greeks; who controlled the external trade of the region.

When the mercenaries enlisted, paid by the Pope for the Second Crusade (1180 A.D.), there was a massacre of Jews in Vienna, something like a pre-crusade. Afterwards, in spite of everything, the Jewish families returned. By 1400, the Viennese community resurfaced, coinciding with the beginning of the reign of the Habsburgs, originally from a small principality called Babenberg.

At this time there was in Vienna, there lived Richard the Lionheart who had been rescued from the hands of the Saracens. It seems to be that he was rescued at the request of the Baberberg family, through Salomon Ben David, a Jewish banker.

In 1421 Jews lived in several blocks around Judenplatz -blocks that still exist today- around Graben in the center of the city.

This particular year was tragic for the Jews that lived in Vienna. Many were expelled. Eight hundred of them, the most notable, led by the Rabbi,— the Dayan, and the Cantor, were taken by force to the edge of the Danube and massacred. However, twelve of the most devoted locked themselves in the Or-Zarua Synagogue, situated on the Judenplatz, and refused to be evicted. The mob set fire to the place and the *Kadoshim* died in the flames, and with them burned the sacred scrolls of the Torah. This massacre is known as the -*"Gezerz"* - of Vienna.

In 1683, the Turkish siege began around Vienna. But they never took the city, for it was well-defended by 26,000 Poles under the command of Prince Jan Sobiesky, who threw the Turks from Vienna, Austria, and Hungary.

The Jews used to negotiate with the Turks. At different times, the Turks even supplied them with coffee beans for the city. The first *Kaffehaus* or Viennese café was established during Joseph I and Prince Eugene's reign. Silvio Piccolomini (1441 A.D.), the future Roman Pope, who visited Vienna, attests to the riches of the city and relates that there was an active Jewish community.

In the time of Maria Theresa, who was openly anti-Semitic, the Jews were expelled once again from the city. Her son, Joseph II, invited them to return, giving them back their property. Under his rule, for the first time in the city's history, they were recognized as citizens. For us, this was freedom, the emancipation a reality.

In this era the first temple, Stadttempel, was constructed on Judengasse, a street within Seitenstaetengasse, built between 1824 and 1826. It was a symbol of a growing community, vigorous and powerful, but nonetheless reserved.

The Temple boasted an ordinary façade and contained the offices of the community, or *Kultusgemeinde*. Inside, beyond the patio, arose the temple, beautifully ornamented, with seating for 1,600 people.

The emancipation was issued under Joseph II, Joseph der Zweite, under whom all citizens enjoyed the same rights, including the Jews. Hence, they were able to construct an elegant and lavish temple for one of 1830s Europe's most buoyant communities.

Behind this decision there was a logic determined by then *Rosh Kehila*, or Community Leader, Bernard von Eskeles—and it was very simple. The less you caught the attention of the Goyim gentiles, the better. No need to open their eyes, he said. For the leaders of the community in those days, *Prunk*, to be lavish and *Prozen* to show off, was in poor taste and by definition anathema. No doubt his wisdom brought great advantages to the community. Under the leadership of the young emperor Franz Joseph the communities throughout the empire—not just in Vienna—enjoyed colossal growth, thanks an official policy of tolerance and benevolence shown toward the Jews. Meine Juden, My Jews, the emperor called them. Eskeles was the Haupt of the community. He was ennobled, *"Freiherr Von Eskeles."*

Thereafter (1820 A.D.) tolerance shone bright: Jews could study in universities, they became magistrates and soldiers. Some even adopted German names that were subsequently renowned in the history of the city. Others received noble titles. It was the era in which Ludwig van Beethoven, Gluck, Schubert, and Wolfgang Amadeus Mozart lived in Vienna, and the city became the European capital of the arts.

The emancipated Jews were refined and cultured, rubbing shoulders with nobility and the *Grossbuergertum*, the genteel upper middle class.

Jews breached the upper echelons of society, but also sympathized with the working class. The founder of the socialist party, Victor Adler, was Jewish. The majority of the socialist leaders between 1890 and 1934 were Jewish. They fought with vehemence to improve the situation of the working class. Between 1921 and 1934, Vienna was at the head of all the European countries, including the Soviet Union, in the construction of public housing financed by the government. These endeavors were spearheaded by Jewish administration. Credits were typically 35 year credit, with no interest. For that time, this was a big attraction. This auspicious situation was valid until the Anschluss (1938). No one harbored ill will against the Jewish directors, on the contrary, they were very popular.

My grandparents settled in the Kochgasse with their eight children. Grandmother Rivka, without knowing anything but Yiddish, put herself to work selling clothing on credit in working class neighborhoods. She moved by tram throughout the city, visiting her clients, selling and collecting.

Her husband sought a small *Stieberl Shul* where he could continue studying the Talmud and the Torah. Newcomers were easily integrated into the Viennese Jewish community life by the end of the century.

The *Shtibl* was Grandfather's whole world. He attended every single day. The other parishioners, the *Mitpalelim*, were his friends, and together they formed a *Chevrah*.

Grandfather didn't go to Temple. He went to the *Shtibl*, and to get there he crossed the Danube *Donaukanal*, entering Leopoldstadt, the Jewish neighborhood. The *Shtibl* was a relatively large room with long tables. At each table were two long benches, one on each side. At the base was a platform with a kind of cupboard, covered with a curtain, in which the rolls of the Torah were kept. The whitewashed walls bore no decoration whatsoever.

Everything was austere, *Vi es bedarf tzu sain*, as it should be. *Der Oibershter*, Lord of the Heavens, did not want lights or amenities for his observants. Although Grandfather was not a Hasid, he was extremely religious and complied with all the *Mitzvot* or precept. He was ever vigilant of the laws, even more so than the others. He was *Cohen Tzedek*, descendent of the Cohanim, high priests of the *Bet-ha Mikdash*, the Temple in Jerusalem.

Grandfather wasn't concerned with earthly matters. He left that to Grandmother Rivka, earning money for family necessities—paying rent, educating, dressing, and otherwise providing for the children. He occupied himself with "his" world, the world of *Olam Haba.* Sometimes he spoke with his *Rebbe* but, more importantly, he spoke with G-d.

Although the Katz family earnings were not large at that time, Grandfather demanded that Grandmother give him *gelt,* money for his causes. For the *Chevra Kadisha,* those that prepare bodies for burial. The *Chevra* that occupy themselves with gathering the *Nedunya,* or dowry for marriageable girls. The *Chevra* that cares for refugees, that occupy themselves with the sick and their needs.

They also had to help the *Bocherim,* or young children that were studying to become part of the *Hevra.*

Erev Yom Kippur, the eve of the Day of Atonement, Grandfather spent all night in the *Shtibl.* At sunrise, he continued to pray. He wore a white *kitl,* a type of coat, and slippers, no shoes. In this element, he was happy. He felt accomplished enough to follow these precepts, the *Mitzvot,* and near to G-d.

So I say that he was a *Tzaddik,* and a fair one. Grandfather never occupied himself with politics. He was not a Zionist, nor did he adhere to any other "ism." It was enough for him to be a Jew and a righteous man.

By 1912, there were two hundred thousand Jews in Vienna. And by 1920, the Jewish population was part of and contributed to areas like culture, corporations, medicine, musical, theatre, industry, and commerce. The Viennese Jews felt part of the city.

Despite anti-Semitism from Austrians, the tolerant government under Emperor Franz Joseph allowed reason and benevolence to prevail, and this good will was extended throughout the empire.

By the end of the nineteenth century—a golden age for the Austro-Hungarian Monarchy—just one generation after immigrating to Vienna, Jews had become extremely prominent intellectuals, researchers, writers, composers, musicians, bankers, and politicians.

Writers like Hugo Von Hoffmansthal, Arthur Schnitzler, Franz Kafka, Stefan Zweig and Franz Werfel. Theodor Herzl, father of Zionism. Great playwrights like Franz Molnar, Fritz Kortner and Alfred Polgar. Directors like Max Reinhardt and Rudolf Beer. Composers like Gustav Mahler, Arnold Schonberg. Conductors like Bruno Walter (Schlesinger), Ernest Kleiber, Otto Klemperer. Sigmund Freud, father of psychoanalysis. Victor Adler, Otto Bauer, socialist leaders. And many others.

The children grew, the daughters were married, Grandfather Juer died relatively young at seventy-six. Grandmother Rivka lived until 1931, and her house remained a communal space for the many Katz family members until the last day of her life. She was loved, adored, and respected by all. She reigned as a family matriarch, and there was a general acceptance of her power.

As I've already mentioned, Grandparents Juer and Rivka Katz had eight children, three boys and five girls. The men were Marcus Asher (Max), Leib (Leo), my father, and Poldi, the only one who was born in Vienna. The women were Sophie, Zilly, Julie, and Anna, all born in Brody.

Sophie, who was the oldest, was the first to marry. She married Mr. Wolfthal, and they had five children, four boys—Heinrich, Otto, Bubi, Karl—and one daughter named Blanka.

Afterwards Aunt Zilly was wed to Samuel Bieber, and according to photographs she was the prettiest and also the most devoted. They had four children: two boys—Ernest and Louis—and two girls, Else and Hilde.

Uncle Max, the first of the men to marry, was wed to Yette Kokisch, originally from Brody. They had two sons, Fritz and Paul.

Ida married with Mr. Mordkovich and they had one boy, Hugo.

Julie married Daniel Stark and they had three sons: Karl, Sigi, and Louis.

My father married Grete Bachruch and had me.

Anna married Heinrich Tiebert, and they had no children.

And lastly, Poldi, the youngest of the children, married Bertl Chaiyess, who came from a family of famous orthodox rabbis.

The Bachruchs lived in Temesvar, Transylvania, Hungary, now Romania, walking distance from Arad.

I don't have much information on Grandfather Berthold. But it seems that he came to Vienna around 1860. He enlisted in the imperial army and became a lieutenant captain of the Hussars—namely, the emperor's guard. I remember perfectly a large photograph of him, in my Grandmother Caroline's house: in his uniform regalia, with his sword and helmet with its ostrich plume. His brother Ignaz Bachruch settled in Budapest and was a well known jeweler, a supplier to the Court, patended K&K, meaning Kaiserlich & Koniglich.

The Gruenfelds were from Nitra, Slovakia. They arrived in Vienna around

1860. Grandmother Caroline was born in the city. She had two sisters, Rosa and Sidonie and two brothers, Leopold and Shandor.

Grandmother Caroline was a seamstress, at the time a common profession for young women. She worked in various workshops in Vienna as an employee, and at thirty-five, after gaining sufficient experience, she opened her own shop for women at Wollzeile no. 17. This building still exists. She became an authorized provider, purveyor to the court, and was allowed to use the K & K.

Berthold and Caroline met in Vienna and married in 1892, with the blessing of their respective parents, but with reservations from the Gruenfelds, as being a soldier was not a lucrative profession, or deemed worthy for a Jewish youth. Anyways, Grandmother Caroline earned well at her well-renowned shop so that Grandfather Berthold could continue in the militia. He dedicated his leisure time to *dolce far niente*. They had three girls and one boy, all born between 1895 and 1902. The youngest was my mother.

I return now to the Katz family. Grandmother Rivka was from Odessa. The Jewish neighborhood there was called Moldavanka. With 140,000 souls—35% of the total population—Odessa was the most populous Jewish city, and after Warsaw and Vienna the most important Jewish population in the Russian empire, and with an intensely close-knit and intellectual community.

The Jews arrived in Crimea, part of Ukraine, around 1740 when it was still under the dominion of the Muslims and was not yet part of the Russian Empire.

I don't know much about the Kleitnik family, my grandmother Rivka's family name, but I will talk about Otto, one of my grandmother's brothers, much beloved by the Katz family. Liberal and cultured—prototypical of an emancipated Jew—he was admired and idolized by my father Leo, my cousin Hilde, and by other young people in the family.

Uncle Otto went to the gymnasium in Odessa. Later, he went to Vienna and won the representation for Russia, of Thonet, the most prestigious furniture maker in Austria. He was a businessman and received permission—back then this was a privilege—to live in St. Petersburg. When he arrived in Vienna, he always visited his sister Rivka and spent time with the Katz family children that admired him very much, as a *Maskil, a liberal,* as they were taught as traditional Orthodox or *Strenge Orthodoxen*.

The Gruenfelds from Nitra, my maternal grandmother's parents, were: Hermann Gruenfeld, who was born in Topolschav Slovakia in 1846 and died of natural causes in Vienna at seventy-five years of age. His wife Rosa Gruenfeld—

they were cousins—was born in Nitra in 1869 and died in Vienna in 1932.

They had three children: one daughter, my grandmother Carolina, and two boys, Leopold and Shandor.

My great grandfather Hermann Gruenfeld—I've mentioned him already—arrived in Vienna in 1872. My grandmother Caroline was born in Vienna and married, Berthold Bachruch, in 1893. He arrived in Vienna in 1860. The last name Bachruch is probably Bachrach mispronounced. The Bachrach are named after Bacharach, a town near the Rhine, in Germany.

Leopold Gruenfeld married a woman from the Ehrenfeld family, who were very religious. The father was a slaughterer, or *Shochet*. They had five children: Josef Joshy, Friedrich—who died in the Austrian military ranks during the Battle of Oleka, Russia, in 1915—and Emil, Oscar, and Poldi.

I don't know much about Shandor, the other child of my maternal great grandparents. I only remember meeting him in my grandparent's house in Vienna when I was very young.

Joshy married Emma Silberbauer—who was not Jewish—and they had a daughter Gertrude (Gerty), who lived in Scarsdale, New York. Oscar married Bertl in Vienna and they had a daughter Erika who lives in London.

Emil married Eleonore, in Trenton, New Jersey and they had two sons. Poldi married Paula in Vienna, and they had no children.

Caroline and Berthold Bachruch, my maternal grandparents, had four children, three girls and a boy.

Julius was born in Vienna in 1895, married Ida Steimer in 1930. She was a Swiss woman, and a gentile. They had a daughter Ruth, who lives in Basel, Switzerland. Ruth was born in 1932, and is married to Wilfried Eichenberger.

Else, who was born in Vienna in 1897, was married in 1925 to Moritz Lazar Ellenbogen, and they had a daughter Daisy, who died in Mexico in 1943.

Isabella, born in Vienna in 1898, died at the age of 12 and is buried in the Jewish cemetery in Vienna, next to my grandfather.

Finally, Grete (Margarete), my mother, was born in Vienna in 1902, and was married, also in Vienna, in 1925, to Leo Katz, my father. They had me in 1930. My mother was eighteen years younger than my father.

In Odessa, where Grandmother Rivka grew up, the Zionist movement began to emerge long before Theodor Herzl, with notable figures like Bilu Usishkin, Achad Ha Am, founders of Petach Tikva; writers like Chaim Nachman Bialik, Mendele Mocher Sforim, Josef Klausner and Simon Dubnov, the last historian both born in Mstislav,

Odessa also gave to the Jewish people and its rebirth in Eretz Israel men like Lilienblum, Diezengoff, Borojov, Zabotnisky, the founder of Betar and Trumpeldor, the hero of Tel Chai, among many others.

Odessa gave to Russian literature Babel and Yuskevich. To the Socialist Revolution, Lev Bronstein Trotsky, who was assassinated in Mexico in 1940.

From what I've read and has been told to me aloud, there existed a strong bond between the communities of Brody and Odessa. I don't know how it came about, but by 1830, many families from Brody lived in Odessa. Communication was easy, as both cities were in the territory designated as the Pale of Settlement.

By 1880, the most famous banker in Odessa was V. Brodsky, frequently mentioned in the novels of Sholem Aleichem. There was a circle of *Brodskists*. Orthodox Jews who opposed the liberal *Maskilim*. Probably a *Shadchan* offered my grandfather's family the hand of this young woman from Odessa. The wedding was celebrated in Brody, with the approval of the Katz and Kleitnick families. The young pair settled in Brody, but afterwards moved to Vienna.

The Katz youth, Asher Marcus (Max), my father Leo, and the youngest, Poldi, who was born in Vienna, grew up, went to school and to gymnasium, lived in an environment rich culture in this fin de siècle era in Vienna.

My father was a traveling textile salesman. He visited clients in Galicia and in the Russian Empire. He had much success, and spoke six languages: Yiddish, German, Russian, Italian, and French. He was an assiduous Hebraist, and an autodidact.

Later on, my father became the representative of two famous factories that manufactured Lyon silk, and he traveled twice per year to France.

At the age of thirty-five, he became independent, and set up his first store, Leo Katz & Co., in the Seilergasse no. 4, in downtown Vienna.

The Katz boys, like the majority of young Jewish boys at that time, were regulars at the tea dances, *Funfuhr Tee*, held at salons and nicer hotels. These dances were frequented by Jewish girls from prominent families. They would tell me the story of how my father, who was 25 at the time, invited his mother, grandmother Rivka, to a dance in Baden, a recreational spot near Vienna. Everyone there was talking about Leo Katz, dancing with his mother.

Most likely, at one of those dances, my father fixated on a beautiful young girl of only twenty. He was eighteen years older, but he began to court her.

Going to dance the Foxtrot, the Waltz, and the Polka, was a common activity for young single men in Vienna. This was frowned upon by their elders. The *Shadchanim* were still very active in the Vienna of the 1920's, but in the case of my parents, they seemed to think it was love. My father idolized my mother, and was incredibly proud of his young, gorgeous girlfriend.

During World War I (1914-18), my father, who was thirty at the time, enlisted in the Imperial Army, like most of the young Jewish men of age. He was moved rapidly to the Eastern Front. And as *Feldwebel* sergeant he served as army translator, or *Dollmetscher*. They were demobilized in 1917, when the Austro-Hungarian Empire crumpled with the abdication of the young emperor Karl the Habsburg.

After losing the war, according to the Treaty of Versailles, the Austrian Republic was born in 1918 amid social and political unrest.

The situation in Vienna was chaotic. The war had been lost. Emperor Franz Joseph, who had reigned for fifty-eight years, was dead. His son Karl, heir to the throne, sought refuge in Switzerland. A National Provisional Assembly was formed, and proclaimed the Republic. Meanwhile on the steps of Parliament—an imposing building in Greek Classical style—the Communists, who had already formed their *Rote Garde*, or Red Guard, began attempting to take power. Among the leaders were Egon Erwin Kish and Franz Werfel, both young Jewish writers from Prague. At that time Bela Kuhn, a Hungarian Jew, had begun taking power in Hungary, proclaiming the Republic in Budapest, *Magyar Nepkosztartasag*. The *Spartakists*, with Rosa Luxemburg and Karl Liebknecht at the forefront, wanted to do the same in Germany. The Viennese social democrats, led by the Jew Otto Bauer and Victor Adler, foiled the attempts of the Communists (1919).

In Vienna, there was famine, and a shortage of coal. The municipality could no longer produce the gas necessary to supply the network (pipeline) Vienna had had since 1890. The population had to turn to farmers from the provinces in order to find food at exorbitant prices.

The famine between 1918 and 1920 caused anti-Semitic outbreaks in Vienna, directed especially at the *Ostjuden*, Jews from the East, who had arrived in huge numbers from the provinces lost by the Empire: Galicia, Ruthenia, and Bukovina.

"The Jews take the food from our mouths," they said.

Of course, not only Jews had arrived in Vienna. Many senior officials of the lost provinces took refuge with their families in the capital in order to resume their usual lifestyle and continue to receive their pensions. The Empire was lost.

The Black market surged, and the *Schieber* traffickers, earned fortunes. They conducted themselves like typical *Noveaux Riches*, and strengthened the people's hatred. Among the *Schieber* traffickers there were of course Jews, but also those who fostered anti-Semitism. No one took into account that the starving populace also included many Jewish families, who in order to feed their children depended on the charity of the *Kultusgemeinde*.

They opened kosher kitchens where they prepared *Eintopfgericht*, a mixture of potatoes, vegetables, and sometimes meat. These kitchens operated until 1922, and were indispensable for many of the poorest in the community.

My parents, Leo and Grete, were married in Vienna in 1925. I was born five years later. These were difficult times for Austria, which after the war was lost, was dismembered, its territory diminished. The misery was all-encompassing, and anti-Semitism grew with each passing day. In Versailles, the victorious Allies created Czechoslovakia, Yugoslavia, and Romania won part of Transylvania, Bessarabia and Moldova, Poland reborn as a nation, at the expense of Russia, in Brestlitovsk (1919). It's interesting to note that these nations granted rights for the first time to the Jewish minority—which was, of course, to no avail once the Germans and Fascists occupied these countries during the Second World War (1939). The efforts of Franklin Roosevelt, then president of the United States, did nothing to prevent the abuse that was to follow.

Soon after they married, my father opened his silk shop, as I've already recounted. He also sold ribbons and other sewing supplies for women's clothing, in the Seilergasse no. 4. This location still exists, although now all you'll find there is a bank a half block from the Graben, the premier commercial zone in downtown Vienna.

Anxious to please my mother, his young wife, he rented a tiny apartment for the two of them—I had not yet been born—on the Opernring, the oldest district of the city, near the Opera, the Burgteather and the Burg, Imperial residence

Soon after I was born they moved to a larger apartment, with a *Kinderzimmer*—a nursery—at the Dominikaner Bastei no. 10, also in the first district, Erster Berzirk, near the *Hauptpost*, or post office, and the *Sparkasse* designed by the architect Otto Wagner.

That someone from the Katz family lived in this first district was something new and unusual. The rest of the family lived in neighborhoods much more modest, like Leopoldstadt, the Jewish neighborhood. Although Uncle Max—father of Paul and Fritz—lived in the Berggasse two houses away, and on the same side of the street as Sigmund Freud.

Uncle Heinrich Tiebert—Teitelbaum—had a jewelry shop in the Wehringerstrasse in front of the Church Votive (*Votivkirche*), a very elegant section of Vienna. The family nicknamed him Tibbik.

In this Vienna full of vibrant cultural and intellectual activity worked the doctor Theodor Herzl. Although he was born in Budapest in 1860, his formal education was in German. In monarchical Hungary, under Franz Josef, the Jews of the bourgeoisie spoke German, and this was also the case in Prague, Trieste, Fiume, and Chernowitz. The Jews were the promoters of German culture: theater, lectures, newspapers, and publishing.

Herzl's mother, Jeanette Diamant, was the product of assimilated parents. Herzl grew up amid this assimilation. When he did his Bar-Mitzvah, his parents said he'd completed his "confirmation."

In Vienna, many Jews had assimilated, and some had even converted to Christianity. They firmly believed themselves Austrian, just like everyone else, but professed from the Israelite religion *Mosaische Konfession*. For the others there were merely *Juden*, Jews. They could not erase this through conversion. The Spanish considered Jews differently, like "new Christians" and later as Marranos.

Herzl found work as a Feuilletonist in the liberal newspaper *Die Neue Freie Presse*, and was sent to Paris. He traveled to France with illusions about the *Grande Démocratie Francaise*, heir to the innovative ideas born from the world's first social revolution, and promulgator of the *Liberté, Egalité,* and *Fraternité*. But he was immediately conscious of the reigning anti-Semitism of the French right. In 1885, the pasquinade *La France Juive* of Edouard Drumont appeared, criticizing the extreme Jewish influence in politics. Definitive for Herzl was the trial of Captain Alfred Dreyfuss, falsely accused; from this, he saw clearly the gravity of anti-Semitism throughout Europe.

It was then, out of conviction, that he became consciously and openly a Jewish activist. Upon returning to Vienna, he wrote *Der Judenstaat* (1896), in which he said: "If we want to have our own Jewish State, we have to gain it by pulse." Later on, in 1900, he published the utopian novel *Altneuland*, with a phrase "If you really want it, it will not be a fairy tale."

For the first Zionist Congress, celebrated in Basel, Switzerland, Herzl rented the elegant municipal casino, asking that all the representatives—the majority being Russian and Polish Jews—to wear coats with tails. Max Nordau was then his loyal right hand man. Herzl, more than being a master of ceremonies, longed to impress the delegates from the *Stetlach*, not to mention the intellectuals from Odessa, Prague, Warsaw, Jassy, and Chernovitz, the pious Jews of Sofia, Salonika, Smyrna, and Istanbul. And he succeeded. The delegates gave him a standing ovation that lasted for twenty minutes, declaring him a king with a *Yechi La-Melech*, Long live the king! This First Zionist Congress was the rebirth of the Jewish people, now still in the Diaspora.

Hope was reborn, *Ha-tikva*, amongst a people in exile, where desperation reigned, their collective history riddled with pogroms, *Numerus Clausus*. A people that faced daily discrimination and constant vexation.

There was a resurgence of pride and national sentiment: *Am Israel Chai!* The Jewish people had been reborn. A tall, handsome Viennese man with a black beard more closely resembling the Emperor Darius of Persepolis than King David of Jerusalem, had given the people an ideology and a project: Zionism. This political movement advocating national vindication in the 19th century gained international recognition.

The Katz family was very close, the sons visited their mother every day. Without having read Karl Marx or Friedrich Engels, but operating on Biblical principles, her single children handed over their salaries, so that she could distribute them according to everybody's needs. This was very common among Jewish families back then.

The economic crisis culminated in a drop in the stock market, resulting in catastrophic diminution, inflation, and devaluation of personal savings. This was fertile soil for growing anti-Semitism in Vienna

The population was divided between the *Rote*, or socialists, and *Schwartz*, for conservatives. The majority was Catholic, although there was a growing number of Protestants.

Ten percent of the Viennese population was Jewish, and their situation was very tense. In the provinces, it was abysmal. In 1934, Chancellor Dollfuss was assassinated. The Nazis tried in vain to take power. This was a warning to Jews. The German Nazis were our immediate neighbors, but no one in Vienna paid attention. Viennese life was *gemuetlich*, too cozy, the Jews were well organized in the *Kultusgemeinde*. They had Zionist organizations of all shades, from Betar to Shomer Ha-Tzair.

A cousin of my mother's, Joshy Gruenfeld, father of Gerty--who now lies in Scarsdale, in Westchester, New York—was a soccer player in Hakoach, the Jewish soccer team, that won the Austrian championship in 1923. Anti-Semitism was growing, but nonetheless, no one even imagined what was coming.

I forgot to mention that I was born on the 19th of May, in 1930, in a clinic in the Landstrasse, in the Third District, near the Hilton Hotel and Stadtpark, or city park. My parents brought me to the new apartment that they had just rented, in the Dominikaner Bastei 10, where it's certain a psychoanalyst and Freudian disciple Max Adler also resided. I discovered this fact during my first visit to Vienna after the Holocaust, in 1958.

My mother was extremely protective of me. Whoever wanted to see me had to call first, or make an appointment. Only one person could enter the nursery, with my mother and the nanny present. The visitor had to cover their mouth, to avoid contagion. My father's family, in contrast to these restrictions, flocked to greet the first son of Leo Katz, who was highly appreciated. They proudly and affectionately nicknamed me *Der Kleine Prinz*, "The Little Prince."

My mother was considered very modern for 1930. She adopted the latest medical innovations, education ideas, psychology and social behavior en vogue in post-war Vienna. I had a nanny with a uniform, which was unusual for the Katz family.

There was a very intense intellectual life in Vienna. The theaters were showing at least three or four new works each season. There were conferences about a plethora of subjects, and these drew huge audiences.

Opera season was lengthened for a month. There were four symphony halls, and Sunday concerts were initiated for the youth. Concerts were given in public parks. Operettas were performed in small surrounding towns like Baden, among others. The leading actors of the *Burgtheater* were national heroes. Those that didn't live in the capital listened to theatrical works broadcast on the radio.

In 1930's Vienna, up until the Anschluss or German occupation, Jewish cultural activity was alive and growing. The percentage of Jewish intellectuals was incredible in proportion to the general population.

At the University, in the field of medicine, Jewish students occupied 34%, and in the humanities, 23% of the classes, thanks to the insistence of Jewish families that their children have at least one academic degree. It stands to reason, then, that the percentage of Jewish professors was also quite high.

At that time arose Arnold Shonberg, Franz Lehar, Imre Kalman, authors of operetta. Fritz Kortner was a theatrical producer. Satirical *Kabarett Simplicissimus* was the most popular, performed night after night, by Fritz Grunbaum—later beaten to death at Dachau—and Karl Farkas. Other *kabaretts* included Hermann Leoopoldi, Hugo Wiener, Szoeke Szakal, and many others.

Franz Werfel, Josef Roth, Elias Canetti, Erwin Kish, and Beer Hoffman were all very prominent writers. Some of them translated in different languages.

Most of the editors of magazines in high circulation were Jewish. Karl Krauss, critic from *Die Fackel*, was very popular. Of course, widespread Jewish prominence provoked strong anti-Semitism and more than a little resentment among the gentiles, their hatred given free reign when Hitler marched triumphantly through Vienna on March 13, 1938.

In 1931, Jewish writer Hugo Bettauer published *Die Stadt Ohne Juden*, or *The City without Jews*, a science fiction book about Vienna without Jews. This was an unexpected success, and the first edition sold out. It was reprinted four times before going out of print.

World-renowned medical doctors founded what was known in the 1920's as *Die Wiener Schule,* the Viennese School of Medicine.

Josef Brauer, Sigmund Freud, Max Adler, and Victor Frankl were recognized psychoanlaysts. Doctors like Carl Sternberg, Julius Schnitzler, Ernest Loewenstein, Josef Halbhans, Robert Barany, and Otto Loewy, these last two recipients of the Nobel Prize—1914 and 1936, respectively—attracted colleagues from around the world to come to Vienna and study with them.

Philosophers and humanists like Karl Poppe—who immigrated to England—Martin Buber—who settled in Palestine—and Ludwig Wittgenstein, brought fame and renown to Vienna.

The Jews in Vienna lived through these years without any worry, even when Jewish refugees from Nazi Germany began arriving. The Nazis assembled at huge public meetings, donning brown uniforms and swastikas, under the direction of Seiss Inquart, the future "Gauleiter," well known and feared by many.

I was educated by my mother and nanny in her neat and tidy uniform. On weekends we almost always went to Baden, where Uncle Leopold Gruenfeld had a house with a big garden, and many water fountains of varying size and style. I don't remember whether my father had a car or knew how to drive. We probably traveled by electric tram, which took around forty-five minutes from downtown Vienna.

Although the health club, or country club Hakoach was founded in Vienna in 1909, the anti-Semitism and economic collapse that erupted after the First World War—essentially, the fall of the Austro-Hungarian monarchy—were instrumental in its growth.

Sports were of great interest among the Jewish youth in Vienna. Around the time the Second Zionist Conference was held in 1898 in Basel, Switzerland, Max Nordau, a writer from Prague, appealed for the physical regeneration of the Jewish people. Hence, the health club Bar Kochba was founded in Germany. In Hungary and Czechoslovakia, Club Macabi. Over time, Hakoach gained many adherents due to the introduction of exceptions clauses by most Austrian sporting associations, which excluded Jews from becoming members.

Anti-Semitism also had its advantages. The Hakoach had excellent athletes like Miki Hirschel, winner of two bronze medals in weightlifting at the Los Angeles Olympics in 1932. Likewise noteworthy was the swimmer Idy Kohn, Austrian national champion of the 100 meter backstroke in 1930. Hedy Wertheimer, another swimmer, was national champion in 1932. Zigo Wertheimer was their coach.

Their first division soccer team won the Austrian championship in 1924-25, and during that time my mother's cousin Joshy Gruenfeld was the trainer for the team. They also had a good tennis team, and their best player was Willy Ehrenreich, still alive in 1990.

The athletic success of Hakoach exasperated the anti-Semites, who could not accept that the Jews, who had *Kaffehauskultur* and visited the traditional Viennese cafes, could have healthy bodies and healthy minds.

By 1934, anti-Semitism in Austria had escalated to extremes. Jews could no longer stay in some hotels in the Tirol, Salzburg, Mondsee, Kitzbuehl and Badischl, among others. Although many Jews preferred to vacation in places like Karlsbad, Marienbad, and Badgastein.

In that same year, the restrictive *Numerus Clausus* was introduced for Jews in universities and other institutions of higher education.

At age seven, I traveled with my mother to Hungary, an experience I remember perfectly.

We spent our time primarily in Budapest, in a centrally-located hotel, which was very elegant, in the Erzebetkorut. For me, this was something new and exciting.

We went to concerts, to the theater to see operettas, to Margarita Island. My mother, solicitous, explained everything. I remember she spoke some Hungarian.

We also went to Uncle Ignaz Bachruch's jewelry store, a visit I had erased from my memory. I don't know why. When I visited Budapest after the war, in 1960, I had to leave my passport with an elderly woman, an officer of the Communist Police Station, for a renewal of my visa. Upon reading my last name, Bachruch, she asked me if I knew Ignaz Bachruch. He was the most well-regarded jeweler in Budapest before the war, and was deported and killed, probably in Majdanek-Sobibor Concentration camp

After a week in Budapest, we spent a month at Lake Balaton, in the small village of Balatonlelle, in a guesthouse. There, I learned my first Hungarian words. I remember we ate a great deal of *kukurusza*: corn.

A swimming teacher made great efforts to teach me to swim, but with little success. I also remember another vacation to Bodensee—where Switzerland, Austria, and Germany meet—always without my father, who remained in Vienna, or traveled to Lyon on business.

For the Jewish holidays—Passover, Sukkot, and Purim—we always went to our Aunt Zilly Bieber's house. The entire Katz family gathered there. It was a large house, as Uncle Bieber was the most prominent furrier in Austria. They had four children, Ernest, Luis, Else, and Hilde. They were very hospitable.

At the Biebers, we'd see the Starks, the Wolfthals, the Mordkovitschs, and Uncle Max and his two sons Paul and Fritz, and Uncle Poldi and his beautiful wife, Bertl Chayess, and my youngest Aunt Anna and her husband Heinrich Thiebert. These reunions were happy and spirited, with thirty or forty people. There was always food in abundance. From these gatherings, I learned the significance of Jewish holidays.

My parents belonged to the liberal Orthodox congregation of the Seitenstattengasse Temple. My father sometimes brought me to *Haupttempel*, a stricter Orthodox temple located in Leopoldstadt, the Jewish neighborhood.

My grandmother Carolina attended *Musikverein*, the concert hall, which was transformed into a temple during the major holidays. My father refused to set foot in this temple, for it was far too liberal for him.

Indeed, when we visited we brought her flowers, something unusual for an Orthodox Jew.

I also remember my Uncle Max's clothing store, in the Nussdorfer Strasse.

I remember very clearly my Grandmother Caroline's house, and her sewing shop. My grandfather Berthold was always smoking thin cigars, which were rare and made with tobacco from the Balkans. He took me with him to buy his cigars, marked Piccolo.

In the apartment at Wollzeile 17, we saw Aunt Sidonia, or Sidi as we called her, and our uncles Leopold and Shandor. Uncle Leopold owned an antique store on the Kertnerstrasse, on the corner of the Graben. This corner was called Stock im Eisen and still existed in 1958 when I visited Vienna.

The Gruenfelds were decidedly assimilated, non-practicing Jews. Yet they were, without a doubt, good Jews. Brothers Joshy and Emil were huge soccer fans, players on the Hakoach team. It was easy for them to become absorbed in soccer for four months out of the year. Oscar was a well-known public accountant and Poldi was a banker.

I already mentioned that the only son of the Bachruchs, Uncle Julius, married a non-Jewish Swiss woman, and they had a daughter Ruth, who lives in Switzerland. He became a captain in the Austrian army, and fought at the Italian front in Alto-Aidge, during the First World War (1914-18).

I remember Uncle Leopold's house in Baden very well, as we spent many weekends there.

I also remember having my tonsils removed: I stayed in my grandmother's house for days, and she fed me lots of ice cream.

These are my memories from before March 13, 1938, when the inevitable happened, the triumphant entrance of the German Army into Vienna. I will never forget the joy felt by the populace. My father brought me to the Heldenplatz, to await and witness the arrival of Adolf Hitler. The Viennese police, still in their dark green uniforms, tried to keep order among so many hundreds of people. Hitler's army wore their symbolic armbands, with the *hakenkreuz*, the swastika, as if everything had been rehearsed before. The Nazis, of whom there were many among the Austrians, were already showing off their S.S. uniforms. It was like a staged affair.

When Hitler entered the Hero's Plaza, the people cheered until they lost their voices. Hitler was surrounded by the Austrian generals who had already become part of his staff. They began doing the Nazi salute. My father, and I at his side, standing together with other Jews in the plaza, was flabbergasted at the prospect of what was to happen. This was a horrifying preview of something we never thought would be possible. The fate of European Jews between 1938 and 1945 was beyond all human imagining.

That freezing March 13, the capital of the Austrian Republic ceased to be free, sovereign, and independent. Gray clouds blanketed the city, omens of a deep upheaval looming over all of Europe: the degradation of human beings, slaughters in cold blood, the creation of concentration camps.

Although I was only eight years old, I sensed that something terrible was threatening my parents and me. I didn't know for certain what it was. When we returned home, my father, my mother, and I kept our ears open for news on the radio. We sat and ate dinner at the dining room table. My parents didn't utter a single word. I don't remember feeling such sadness in all my life.

I'm sure in the city of Vienna—with a Jewish population of two hundred thousand—there were many similar experiences. The situation was one of collective incredulity and astonishment. The Jews, in their minds, were reluctant to believe and accept what they had seen that 13th of March in 1938.

The following day, the news appeared on front pages around the world: Hitler had seized his native country, that the German army units invaded the Republic in a record time of 24 hours.

Powerful nations like Great Britain, France, the Soviet Union, and the United States remained silent, and their silence could only be interpreted as a sign of approval for what had just happened. *Finis Austriae*, the end of Austria.

Interesting to note is that during the meetings of the League of Nations, the United Nations of that time, Mexico protested the annexation of the Austrian Republic. Isidro Fabela was the Mexican representative in Geneva, Switzerland. This was a courageous and humane stance taken by the government of General Lázaro Cárdenas, who understood very clearly—and with a historical perspective—what was happening in Europe.

Earlier, in 1936, Mexico aided the Spanish Republican Government by sending them weapons. Mexico was a poor country. But Cárdenas reacted by immediately shipping 12,000 rifles and 200 field cannons to the Puerto de Vigo campaign. When the Republicans were defeated in 1939, he opened the doors of the Mexican Republic to more than forty eight thousand Spanish refugees.

With a gesture that nations much wealthier and more powerful, like the United States, Great Britain, and France, could have imitated, Mexico demonstrated to the world its humanitarianism, and greatly benefitted from the wave of immigrants fleeing from Fascism, among them university professors, researchers, progressive scientists, writers, doctors, or just plain hardworking people.

Later on Mexico opened its doors to Austrian Jewish immigrants—among them my uncle—as well as German Jews, Czechoslovakians, Hungarians.

After the German army invaded Vienna and the Nazis took power, a cataclysm befell the Jewish population. Everything happened very rapidly. Contrary to what had been happening gradually in Germany since 1933, in Austria the National Socialists took charge in just a few weeks.

After the invasion, the state declared two days of public festivities. I attended Hegelgasse school, which was a public school, as usual. Classes began normally, but at around noon several S.A. uniformed officers arrived, going with the principal from classroom to classroom with a list in their hands.

They summoned us—all the Jewish students—to the principal's ffice. Assembled there, we were notified that we could no longer attend school, because it was for Aryan children only. But we were to continue studying in a school for Jewish children in the Boersegasse, once it was organized and ready to receive us, with Jewish teachers, of course.

The school secretary called our parents so that they could come pick us up. We were not allowed to return to our classrooms to say goodbye to our other classmates.

About forty of us were quarantined until my mother arrived, frantic and worried. She took me home. Then, days of forced vacation followed, until the primary school for Jews opened its doors.

In just one day, the relationship I'd had for years with my classmates was abruptly terminated. Childhood friendships became filled with suspicion; Austrian youths were brainwashed and, hence, they despised their Jewish classmates, deeming them unworthy of friendship. They no longer spoke to us, but instead insulted us, without knowing for sure why. Those who were once my friends refused to speak with me, unless it was to call me a Jew. The minds of the children had been poisoned. The new ideal was to be an active Aryan, to enroll in the *Hitlerjugend*, Hitler Youth—HAYOT its acronym. The banks in Stadtpark and in other parks were painted with graphic precision: *"Nicht Fur Juden."*

In the Taborstrasse, the main street of Leopoldstadt, the Jewish neighborhood, a humiliating incident transpired: Jewish intellectuals, rabbis, *Gayim, Shamoshim*, community officials, gym teachers, and university professors were forced by the S.A. officers to clean the street with brushes, amid the laughter of passersby. The Viennese police watched impassively. In typical Viennese style, no one tried to stop this act of degradation. In Germany it had not yet come to that.

The Jews were kicked as they were forced to degrade themselves by performing squats unto exhaustion.

In the Rotenturmstrasse near the temple there was a similar spectacle, and the onlookers were equally indifferent. The police did not intervene. Every day there were more Viennese Nazis in uniform in the streets, in the S.A. café, or *Sturm Abteilung.* They began arresting prominent Jews, or simply Jews reported by envious coworkers who sought their jobs. It was sufficient just to point the finger at someone and say "This man is a *Saujud*" to have him arrested for interrogation.

The committees worked on all the streets in the city. Many of the people were trained. The prisoners were assembled in a school for these purposes. Later they were sent to the camps K.Z. Dachau in Bavaria and to Buchenwald near Weimar. Mauthausen, the camp of sad memories in Austria, which opened later. Concentration camps from which many did not emerge alive, or if they did, they were disabled for the rest of their lives.

From our family, Joshy Gruenfeld—Gerty's father, former soccer player from the Hakoach team in Vienna, a veteran injured in the First World War—was arrested. He spent one year in Dachau. One of his customers denounced him, because the customer owed money to the "Jewish money lender." Of course the debt was cancelled. Joshy Gruenfeld was a banker. Karl Stark, Sigi's brother, was also sent to Dachau for the "crime" *Rassenschande*: living with an Austrian woman, not a Jew.

Bubi Wolfthal was sent to Buchenwald. He spent a year in the camp and later managed to escape by jumping from a train taking other prisoners to another concentration camp.

In 1938 the word "transport" was incorporated into the Jewish lexicon of martyrdom side by side with "*Kidush Ha-Shem*," or act of faith in different eras. Also, "*Austrottung*" during the Medieval Crusades and "*Pogroms*" of Tsarist Russia. The Jews were transported in train cars normally used to transport animals. Passenger coaches were reserved for Aryans and military personnel. Germany built an army of eight million soldiers, over time the most powerful army in all of Europe and the rest of the world. Highly mechanized and with excellent combat morale, the German army metamorphosed into a formidable war machine between 1935 and 1945.

The Germans had achieved a certain level of combat expertise in the Spanish Civil War (1936-38). The Spanish fell against the Germans like blades of grass, in Guernica, Albacete, Extremadura, Teruel and Badajoz. By 1939, no European army was in any condition to confront the Germans and their airplanes.

The Jewish people in Vienna were on the hunt for visas from any and all foreign consulates, beginning with the United States, but also to exotic countries like Cuba, Mexico, Guatemala, Brazil, Santo Domingo, Bolivia, Japan, China, Turkey, and any country who would let them in. They stood in long lines trying to obtain visas to leave as soon as possible, before all hell broke loose.

If one was not able to be received by the consul during office hours, he would queue again the following day. And again and again. Others, like my father, left the country illegally, crossing the borders of *Grosses Deutsches Reich*, at night or with the help of a *sheliach*, the "coyotes" of that time. They bribed the German border guards, who turned a blind eye at their *schmiergeld*. Corruption was rampant among the Germans.

In this first stage of the "Solution to the Jewish Problem," the Germans attempted to expel the majority of Jews, forcing them to leave and bequeath their belongings and fortunes to the Reich. Germany became heir to their money, their property, bank accounts—especially those domiciled abroad—and their art collections Whatever wealth they possessed had to be left to the German state.

Large transactions were conducted, in which venerable institutions—Deutsche Bank, Deutsche Sudamerikanische Bank, Credit Anstalt (this last one expropriated from the Rothschilds)—directly intervened, putting extreme pressure on Jewish clients, once they had complied with the documents necessary to leave Austria *Auswanderung Nachweis*. Without this document, it was impossible to emigrate.

Eichmann had been installed in Vienna. Alois Brunner—his lieutenant, today living freely in Syria—was commandant of the concentration camp Maidanek Sobibor. The Final Solution, or *Endloesung*, was agreed upon in January 1942, in a conference of high-ranking German government officials and the S.S. Chief of Staff, Richard Heydrich, in Wannsee near Berlin. Here, they issued orders from several German companies: I.G. Farben Bayer for zyclon gas, Gerbrueder Topf Mashinenbau for crematoriums, BMW (*Bayrische Motorwerke*), and Maximilian Porsche AG of Austria for trucks equipped to produce deadly gas. This was not until the year 1942, beginning of the Final Solution.

Here in Wannsee, a beautiful village meant for lakeside summering, plans for the Final Solution were devised, and logistics of the technical matters were set in stone. This was the beginning of a new chapter in the war against the

Jews. It was to be final and definitive destruction of the Jews.

I visited this peaceful country house, constructed for a wealthy German industrialist at the beginning of the century, a place to spend weekends and summers. The villa is at the edge of a pristine natural lake, situated between Potsdam and Berlin. It's difficult to conceive of a better environmental antithesis for what was decided there. Such an idyllic setting for the genesis of the most horrific mass murders in all of human history, the Holocaust.

I began attending the school designated for Jews, Boersegasse, in May of 1938. The teachers were, of course, also Jewish. The subjects were the same as they were in the Hegelgasse School.

The first few days, at the end of classes, groups of non-Jewish children waited outside and threw *kieselsteine*—stones of varying sizes—at us. We shielded ourselves as best we could with our backpacks and ran towards home. Sometimes we would pick the stones up and throw them back at our attackers. But for the most part we ran as fast as we could. These attacks lasted for fifteen more days, then disappeared as if by magic. Most likely the attackers had simply grown tired of bothering us, for there were certainly no policemen to deter them.

Schoenschreiben, or calligraphy, was added to our curriculum, and it was taught by a teacher who was jovial, but also very demanding. We had to write with fountain pens, which often stained the paper. When this would happen, we had to repeat the entire page, for our teacher accepted nothing less than perfection. And so went calligraphy class and the rest of the subjects.

Tension and sadness pervaded at home. My father would walk in the door, sit down in his chair without speaking, staring forlornly into space. My mother tried to brighten the mood, talking of lighthearted, trivial matters. She also spoke about the Bachruch-Gruenfeld family, surely to be immune because of the services they provided to their country. Or so she thought.

Then there were *Aussnahmejuden*, Jews who enjoyed, or at least hoped to enjoy, special privileges. Similar to the *Hofjuden* of the Middle Ages, Jews who were part of the court. The *Mischlinge*—literally "mixed"—occupied a very important category. These were people who were products of mixed marriages, and classified in varying degrees, according to the racial laws of Nuremberg. At the beginning they were protected, but by 1943, they were deported like everyone else.

For my father, a traditional Jew, it was easier to accept the idea of emigrating. It wouldn't be his first time or his last. Lech, Lecha, said G-d to Abraham Ovinu. The possibility of reconstructing a new life abroad did not scare him—in fact, it appealed to him despite the effort and uncertainty it entailed.

My mother could not have felt more differently. She was unable to comprehend, much less accept, what was happening. She was second-generation Viennese, and accepted and integrated into gentile society—or at least she believed she was. She was the daughter of a lieutenant of the Imperial Army; sister of a Republican army official, who had served in the First World War, my uncle Julius Bachruch; cousin of a colonel in that same army, Joshy Gruenfeld; daughter of a dressmaker for the court.

In her view, she and her family would certainly be exempt from danger. She couldn't see things any other way, simply because it was inconceivable, contrary to logic. And in Vienna...*Logica Imperat*. And just like my mother, thousands of other Austrian Jews, who were "fully accepted and integrated" into Austrian society up until March of 1938, believed the exact same thing.

The wealthiest Jewish family in Vienna was without a doubt the Rothschilds. Baron Louis Nathaniel Rothschild was head of the Austrian branch of his family's bank, headquartered in Frankfurt. A third-generation Austrian, he was well-educated, and could easily pass for an intellectual. Those who knew him said he appeared and conducted himself more like an English Lord, and less like the heir to one of the largest fortunes in Central Europe.

Extremely dedicated to philanthropy, he sustained a great, modern hospital in the city, open to Jews and non-Jews alike, so that everyone could receive medical attention free of cost. The people loved him, and it became customary to say *"Meine Sorgen Und Rothschild's Geld,"* or my concerns and Rothschild's money. The day after Anschluss he was visited by two S.S. officials, who took away his passport.

After a long interrogation, Louis Nathaniel was imprisoned in the cellar of his own castle until he was taken to the infamous prison Hotel Metropole, at the shore of the Donaukanal, which had become headquarters of the Gestapo. Although Adolf Eichmann had dealt with his case personally, the Nazis had a vested interest in Rothschild. Himmler visited him in his cell, which was next to that of Kurt Von Schuschnigg, the deposed Austrian Chancellor.

Rothschild was imprisoned for more than a year. There were lengthy negotiations with his family in Paris and London in which they ceded all of their property in Austria, as well as Moravska Ostrava, the most preeminent steel foundry in all of Central Europe, and certainly very generous bribes to high-ranking S.S. officials. He was set free in May of 1939, with an *Ausreisebewilligung*—permission to leave the German Reich—and managed to escape to England, and afterwards he resided in Vermont, in the United States. He never returned to

Vienna, but at least he managed to survive. He was fifty-six years old.

The Reich's Ministry of Finance had a special division called *Devisenschutz* that worked hand in hand with the Gestapo and the S.S. to "dip" into the substantial fortunes of the Jews. This division was directed by Halmar Schacht, Hitler's Minister of Finance.

Many people committed suicide in Vienna during this time. A university professor threw himself from a fourth floor window. A writer killed himself by lighting the gas on his kitchen stove and hermetically sealing the doors and windows of his apartment.

It ran in the news that a political cabinet *conferencier*, wanting to jump from his balcony, respectfully asked passerby to back away so that he would not crush them in his fall. Such was Viennese etiquette. Suicide cases multiplied between May and November of 1938.

I mention these suicides because they indicate a response to tragedy so typically Viennese. *Anschluss*, and what was to come afterwards, represented the end of their lives as they knew them; the death of their beliefs, their personal history.

We will now speak of the converts who had broken from their family and transformed themselves into *Geschmatte*, removed from their community.

Many of these suicide cases involved Jews who converted and were baptized into Catholicism. The issuing of the Nuremburg Laws in Austria that terrible thirteenth of March, 1938 rendered baptisms worthless, less valuable than the papers on which they were written.

Between March and November, after *Kristallnacht*, Night of Broken Glass, 548 people committed suicide in Vienna alone. Among the most notable were well-known author Egon Friedell, Karl Brody, editor in chief of the *Telegraf*, Army Major Emil Fey, Infantry General Wilhelm Zehner. Bankers, professors and judges became Jews again overnight, according to the Nuremberg Laws.

The Austrian S.A. had another pastime: capturing various devout Jews, preferably those with beards, providing them with paint and brushes, and forcing them to paint Stars of David and the word *"Jude"* above the doors and shop windows of stores owned by Jews.

My cousin Sigi Stark, who had worked abroad as a diamond setter, took the train to Belgium as the people celebrated Hitler in the Helden Platz. He had no problem crossing the border with his Austrian passport. One day later, on March

14, 1938, Austrian passports were invalidated.

My father's store in the Seilergasse 4 was seized—rather, it was "officially expropriated," and here's how it happened: An Austrian man appeared at the door, my father's supplier for many years, a ribbon manufacturer in Gumpoldskirchen who delivered materials to his client, Katz the Jew. He arrived accompanied by three men from the S.A. and a notary public. They drew up a contract, in which they named the Austrian manufacturer *Komisar* and threw my father and three other Jewish employees out on the street. This was consummated as fact, and appears as such in the archives of the Presidium of the Viennese police, in Ballhaus Platz. I found this out on a visit to Vienna in 1958. Things were done correctly in the Vienna of 1938.

In effect, the Germans and Austrians alike wrote documents and made them "official." Of course, there was no compensation whatsoever, or anything of the sort.

My father opened another, smaller store, in the Singerstrasse, to cater to his clients. Nothing could compare with his elegant establishment in the Seilergasse. This new store was destroyed by the mobs on *Kristallnacht*.

Paul Katz, later Curzon, together with his girlfriend Bertl Kokish—whose family also came from Brody—were able to obtain employment as butler and chef in the home of an English family in Yorkshire, and hence they received two visas to immigrate to England where they worked until the war broke out in September 1939.

As a result of that situation they were declared Enemy Aliens. Fortunately, they were able to remain in Great Britain. Afterwards Paul was able to bring his parents, my Uncle Max and Aunt Yetti, out of Vienna.

My cousins Ernest and Louis Biber were also able to leave Vienna, after leaving all of their property to the government. They went to England, where they had a family owned subsidiary since 1930.

My uncle Poldi, my father's younger brother, immigrated to Bolivia with his wife Bertl in 1938.

Fritz, my father's oldest brother, was a musician in a jazz orchestra. The *Anschluss* surprised him while he was on tour with his orchestra in Damascus, Syria. Obviously he did not return to Vienna. After performing in Istanbul and Casablanca, he arrived in England in August of 1939, just before the war began.

Little by little, Jews who could obtain visas, or risked travelling illegally, left the city.

Little by little, the city was being emptied of Jews as concentration camps were filling. Jewish corpses were arriving in morgues. There was not a Jewish family in all of Vienna that couldn't speak of an emigration or a deportation. The same situation prevailed in Germany.

For the most part, the immigrants were a welcome addition to the countries that received them. Among them were hard-working professionals, engineers, doctors, orchestral conductors, movie directors, jewelers, and experienced manufacturers with extensive knowledge of their products.

Among the architects who left were Richard Neutra, trained in the Bauhaus School of Weimar. Josef Franz, who had built Karl Marx Hof, a rent-controlled housing complex for workers—rent could not exceed 35% of the salary of the *Pater Familias*. Oskar Kaufmann, builder of the *Volksbuhene,* or People's Theater, in Berlin. Erich Mendelsoh, Rudolf Schindler, Oskar Strand, and Bruno Sevi. Sevi, a Jew from Padua, Italy, developed foundational architectural theories applied throughout Europe and America. Robert van't Hoff, Josef Neufeld and Jakob Orenstein, who were also from the Bauhaus School, immigrated to Palestine, where they built the first Art Deco modernist buildings in Tel Aviv between 1936 and 1939.

People like Otto Preminger, Billy Wilder, Heddy Lamar, Louise Reiner, Paul Muni and Theodor Bickel arrived in Hollywood. Lotte Lehman and Richard Tauber to the opera in New York. Max Reinhardt to the theater in Switzerland. Sigmund Freud to England. Egon Kis, Hans and Louise Rohner to Mexico. Paul Kleiber, Bruno Walter to New York. James Rohatin the banker to London. Teddy Kollek, future mayor of Jerusalem, arrived in Palestine. Many others, more or less important, each contributing a grain of sand to the development of the countries that welcomed them. Let's not forget the Cardinal Jean Marie Lustiger of France, possible candidate for the papacy—a Viennese Jew. Or Michael Blumenthal of Unisys and Steven Bloodhound of Twentieth Century Fox, also Viennese Jews.

As were Henry Grunwald, editor of *Time Magazine* for more than twenty years, and afterwards United States ambassador in Vienna, and Fred Lauder, president of Estee Lauder and later ambassador of his adopted country in Vienna.

I will now speak further about the *Kristallnacht,* which I've already mentioned. On November 11, 1938, well-organized mobs with a preapproved plan devoted the entire night to breaking the windows of Jewish stores and looting them. Hence, "night of broken glass." They burned synagogues and Jewish community centers, and beat to death any Jew who stood in their way.

There were many victims. This same kind of vandalism was happening to the Jewish populations in the cities and towns throughout the German Reich.

This led to retaliation, such as the murder of a secretary in the German Embassy in Paris, perpetrated by a Polish Jew, Henryk Greenspan, who was later apprehended by the Paris police.

It's not difficult to see the logic in this. It was a plan premeditated by the highest German government officials, executed by the subordinates of Heydrich, Himmler, and Eichmann. There was scarcely a synagogue standing; all burned throughout the Reich. The police looked on, but never intervened. Press from worldwide news outlets, with reporters stationed in Vienna, Berlin, Salzburg, Munich, Frankfurt, Hamburg and Leipzig, reported on facts but nothing more. The world remained silent. The Jews, Armenians, Kurds, and Gypsies were not, after all, relevant news for readers. Everyone else had their own problems, or so they believed. Of course, these "problems" in 1938 and 1939 were created in one form or another by Adolf Hitler himself. But no one wanted to believe it: Neville Chamberlain, while attempting to execute his Shuttle Diplomacy with such dedication. "I will try and try again," declared the press. They tried at all costs to calm Hitler, never to curb or counteract his rapid expansion, for Germany and for his ideas.

Kristallnacht finally convinced my father—who was, up to that point, indecisive—to leave Austria. He chose France as his destination. He had, after all, good friends in Lyon. He thought surely they would help him out after many years of good business partnership. He figured he would leave first, and afterwards would send for us to join him.

I'm sure that my father weighed the possibilities again and again. It was not easy to abandon Vienna and leave my mother and me in such hellishness. He had always been a family man. He lived and worked for our sustenance. Life without us made no sense to him. Nonetheless he decided that he must act, and fight against fate, in spite of doubts and anguish.

He went to Lyon, where he would send for us with the help of his French friends. Or so we thought. He went alone by train to Achen Aix la Chapelle. In 1938 it was still possible to travel without a problem. Sigi Stark, already in Brussels, had hired a *Sheliaj* who waited for him at the border of Germany and Belgium at night, at a time they'd previously arranged.

To cross the German border and achieve freedom, one usually had to bribe the German border guards. My father arrived at his lodging in Aix la Chapelle and began talking with the *Grenzpolizei* official. After an hour and a half, he was able to go without having to pay a single cent, a singular experience. My cousin Sigi told me this many years later.

My father had the gift of conversation, of telling little stories and rendering them very interesting for the interlocutor. On this occasion after illegally crossing the border between Germany and Belgium, he accessed his gift with excellent result.

He arrived in Belgium and stayed for several days with my cousin Sigi, and saw his brother Louis and my cousin Hugo Mordkovitsch. After Brussels, he once again had to cross the border between Belgium and France. Similarly dangerous, but fortunately he would not be apprehended by the Germans.

Back in Vienna, my mother spent her days ridden with anxiety until she received word that my father had finally arrived in Paris.

I was nine years old, and there were many things I remained unaware of although I knew more than my mother thought I did. I was consciously aware of my father's absence. What I did not know is that I'd never see him again.

Sadness reigned in our home. Life without my father was not the same. We barely went out in the afternoons to play in the park. Jews were prohibited from doing so. My mother limited the number of times she went out to buy groceries. It was dangerous: she never knew who would recognize her and insult her in the street, or who would make nasty comments in a store, like "The food here is for us and not for Jews" or "Look at this Jewess, who still dares to go shopping."

There were no longer social functions, parties, or visits among family friends in which there were boys and girls my age with whom I could play.

There was no going to Temple to socialize; it was destroyed. Jews didn't dare walk in the street in groups for fear of Nazis, or even average citizens, ready to beat them with truncheons they'd stolen from the police.

We never visited my father's family; all the youth had left: *Lech, Lecha.*

We only visited my grandmother Caroline, in her house at Wollzeile 17, of which I have many memories. My grandmother lived in the first floor of a building in the *Jugendstil* style, constructed during a period of great urban change between 1860 and 1890. In this era many medieval walls and gates that had protected Vienna during the Turkish siege were destroyed, or collapsed.

In its place, the Ring was constructed, a wide avenue following the trace of the walls and gates of antiquity, called *basteien,* or bastions. Vienna was enriched with sumptuous buildings five stories tall, with ten-room apartments, housing for the high bourgeoisie. Buildings like the Parliament, the Opera, and the Municipality were constructed, this one in Gothic style that clashed with the Baroque and Neoclassical Viennese styles that dominated the city. Other buildings constructed around this time were the *Boerse*, or Stock Exchange, the University, the Votive Church *Votivkirche*, the Ministry of Defense, and the *Musikverein*, the finest concert hall in the city.

This was the era of architect Otto Wagner, who constructed the *Sparkasse*, or savings bank, two short blocks from our apartment. He also designed buildings in *Jugendstil* or Art Nouveau, in the Wienzeile, such as the Mayolica House.

In that time, there was an outpouring of unique artistry like Vienna had never seen before. This era gave birth to the Secessionist movement, which included the architect Olbrich, and painters like Gustav Klimt, Egon Schiele, Oscar Kokoschkla and Koloman Moser. They exposed their scandalous work to Viennese society until the Emperor Franz Joseph accepted and inaugurated it. This calmed things down, and quite a few young painters from the Versacrum group were accepted into Viennese society.

My grandmother's apartment and sewing shop were on the first floor of a building from that time period. I remember what seemed to me at the time an enormous photograph of my Bachruch grandfather in full Hussar regalia, standing on a low table. My grandfather Berthold had passed away from natural causes before Hitler had invaded Austria. My grandmother was too old to sew, and she had difficulty moving around. She was very vivacious, and would tell us that she had taken photographs for a visa. Those famous visas of salvation. She never got one. Foreign countries did not want Jews, much less the "old and unproductive" ones.

I still have one of these photographs: a portrait of a dignified woman, full of goodness, but very sad. My grandmother, like my mother, would leave Vienna only to be sent to a concentration camp, Theresienstadt, a *Sonderlager fur Sonderjuden*, or "special camp for special Jews," devised by Heydrich and Himmler as a "model camp." The Germans allowed visits from heads of state like Count Ciano, Admiral Horty, and Catholic Bishop Tisza of Slovakia. On occasion a delegation of Vatican cardinals would attend. Hitler, with great insistence, "commended" Pope Pious XII.

The reality is that the *Curia Romana* during those terrible years (1933-45) did not protest what was happening in the name of humanity, or even in the name of the Roman Catholic Church. History remembers Pious XII as the Silent Pope who never had the courage to assert his moral authority, which was, or should have been, strongly opposed to the Fuhrer Hitler and the German nation. Not even in Italy, where he concluded his *concordat* with Mussolini.

The International Red Cross was also given permission to enter Theresienstadt. Here the Germans made two full-length propaganda films, one of them by Leni Riefenstahl, famous for her documentary on "The Berlin Olympic Games" (1936).

Theresienstadt was situated in the barracks of the imperial army, constructed during the reign of Empress Maria Theresa around 1810. Recruits were trained here, including those from the Czech Republic, when Mazarik and Benes were presidents. Cvjetko Popovic, who assassinated Archduke Franz in Sarajevo, was held here for a while. This attack was the catalyst of the First World War, in 1914.

The camp was exclusively for Jews. There were no gypsies, political prisoners, or allied prisoners of war. Only *sonderjuden*. Renowned intellectuals were sent there, as well as actors from the cinema and the theater, musicians, opera singers, high-level Jewish leaders, rabbis, university professors . . . the idea was to have a "model camp" to demonstrate the magnanimity of German civilization, of the "new order." Any infraction was punished with solitary confinement in a dungeon, with meager rations that consisted of watery soup, a piece of bread, coffee from burnt beans, and rutabaga, a type of tuber similar to a potato. Meat was only for public meals witnessed by foreign delegations and filmed for news in Germany and abroad.

There were organized concerts of Classical music by the camp's symphonic orchestra, which included world-renowned soloists. The public, the other inmates, were obligated to applaud. Theatrical works were performed with well-regarded actors, directed by experienced directors, plays written by Jews and non-Jews: Shakespeare, Racine, Moliere, Hauptmann, Schnitzler, Brecht, Trugenyev, Tolstoy . . . every day there were rehearsals and presentations in the event dignitaries were to visit.

There was even a synagogue, with a Torah, Aron Kodesh, a rabbi and cantor, a full display of "happy Jews."

Jews were imprisoned here from August 1941 onward. The majority came from Germany, Austria, Czechoslovakia, Hungary, and Romania. There were no Polish, Russian, or Lithuanian Jews. They were sent directly to extermination camps.

Murmelstein, a Viennese community leader, lived and died in Theresienstadt. Likewise, the Rabbi Guedemann from the *Haupt Tempel*, or "Main

Temple"; in Leopoldstadt, the cantor from the *Seitestaettegasse* Temple; Viennese Zionist leaders, among them Josef Stricker.
The managers of the Deutsches Theater in Prague, the rabbi from the temple Dohanyi Utza in Budapest; judges from Jassy, Bukovina, community leaders from Bucharest were also imprisoned here. As was Leo Beck the *Oberrabiner*, great rabbi of Berlin.

Inmates died at the rate of eight thousand per month, mostly from malnutrition, tuberculosis, diabetes, typhus, or from being beaten by the S.S.

My grandmother Caroline was imprisoned in the camp until early 1943. In February of that year the Germans organized the transportation of elderly Viennese Jews to Maly Trostinek, formerly a Russian military training ground for tankers. Here, mass graves were dug. The train carrying my grandmother arrived on February 14, 1943. Many of the elderly prisoners needed assistance getting out, since many could barely move. Under the hostile watch of the S.S. guards and their dogs, they were forced to walk to the edge of the pits, aligning themselves forty at a time, some standing, some kneeling, as two soldiers, each with a machine gun mounted on a tripod, riddled them with bullets.

The deafening cacophony of the machine guns was perhaps worse than death. The elderly people were terrified as they waited for their turn to be riddled with bullets.

This military camp existed since the time of the Tsars, and was then reconditioned by the Red army. It's located about forty kilometers from Minsk, in Belarus.

In Vienna, after visiting my grandmother's house, my mother and I would wait until it grew dark before returning home. For me, this was an adventure; I enjoyed it. Beforehand, we never went out at night. I was usually in the apartment, already bathed and waiting for dinner by nightfall. Now it was the opposite; the darkness provided security for the Jews, made us more difficult to recognize. Vienna in 1938 was a crazy, interesting world, full of adventure, at least for an eight year old boy, like me.

One afternoon my mother arrived with important news: the Viennese Jewish community, with supervision of the Gestapo, had organized a transport for children under the banner of the International Red Cross, who had already negotiated with the Germans to transport and save both Republican Spanish and German Jewish chidren. This was all approved.

The first transport would leave Vienna on December 20th. The Nazis guaranteed that the wagons would be sterilized for the children's safety. They would arrive in Belgium with four hundred and fifty Jewish children. Each child could bring one suitcase, which could not exceed 15 kilograms, and food for the three-day journey. My mother saw to the preparations for my trip: she selected clothing I was to wear, and on each garment she sewed a cotton tag with my name on it. As if her son was going to summer camp.

My mother chose several books: a *Siddur* of my father's, an illustrated book of Bible stories, a Hebrew lesson book from school. She also gave me an envelope of photos of my father, herself, and me when I was younger.

Later on, I came to the conclusion that my mother, although not necessarily a traditional believer like my father, did what he would have done, choosing Jewish books for her son as he ventured from his paternal home.

The departure date for the *Kindertransport* was delayed twice, but our orders finally arrived. My mother took me to what was left of the Seitenstaettengasse Temple, in the Judengasse: blackened walls, remains of the Beth Midrash cast aside.

Here, children my age and younger were assembled, each of us carrying a suitcase. Gestapo agents in charge of the transport verified the lists prepared by the *Kultusgemeinde*, or community. Officials wearing yellow arm bands were attempting to help the children, their parents and their older siblings.

After three or four hours of "arduous toil"—doing things "correctly" when it came to these 450 Jewish children—German soldiers from the Wehrmacht boarded us one by one into the army trucks, painted dark green, with benches on either side, and aisles where our belongings were stored.

There were little girls with their favorite dolls, and boys with teddy bears. I went with a thick coat, as it was winter. In order to identify ourselves, we each wore a card pinned to our clothing, which included our names, ages, where we came from, and each of us was assigned a number.

This was the last time my mother and I laid eyes on each other. The army trucks set out in the direction of the Maria-Hilferstrasse, towards the Westbahnhof Station. I never saw my mother again.

The train we took traversed the entire length of Germany until we reached the city of Cologne. We stopped several times; never at a station, but rather in open fields. There was little supervision from the German soldiers; occasionally an official would pass by without saying a word to us.

We ate at a schedule determined by the position of the sun, since none of us had a watch. There were no adults on the train. I remember sleeping most of the time, lulled by the sound of the wheels on the tracks. We also slept at night, of course. Lights out until we were awakened by the sunrise.

We reached the station in Cologne. Here we waited for the army trucks, just like in Vienna. We boarded, escorted by the German soldiers, only now at the head of each bench was seated an army official wearing a black band emblazoned with a skull and crossbones that looked as though it were made of silver. No one said a word, nor did we know where we were being taken.

After a half hour, our truck—part of a convoy of about ten other trucks—entered a grand courtyard, and stopped. We learned that we'd come to a refuge for Jewish orphans. Here we spent the night, lying as best we could, five children to a bed. But beforehand we were served dinner. Hot, delicious dinner! Our first hot meal in three days, prepared by the Jewish community, or what was left of them. There were no guards; they were probably outside the main gate.

Some very nice ladies tried to calm us, asking us if we needed anything. "More food!" we said, and they served us. We were happy, if very tired, though we'd slept most of the trip. After we showered—something I'd never done before—we squeezed into our beds and fell asleep immediately.

We stayed here two days and two nights. And we were well cared for! Later we found some missing paperwork that the Belgian authorities required for our admittance into the country.

We returned to the station, where we took another train. Cologne was very close to the border—we could see Belgian cars—and before we knew it, we were in Belgium. The train stopped, and men got on wearing khaki uniforms different from the German green ones.

They opened the windows to let in fresh air. We were happy, although we couldn't understand what they were saying, as they were speaking Flemish. After a few minutes, pretty nurses wearing gray and white uniforms gave us sweets. They stayed with us until we arrived at an immense, beautiful palace, like in a fairy tale. Each of us had our own bed. We ate again, attended by the nurses, and seated at long tables with white tablecloths.I remained here for four days, until Sigi Stark, whom I've mentioned before, came to pick me up. He lived in Brussels. The other children remained there.

The castle was located half an hour from the capital. My cousin came for me in a taxi, and we rode to Brussels. I was extremely happy to be with family.

My cousin had received permission to bring me home, on the condition that he would return me in three weeks, when we were to be delivered to local Jewish families.

And so I was able to stay with Sigi, who lived in a Belgian family's home. They had one son, a year older than me. It was fantastic to have someone to play with. And I learned some French.

Sigi went to a jewelry shop every day. He also worked at home. His work consisted of setting diamonds onto rings, earrings, necklaces or brooches made of silver and gold. It was meticulous work, a trade he'd learned in Vienna and London. In Vienna he worked with Halpert, a famous European jeweler, who had emigrated from Russia at the outbreak of the Revolution in 1917.

Mr. Halpert reconstructed his business in Vienna, essentially with the same employees he'd worked with in St. Petersburg. He had great success thanks to the famous technique of Faberge, jewelers of the Tsar and Russian nobility. Thus, he exhibited the innate and formidable Jewish ability to adapt and survive.

I spent three very happy weeks with Sigi. He was my tour guide around the city—he showed me everything, and made me forget my homesickness. He was like a father to me. We were cousins, but he was twenty years older. He made me write a letter to my father in Paris, and another to my mother, from whom I received weekly correspondence. Papa wrote me every two weeks. It was better to have parents by proxy than none at all.

My mother asked me about practical details, like whether I bathed each day, if I folded my clothing after washing and drying it. Things of this nature. Ah! She asked if I got on well with Sigi, if I thanked him for everything he'd done for me. That she wanted to feel proud of having raised me well, *guterzogen*.

My father, on his part, felt the need to impart upon me Jewish values; our unwavering belief in justice. He would write me stories steeped in Judiasm, that expressed a rich symbolism, and in which I saw myself reflected. I received these missives without a problem until the outbreak of the Second World War in September of 1939. My father's letters, with their symbolic and illustrative content, should have been aimed at a boy much older than I. But nonetheless they were sent to me, helping me become conscious of being Jewish, and certainly a better human being.

The time came for Sigi to return me to the castle to be with my fellow travelers & friends from Vienna.

The first day of February, 1939, we were brought to downtown Brussels, to the Hotel Albert Premier, so that interested Jewish families could meet us and welcome us into their homes.

The previous night the project organizer came to speak to us. She was the Baroness Lilianne Rothschild from the French branch, who together with the International Red Cross in Geneva had worked diligently on this project, which functioned effectively until the war began. They were fortunately able to save some thousands of Jewish children from Germany and Austria, known as the Kindertransports.

She asked that we be well-groomed and wearing our best clothes. She wished with all her heart that we find safe homes within these Jewish families selected by the communities of Brussels and Antwerp.

At 8 A.M. the elegant Pullman trucks arrived, and we were driven to the grand ballroom of the hotel. The women and nurses lined us up, leaving room for us to turn. I'm sure we looked like pawns on a giant chessboard.

The people began arriving at around ten. I was wearing my nicest clothes, ready for inspection. A navy suit with shorts, a starched white shirt, and my hair, which back then was abundant, was combed with brillantine that Sigi had bought for me. I was quite chubby then.

The immense ballroom filled up quickly. Various people passed by, continuing down the hall. And then appeared a well-dressed couple. The woman with an enormous leather purse and hat, the man of dark complexion like the Gypsies I'd seen in Vienna. They stared at me and whispered amongst themselves in a language I could not immediately recognize. I realized later they were speaking Hungarian. After all, I had been to Hungary at age seven and remembered some words.

The couple was still there, not going anywhere; they continued arguing animatedly. Finally, the man asked me in German: "What's your name?" "Hans Peter," I responded, and he said to her: *"Hans Peternek Hiviak Otet."* Meanwhile, she looked at me sideways, inspecting me, I suppose. He left and returned after awhile, accompanied by one of the women from the committee, with a notebook and "order form." He asked his wife for her approval, and then the woman in charge proceeded to fill the order. He signed, and that was the conclusion of the transaction. Afterwards they took me with them.

We went through the dark corridors of the hotel, passing by the kitchen, which gave off a delicious smell, until we came to the courtyard behind the hotel. Here we got into a car. I was so impressed! The man got behind the wheel, the woman in the passenger seat, and me in the back. He started the car and headed for the streets of Brussels. It was the first time I'd ever been in a car that wasn't a taxi. They continued speaking to each other in Hungarian. Afterwards, the man looked at me in the rearview mirror and asked me in German: *Bist du hungrig?* Are you hungry? *Ja*, I answered. This was our entire conversation. We arrived at what appeared to be their home. My future home...he took my tiny suitcase and we climbed a flight of stairs. The staircase was made of wood covered in linoleum. We were in the Rue Des Vierges, no. 10, not far from downtown Brussels. He later told me in German it was *Jungfraugasse*, which didn't mean much to me. I still didn't understand the meaning of *jungfrau*, or virgin.

It was a small apartment in comparison to my parents' spacious apartment in Vienna, but it was full of natural light. It consisted, basically, of three rooms: a dining room, a bedroom, and a small kitchen. The bathroom was on another floor. There was already food on the stove, and later, much later, we got ready to eat. First they gave me a rich chicken soup, then the woman—who I knew now was called Yolanka—brought to the table a serving bowl full of what appeared to be a beige-colored puree sprinkled with something deep red. Without changing the plate the soup was on, we each served ourselves this mash, which turned out to be made of white beans. The red was paprika, which was delicious...we ate it with thick slices of dark bread, fresh from the oven. I had never eaten this sort of food, and enjoyed it immensely.

This encounter was so casual and without any kind of formality; it was as though I'd known them forever, as though I was their child who'd returned from abroad.

Despite the lack of communication—the woman spoke only Hungarian—I immediately felt at home. What a surprise!

They were Adolf and Jolan Lanksner, Hungarian Jews from Nagyvarad, Grosvardein, Transylvania. They immigrated to Belgium in 1930. They had no children. They responded to the notice from the Jewish Committee—truth be told, they wanted a girl. They told me later that when they saw me standing in the hotel without any potential "customers" they felt pity and decided on me.

I was in a new country, where people spoke a language different from my own. I was without parents or family except for Sigi, and without friends. This was exile, and it was the experience of hundreds of thousands of Europeans—a migration in every sense, fleeing from Fascism, from barbarism, from destruction, the firing squad, senseless bombings committed in the name of a "new order," in Spain the Falangist paradigm of backwardness, the blessing of a church that called itself human, and adherent to the teachings of Jesus, a crucified Jew.

The Germans, the third link in this tripartite of civilized nations—the nation of Gutenberg, Goethe, Beethoven, and Roentgen—was now lowered to worshipping the Wotan God of Wagner, and sanctified in the name of the Fuhrer Hitler, who organized book burnings, opened concentration camps to vilify human beings, destroying them. How could a nation so proud of its scientific advances allow itself to be manipulated by a *Niemand*, a nobody?

The Italians, drunk with Roman dreams of conquest—in reality, an inferiority complex—attacked weak countries like Eritrea, Ethiopia, and Lybia in order to demonstrate to the world what they, these "black shirts," were capable of: killing innocent people. The *Negus, Haile Selasie, was unable to defend his people.*

The most powerful nations said nothing against the annexation of Austria and of the Sudetenland, nor did they acknowledge the impossible predicament of the German Jews. There were no protests, save for Mexico. There was no breach in diplomatic relations. Nothing of the sort. The number of Jewish refugees who tried in vain to obtain visas from any country that had an embassy or consulate in the Reich began to trouble the world. Not a great deal, but enough so that the Commissioner for Refugees from the League of Nations—initiated by Franklin Delano Roosevelt and instigated by his counselor Henry Morgentau—held an international conference in Evian, Les Bain France, which took place during the last week of July 1938.

Although many nations were invited, only 32 countries sent representatives. After four days of discussion and presentations by the Joint, or Jewish Agency, and by Hias, formerly Hicem, and by a delegate of the American president, only two countries offered concretely to receive some Jewish refugees and grant with visas: The Dominican Republic and England. The first offered 400 hectares in arable land in Sosua, near Puerto Plata. The second offered arable land in British Guyana in South America. There was a restrictive clause; they admitted only farmers. Of course, Palestine was beyond expectation; the British feared Arab protest.

This happened in Evian in 1938. The delegates returned to their homes. I imagine that they felt a bit bothered by the horror stories they'd heard. But self-satisfied: after all, they'd gone to the conference. They'd fulfilled their obligation and that of their government.

Surely the League of Nations, with headquarters in Geneva, had a "High Commissioner for Refugees," who earned a decent salary. What did this man do after Evian Les Bains? Absolutely nothing.

Immense was the catastrophe that befell the German Jews in May, 1933. And the French with the annexation of Saar in 1936 after a plebiscite, on Austria in March of 1938. And the occupation of the Sudetenland in Czechoslovakia, in July, 1938. This was conceived primarily by the party of Konrad Henlein, local Nazis, and carried out by the German army and the S.S. under the pretext that the majority of the inhabitants in that region were German, *Volksdeutsche*. In reality they were Austrian, as those lands were part of the Austro-Hungarian Empire, ceded to Czechoslovakia in 1919 in the Treaty of Versailles.

In this terrible time there was still a way out for Jews, a possibility for escape: emigration.

To emigrate, a Jew had to bequeath all of his belongings, if he had any. Which is to say, the deed to his house and all its contents; his business with all goods in stock; his shop; his country house…all for the German Reich. The Jew could take only a suitcase with a maximum weight of 30 kilos and ten German marks in his bag, and the clothes on his back. Nothing more. The Germans wanted the Jews to emigrate only if they found a place where they would be accepted.

Of course, the problem remained: who wanted the Jews? In the beginning, when German and Austrian Jews were able to leave, many went to the United States. Others to England and Palestine. Many intellectuals immigrated to Switzerland, where they were accepted because it was a German-speaking country. Others went to Czechoslovakia and France, considered a country that espoused freedom of expression and "liberty, equality, and fraternity."

Others who were braver traveled to Australia, New Zealand, and Shanghai. Some to Argentina, Uruguay, and Chile. When Austria was annexed and Czechoslovakia was invaded, a new crop of German-Jewish immigrants found themselves under the umbrella of the Reich.

Of course, the prospect of emigrating had a human dimension. For many, it was not easy to leave everything behind in one stroke, after earning a fortune through hard work and living amongst gentile neighbors in some cases for the last 700 or 800 years.

"This ignorant corporal is not capable of governing this great nation," said the Jews. *Dass Waere Ganz Unglaubich,* it was inconceivable, they concluded. Some held out remote hope for a miracle.

German-Jewish families, Austrians, and Czechs had lived in the same place in the same city for countless generations. Since the emancipation (1820-48) they had served in the army with great zeal and patriotism. Some had lucrative careers as judges, magistrates, university professors, and notaries. Others became researchers and scientists: Adolf Von Bayer (Nobel Prize 1905), Paul Ehrlich (Nobel Prize 1908), Otto Wallach (Nobel Prize 1910), Alfred Fried (Nobel Prize 1911), Robert Barany (Nobel Prize 1914), Fritz Haber (Nobel Prize 1918), Albert Einstein (Nobel Prize 1921), Gustav Herz (Nobel Prize 1925), Otto Meyerhof

(Nobel Prize 1931), and Otto Loewi (Nobel Prize 1936). An impressive list.

Many Viennese Jews were more Viennese than they were Jewish. The same was true in Berlin, Prague, and many other German cities, thanks to the intimate relationship between creators of culture and public reception, especially in Germany and Austria. In reality the "intellectual climate" in which they lived and developed until Hitler's rise to power in 1933, had created a thirst for culture amongst the German populace.

Dicha Stimmung was brilliantly described by Stefan Zweig, a world-renowned Austrian-Jewish writer. He wrote from exile in Brazil: "It's nearly impossible to measure the contributions of the Jewish bourgeoisie to Viennese culture, nine-tenths of what the world celebrates as 'Viennese culture' of the nineteenth century. It's nothing more than a culture stimulated, nurtured, and in some cases created by the Viennese Jewry. There was no better place than Vienna to be and feel 'European.'"

As in Vienna, there was a clamoring for visas in the areas with a strong Jewish presence within the annexed territories of the Sudetenland, now in the control of the "Great Reich."

Various Jewish organizations tried to help the desperate "candidates" wanting to emigrate. First off, the central organizations, or *Kultusgemeinde* of Berlin, Vienna and Prague. HIAS (Hebrew Immigration and Sheltering Society) and the Joint Distribution Committee began compiling lists of applicants. The destination was not important in order to receive a visa. Once the visas were obtained, these aforementioned organizations sold them some currencies. In the event of a lack of funds, they helped them to obtain visas for transit through the countries they needed to pass through in order to take the boat to their final destination.

The delegations of HIAS in Milan, Zurich, and Marseilles also aided in the transfer of immigrants. They even got them support or temporary shelter for the night.

A small army of Jewish men and women dedicated themselves to helping these immigrants, and they were generally volunteers, without any form of monetary retribution. As a result of the annexation of the Sudetenland and the invasion of Czechoslovakia, the number of immigrants drastically increased.

In Karlsbad, Karlovy Vary, Marienbad Marianskelazne, Reichsberg, Gablonz, as well asin Eger and Tachow, Jewish communities had existed since time immemorial. Together with Prague they formed a zone of German culture, in which the Jews distinguished themselves by making themselves at home. This culture produced Franz Kafka, Egon Erwin Kish, Franz Werfel and Max Brod, writers of worldwide fame.

Karlsbad—the center of the Sudetenland—in addition to hosting a spa, highly celebrated for the quality of its curative waters, was the seat of a populous Jewish community. Here, two Zionist conferences were carried out, in 1921 and 1923. The majority of physicians from Karlsbad, as well as Marienbad—with patients coming from all around Europe—were Jewish.

In the *"Sportsheim"* youth hostel in Keilberg, there were organized conventions for Zionist youth during the 1930's, attended by important delegates from Austria and Germany, and orators such as Chaim Weitzman, Usishkin, Sokolof, and Vladimir Zabotinsky.

Prague, "City of Golden Spires", at the shore of the Vltava River—*Moldau* in German—had a vibrant Jewish community of 45,000. The Jewish presence in Prague dates from the year 1000 A.D. and, in contrast to Vienna, its presence was protected by the Dukes of Bohemia. In the Jewish neighborhood, or *Maizelova*, there still exists the Altneushul synagogue, constructed in 1274, and the adjacent Jewish cemetery, from the same era. There are also other synagogues and community buildings, like that of the Chevra Kadisha. In Pariskova, you can still find apartment buildings in the Art Nouveau style of the 1920s, once occupied by wealthy Jewish families.

Prague was the city in which rabbis "reigned," the likes of Avigdor Kara (15th century), great Hebrew religious poet, and Rav Chaim Loew, renowned cabalist and the creator of the *Golem*, the earthen homunculus (16th century).

Those expelled by the Nazis of Konrad Henlein following the decree of cleaning, or *reinigung*, the Sudetenland, fled mostly to Prague. After, of course, having surrendered their belongings to the Germans.

Suddenly, twenty thousand refugees found themselves in Prague. The list of candidates for emigration eventually grew to 36,000 names.

The defeated Europeans, deprived of their elemental rights day and night, were thrown from their places of origin and forced to seek asylum that no one wanted to provide.

"The League of Nations," "The Congress of Labor," "The Commission for Human Rights." All were incapable of opposing the Germans, or of enforcing the infrastructure that 20th century man had constructed and sustained between the two wars.

The world clung to peace and saw nothing else: they were blind. They saw nothing beyond Neville Chamberlain's travels to Munich. Nonetheless, in September 1939, World War II began with the invasion of Poland, and no one was prepared, save for the Germans.

In Hamburg, a boat from the Hamburg-Amerika Line was chartered, owned by Ballin (a Jew himself), with 945 German-Jewish passengers on board who, having met the proper requirements, set out with round-trip tickets, just in case.

They had visas from the Cuban government, which cost five hundred US dollars, paid to the Cuban consul in Hamburg. The consul had made a good deal, and the nine hundred forty-five passengers thought the same…

The ship captain was of the old school, a decent man; he'd worked twenty years for Ballin. The Gestapo had infiltrated his crew, which was standard for that time. All of the first-class passengers belonged to the upper echelons of German-Jewish society.

The ship set sail and arrived seven days later in Havana. In the port, the passengers were approached by Cuban immigration officers, as was customary. What was not customary was the receipt of a "bribe" from the German ambassador in Cuba, the declaration that the visas expedited by the consulate in Hamburg were invalid. The ship remained anchored in the pier for four days.

To no avail were the protests of the Jewish community in Havana, who assured the Cuban government they'd be financially responsible for the refugees to avoid any expense charged to the Cubans.

Nothing was achieved by an envoy from the North American Jewish Committee, or JOINT, who asked the Cuban authorities to let them disembark while the United States could process their visas.

The Jewish community in Havana, and various North American Jews who had settled in Cuba and had great connections, appealed directly to the President of Cuba, with no success. The boat, which was called "The Saint Louis," was forced to leave the port and sail towards the northwest, along the coast of Florida. The good captain felt compassion for these poor deceived passengers. He knew that if his human cargo was not accepted at any U.S. port, he would have to return to Hamburg. Once they returned to Germany, they would suffer the same fate of those who remained in the hell created by Hitler.

The envoy from the Jewish World Congress, who had arrived in Havana days before, returned immediately to Washington and from there established radio contact with the ship. This Jewish-American man moved heaven, earth, and sea to reach someone with influence; he pressured the department of immigration. The demand came at the hands of Bernard Baruch, Secretary of Treasury and Henry Morgenthau, a Jew who was very influential in the government of President Franklin Delano Roosevelt.

No one could or would do anything: "The quota for German Jews has already been filled," everyone said. The immigrants lacked affidavits or certification, a sort of bond or guarantee that the immigrant would not be a charge of the state.

The ship captain intentionally skirted slowly northward, to give the North American authorities time to react. But it was not to be. After four long days of navigating, the boat was forced to head eastwards in the direction of Germany. The passengers were desperate and ready to riot. There were two suicides on board.

This was how things were in 1939. It was not good to be a refugee with a German passport but without a valid visa. Although these refugees were "first class" and had paid for their tickets in cash, there was a catch: they were Jews. No country wanted Jews!

I liked being in Brussels. I enjoyed this change of pace. I was free from all the methodical regulations to which my mother had subjected me. Things were happening normally, and I liked that. In the mornings, my bath was cursory, as there was no running water or bathroom. We had to bring water from the kitchen, and I washed myself in a *lavoir* as best I could. On Friday afternoons, "Buci"—which is what I called Adolf Lanksner, in place of "Baci" who was my uncle in Hungary—and I would go to the public baths. This was marvelous. High-pressure showers where you could spend as much time as you liked, followed by a steam room, where you couldn't see a thing, and after that the showers again. We were given plush, clean towels to dry ourselves. I'd never experienced anything like this in Vienna.

The food was also completely different from my typical diet in Vienna. I no longer drank the obligatory glass of Ovaltine, a type of cocoa with vitamins and iron, which I'd been forced to drink each day, in the morning and again at night. Here for breakfast we drank coffee with milk, and at midday we ate fresh baguette, vegetable soup and sometimes meat with paprika. At night it was always something different: sausages, salami, sliced tongue, or pastrami. Adolf Lanksner's brother Ignatz was a butcher and he provided us with meat. With this nourishment, I began developing. From a chubby, weak child who'd arrived from Vienna, fortified by my mother with all kinds of vitamins and iron, emerged a strong, even muscular, young man. I thinned out quite a bit through my training with Buci.

On the same floor to the rear of us lived a Greek-Jewish family from Salonika, the Renous.

I made friends with Maurice, the eldest of their three sons, two years older than I. He brought me to school, and from there we discovered the city. I had absolute freedom, never having to ask permission to leave the house to play. I had no curfew, which was unheard of in Vienna, and I loved this aspect of my new life.

Maurice was my first friend in Brussels. He taught me my first French words. He was also my protector. In school, if someone messed with me, they had to deal with him, my *Shomer*, my bodyguard.

The school was a French municipal school, close to the Rue des Vierges, on the Rue des Six Jetons. In Belgium, two languages were spoken: French, spoken in the Valonas provinces adjacent to France, and Flemish, similar to Dutch, in the northern provinces. This linguistic phenomenon goes back to the time of the Hapsburgs, the House of Austria. After gaining independence from the Spanish, the Dutch chose a prince from the Belgian House of Orange, of Celtic origin. They separated from the Low Countries, joined forces with the Walloons, and formed a new country: Belgium. This happened after the defeat of Napoleon at Waterloo (1815). The Belgians appointed king a prince from the German house Coburg. He governed under the name Leopold I (1830). The country had two populations and two official languages. Thus, in Brussels, the capital, there were French schools, and in other schools Flemish was the language of instruction.

I learned French very rapidly. With Maurice's help, I was able to pass my first year in school. I was in third grade, but it was my first year on Belgian soil.

I maintained weekly correspondence with my mother. She proudly took note of my advancements in school, and she encouraged me. She wrote to me with news from Vienna, news of my grandmother Caroline. Each letter reported news increasingly sadder: new restrictions against the Jews, and a dwindling Jewish population. Of course, the letters indicated Sara Grete Katz as the sender. The Germans mandated that all Jews remaining within the Reich add a prefix to their names: Sara for the women, Israel for the men. This decree also specified that newborns—if anyone had the nerve to procreate—had to be registered as Itzig, Isrolik, or Moishe. New Testament names were reserved only for Aryans.

I received letters from my father, too. They were long, sometimes five or six pages. He inquired about my progress in school, asked about my life with the Lanksners—he was happy when I told him they kept a Kosher home—and he made sure that every Friday after the baths Buci and I went to Temple. He hoped that we continued observing all of the Jewish holidays. Finally, he would ask about my health. Every letter contained a Jewish story, usually a classic, always with a moral. For example, the commandment: *"Kabed avicha v'et Imecha."* Honor your father and mother. Each letter was accompanied by a story written in pleasant prose, easy for a nine year old to understand.

La Rue des Vierges was like many streets in Brussels, an amalgam of stores, some specializing in stoves. In Europe at that time, very few buildings had central heating, and those apartment buildings that did were occupied by the wealthy. The rest of the population—which was the majority of people—had stoves in their homes. Every stove was fueled by burning coal, and produced a rich warmth. They were made of polished metal and ceramic tiles in many colors and thus served as decorative objects for the home. The stores on La Rue des Vierges were dedicated to the sale of these stoves. People from all over the city, the provinces, as well as from neighboring countries, came to our street to shop. Nowhere else was there a better selection.

There was also a pub where they served beer. An Italian shoe store, where leather goods were manufactured and repaired—as far as I remember, the owner was the only self-proclaimed Fascist I knew. There was a large portrait of Mussolini hanging in his workshop. A furrier, Rosenzweig, who had a beautiful daughter, Myriam, like Jessica, daughter of Shylok, without a doubt the most beautiful girl in the neighborhood.

One could also find a grocery store, which for me held a specific charm: there was an automated machine that dispensed chocolate bars, *"Cote d'or,"* that operated twenty-four hours a day. I was, doubtless, a steadfast devotee of this marvel of modern technology. There was another, more luxurious pub, with very comfortable padded seating for the regulars, who would be there for hours.

As the reader might imagine, every other store on both sides of those two blocks specialized in stoves, and they had names such as: Vander Brugge, Moelemans, Thielemans, etc.

Practically every day I played ball with other boys on the block. We also played at "gangs": some fought against others, and the losers were made prisoner. I played on the building stairs with Maurice and his two brothers, as well as on the *greniers*, or thatched roofs, and in the cellars where coal was stored. Adolf Lanksner stored *smetene*, or sour cream, eggs, salami, and seasoned calf tongue in the cellar. There were no refrigerators back then.

Maurice was a born leader. While we boys played, the girls would sit watching and laughing...

Yosl Gorshtein also lived on our street, a very erudite and religious Jew, a *Melamed* or teacher—with *tzizit*, fringe, for use in Jewish tradition—although he was not bearded, he taught *tanach*, Bible and Davenen classes, to the Jewish children who came to his house.

He helped prepare me for my Bar-Mitzvah when I turned eleven. But I never put those skills into practice: by the time I turned thirteen, there were no longer Jews in Brussels, all the synagogues were closed, so I never completed my Bar-Mitzvah.

Every day I visited the Renous at their house. The ambiance fascinated me, beginning with the exotic aroma of the Sephardic cuisine. There, I tried lamb, spinach pies, tomatoes filled with rice and pine nuts, stuffed squash, grape leaves, and many other dishes that were new to me. They treated me like a prince. Mrs. Renous spoke to me only in Ladino, though I understood only half of what she said. Mr. Renous was a cabinet maker, and he left the house before dawn and returned late at night. They lived a life full of hardship, arriving in Belgium in 1930, having fled the misery that prevailed in Greece. In 1939, there was a substantial Sephardic community in Belgium, split between Brussels and Antwerp. There were many non-Jewish Greeks who worked in the coalmines in Charleroi. Maurice took me to the synagogue and to the Sepharadic Community offices.

One day Maurice's brothers asked their mother; *"Qui est Hans? Hans? C'est un Vous-Vous."* That was how the Sephardic nicknamed the Ashkenazi. The origin of this name is, I suppose, derogatory, and comes from the way in which Polish Jews asked each other when they didn't understand something: *"Vus?"* which is Yiddish for "What?!"

My first school year flew by. I passed all my subjects. I was already registered for the following year, set to enter the fourth grade.

In September of 1939, Great Britain and France declared war on Germany. Italy allied with the Germans, committing one of the gravest errors in their country's history. Suffice to say Mussolini suffered from megalomania, believing himself a reincarnation of the Roman Caesars.

At the beginning, the war on land was a stalemate. The German army had mobilized and was positioned along the borders of France, Belgium, and Holland. But they didn't attack. There was minimal shooting with small weapons, *drole le guerre*, which is to say "grotesque war."

The French began hurriedly mobilizing their army. The High Command and the government of the Third French Republic had kept abreast of the German mobilization, the construction of the Siegfried line, the efficiency and power of the *messerschmidt* planes and the *stucka*. Yet they'd done nothing to prepare themselves.

How is it possible for a government—responsible for the security and defense of its people—to engage only in childish politics, unveiling the supposed scandals of its ministers, when the security of the nation is in jeopardy? This was the tenor of the government of León Blum, Jewish socialist, who cut off arms support to the Spanish Republicans, cloaking itself in the sacred mantle of neutrality. Thus, the French entrenched themselves behind the Maginot line.

I imagine this scene, in the headquarters of Campeignes. The staff—two marshals and seven generals—are engaged in a discussion. One asks: "How is it possible that the German army has annihilated the well-trained Polish army in only eighteen days?"

The other, I imagine, would answer that the Polish defeat made perfect sense, because the famous cavalry of Marshal Pilzudsky was confronted with armored German tanks in the Radom Plain with only kepi—no helmets—and bandoliers on the tips of their spears, very much in the Polish romantic style. They were utterly unprepared for a war against the highly-mechanized German army.

The horses decimated by the tanks suffered more than the Polish soldiers that survived. Hitler had to suffer the consequences of invading Poland. The Allies declared war. It seems he had calculated everything on his chessboard. He considered his agreement with the Soviet Union to share Poland a success. Those bloodthirsty dictators who don't give any regard to the wellbeing of their people, making pacts over differing ideologies, jeering at idealists. But above all, not preparing for war, nor being able to defend their people.

The German invasion of Poland was a terrible omen for the Jewish community throughout Europe. In Poland alone, there were three and a half million Jews, not counting those who lived in Lithuania, Latvia, and Estonia.

Many fled to save themselves, crossing rivers into Soviet-occupied territory. The majority of the community, whose ancestors were invited to the Rhine and Alsace by the nobility during the year 900 and massacred in the Crusades, these people were trapped. Warsaw had 350,000 Jews, thirty percent of the city population.

The Germans established ghettos in Lodz, a textile hub, where Jews were a majority. Likewise in Krakow, a flourishing Jewish community, a hotbed of great scholarship. In Chelm, a mostly Jewish city, in Radom, Kielce, Bytom, Kattowitz, Kalish, and so many others. Poland, once populated by a huge number of Jews, now all at the mercy of the Germans.

It was 1939, and the Third Reich's victories ocurred one after another. Eichmann was increasingly engaged in his work to annihilate the Jews.

In Brussels, we heard what was happening in the world on the radio. The situation was tense. We feared that the conflict would eventually reach Belgium. The army began preparing itself. King Leopold III made frequent public appearances, dressed in military uniform. Belgium, Holland, and Luxembourg allied as a common army under allied command. Air raid shelters were built, and mandatory practice drills were decreed, in which we all had to participate.

Gas masks were doled out. The streets were filled with propaganda inviting soldiers to enlist in the army.

Buci, a wholesaler specializing in linens, traveled to the interior of the country, selling underwear, socks, stockings, and blankets he bought directly from the factories and distributed to specialty stores nationwide.

Yolanka tended to her house and to me, her adopted son. During the afternoons, she went for coffee with her lady friends with whom she spoke only Hungarian. In Brussels, like Vienna, going out for coffee was a daily ritual. There, they'd share the latest gossip and discuss the situation abroad.

Tension reigned at school, and we feared the worst, that something was going to happen, and quickly. However, months passed, and by December of 1939, nothing had happened.

Daily life had become markedly different. In stores, German goods grew scarce. Only weapons were being produced. People stopped going on vacations to the ocean, but rather preferred to stay at home. *If anything were to happen*, they'd say. Of course, no one traveled abroad, unless it was to emigrate. Yolanka had heard in the café that many Jewish families in Antwerp had left for the United States. Antwerp had a larger Jewish population than the capital city. In 1939 there were 85,000 Jews in all of Belgium. At that time, Antwerp was the European center of diamond cutting. There were hundreds of workshops, large and small, which employed from five to sixty workers, all of them Jewish. Antwerp supplied cut diamonds to jewelers around the world. The stones arrived in their natural state, called *brut*, from places like South Africa, Sierra Leone, the Gold Coast, via London, where they met with the syndicate responsible for regulating price distribution of these precious stones.

The Jewish community in Antwerp was very religious. No one walked in the Pelikanstraat on Fridays after dusk. Shop workers wore *yarmulke* and *Talit Katan*.

The shadow of the Nazi-Fascists spanned from the frigid Arctic to the warm Mediterranean beaches, from the Cantabrian Ocean to the Ural Mountains. Hitler had enthusiastic "henchmen" who willingly offered their services, especially in regard to hunting Jews.

The first was Benito Mussolini in Italy, although I must say he did not take any real action against the Italian Jews, until the Salo Repulic formed after the surrender of the Italian Army to the allies led by Badoglio in 1943.

Then there was Francisco Franco in Spain, who respected the Jews, and even recognized the Spanish citizenship of descendants of the Sephardic living in occupied countries between 1941 and1944. Many lives were saved because of this.

Nicolas Horty protected the 850,000 Jews who lived in Hungary until the arrival of Eichmann in 1944, who took it upon himself to deport them to Auschwitz, just before the end of the war.

Swedish diplomat Wallenberg dedicated his life—which he lost at the hands of the Russians—to the superhuman effort of saving many Jews in Budapest. As did Schindler, a Sudeten German, with "his" twelve hundred Jews, in 1944. Honest people, non- Jews, who saved. They are honored at Yad Vashem in Jerusalem.

The weakness of European democracies began with the demise of the Spanish Republic in 1936. Nothing was done even when the Germans took the Saar territory that same year. Not during the Austrian Anschluss in 1938, nor afterwards with the annexation of the Sudetenland, given to the Czechoslovakian Republic in the Treaty of Versailles.

The invasion of Poland in September 1939 was a well-planned operation, like every campaign the Germans undertook. It was organized by the High Command, every detail perfectly mapped out in the headquarters of Wolfs Schanke. It's interesting to note the respect and devotion Hitler's generals had for him. This breed of soldiers, who just a few years before had despised their leader Hidenburg.

There was a reawakening of the Teutonic spirit, the Prussian military tradition, the notion that with Hitler at the helm it would be possible to execute the old dreams of Bismark: *Deutschland Ueber Alles.* Conquering Europe, and then the world, was a possibility. The reimagining of dreams of glory and conquest that had been destroyed by the German defeat in World War I, by the Treaty of Versailles (1919). The Prussian military caste was reborn like a phoenix from its ashes. This is how their intimate alliance with the Fuhrer was born and lasted.

Hitler was not as terrible as he was portrayed. As it's the human condition to do such things, everyone conformed to the Prussian way, even going so far as to raise their right arms to salute the Fuhrer. A metamorphosis occurred in these generals, many of whom took on surnames beginning with "Von," a distinction extremely revered by the German military class.

A few days before the invasion, known only by its code "Barbarossa," Hitler assembled his military chiefs at his headquarters in Obersalzberg and gave them their final instructions. "I have given orders to my S.S. formations with specific instructions to *liquidate* and *annihilate* without regard for Jewish men, women, and children, nor the detestable Poles. I wish to inspire in you this attitude. Only in this way can we obtain *lebensraum*, living space." This occurred on August 22, 1939, in Obersalzberg.

The invasion of Poland was kicked off by air raids, designed to cause mass panic. This strategy culminated in the bombing of Warsaw. Meanwhile, the German officers pored over detailed maps of Polish cities to coordinate an invasion. They were not, by any means, to advance beyond the line dividing Poland from the territories that would be invaded by Stalin.

It was ordered that the Sonderabteilung occupy themselves specifically with exterminating the Jews with the help of the Polish populace as soon as hostilities had ceased. It was hoped the Germans could obtain Polish cooperation.

First came identifying who was a Jew and who was not, so that Jews could be corralled in the *Marktplatz* and finished off with machine guns. Beforehand, a young, strong group of Jews was selected, and were responsible for burning the bodies after the massacre had been executed.

The actions of the Sonderabteilung began with the small villages. These *shtetlach* contained more than half of the Jewish population. Afterwards, they continued on to mid-sized cities, where they forced the Jews to abandon their homes and belongings, and walk to the nearest big city. Thanks to these tactics, the Germans concentrated the Jewish masses in Warsaw and other large Polish cities, where they established ghettos so as to have complete control over the Jewish population. The harsh and inhumane conditions in these ghettos weakened the Jews with malnutrition and diseases like typhoid and diphtheria. Epidemics were unrelenting and rampant, killing many Jews. Meanwhile, the Germans devised new and more sophisticated extermination techniques, later used in the Concentration camps.

In the *shtetlach* the Sonderabteilung unleashed their extreme hatred for the Jews.

They gathered the men in the village synagogue and closed the doors. They set fire to the walls after dousing them with gasoline. Most of the synagogues in these *shtetlach* were made of wood, and so they burned quickly. The parishioners burned within the ignited synagogues. They forced the men to don their *Taleism* and assassinated them as they said their prayers. Why? First and foremost, for the delight of the Polish public and the Sonderabteilung. The Jews were even convinced of the benefits the ghettos offered, hoping they would find some sense of security, believing those already installed there would be allowed to live.

Ghettos appeared in Warsaw, Lodz, Chenstochowa, Chelmno, Krakow, Radom, Zamosc, Belzec, and Reszow, and after the occupation of eastern Poland in June of 1941, in Lublin, Bialystok, Lvov, Kovno, Vilno, and Grodno.

In each ghetto a *Judenrat* was elected, comprised of representatives of the political parties in each community—either Bund, Communists, or Zionists, like Ha-shomer Ha-tzair, Poale-H Zion, Gordonia, and Betar. There was also a Jewish uniformed police in charge of maintaining order. It was a charade, because the Jews did not have any real power, only the Germans did.

Each ghetto was self-sufficient. But at the same time, paradoxically, they were restricted from access to the rest of the world. They created workshops for textiles, metal sheets, and goldsmithing, creating products that could be sold outside the ghetto and exchanged for basic necessities, like flour, sugar, and tea.

The German soldiers created airtight enforcement ensuring that the Poles could not enter, and the Jews could not leave.

German guards carrying machine guns were stationed at strategic points. At night, in order to prevent Jews from escaping, powerful, moving headlights illuminated walls and doors. Groups of Jewish children—who looked Polish— were smuggled to attempt to make contact with the Polish Resistance, who provided them with weapons for self-defense, or for an uprising. But they never succeeded. No weapons for the Jews, said the Armiya Krayova.

These ghettos housed a cross section of ex-deputies from the *Sejm*, or Polish parliament, as well as judges, those with lifelong military careers, as well as ex-Polish government officials influential in the outside world, many of whom had no other possibility of surviving.

The request for arms on the part of the Jews fell largely on deaf ears. Jews were all but decimated. Why waste weapons to support a cause that's already lost?

From the ghettos, information about the increasing danger and extermination of Polish Jews, was sent to the exiled Polish government, as well as to Jewish organizations based in London, Palestine, and the United States. Emanuel Ringelbum, former Jewish deputy in the *Sejm*, escaped to London. From there, he reported these facts to the Polish ministers in exile, among whom were General Anders, leader of the famous Polish Legion. No one wanted to believe him. They simply could not believe that Poland was being "cleaned" of its Jews. To eliminate a population of three and a half million people? How would one be able to do such a thing? It would be almost impossible, taking into account the logistics and means necessary to exterminate so many people en masse. Besides, the Polish population surely opposed it.

Ringelblum spoke with Chaim Weitzmann, future president of Israel, and with David Ben Gurion, whom he met casually in London. He met with members of the Jewish Agency. The mood was somber. The Jewish Agency, with contacts and envoys in Poland, had already received disastrous reports of the situation. But when it came down to it, everyone was reluctant to fully grasp the true dimensions of the genocide. They simply could not believe it could happen. It seemed like a miracle that anyone could get out of the Warswaw ghetto.

Later on, in 1943, Samuel Zygelboim, representative of Bund in the government in exile, committed suicide in London in protest of the Polish National Council's ambivalence and paralysis.

The distinguished Jewish intellectuals who died in the ghettos, to name a few: Dr. Janusz Korczak, nationally renowned pedagogue Professor Mayer Balaban, historian Dr. Ludwik Hirczfeld, a neurologist with international recognition. Writers like Bruno Schultz, León Berenson, and Izcjac Katzenelson. Painters Maurycy Trebacz, Jaim Tabakman, Marek Holtzer and many other artists and intellectuals of inestimable value to the Jewish world.

When I start to think about this genocide, which by 1945 had taken the lives of a staggering six million people, a million and a half of whom were children—whom the world now put into doubt —the following question comes to mind: How many of these children, lives ended before they had even begun, would, as adults, have become intellectuals, perhaps even going on to receive Nobel Prizes? A grave and irreversible loss for all of humanity.

I employ the generic Niemetzky, Tedeschi, Nemetek, Allemands, Daitsche, etc. when referring to the Germans. I don't call them Nazis or Nazi-Fascists, as many do.
This would condemn the entire German nation, mnot to mention those born in the

generations following the war. Germany is very different now. No other European nation publishes as much or produces as many television shows as Germany, where parents explain to their children their involvement in the events of the period between 1933 and 1945.

However, my first post-war trip to Germany in 1958 made me critical of the fact that this period of history was not sufficiently addressed with school-age children. Now Holocaust studies are mandatory in all high schools in Germany.

Most everyone knew perfectly well what was happening with the Jews, although many now deny they did: the trains to extermination camps were operated by civil conductors. The crematoriums were produced by family-owned companies. Perhaps the factory workers ignored the thousands upon thousands of Zyklon gas cans they prepared—not just in one, but in many plants, owned by I.G. Farben (Bayer)—believing it was mere pesticide, rather than gas meant for exterminating human beings in concentration camps? How is it possible that the German civilization, once a beacon of light for the world, a paragon of scholarship and research, degraded itself so much during this period in history (1933-45)? How could a nation so cultured pervert itself in a "quarrel" of thugs, sully itself with the propaganda of Josef Goebbels?

In pre-Anschluss Vienna, during the 1920's, the Zionist organization Betar was born. Politically, the party leaned toward the right: they loathed the communists and the Zionist left. Betar members, mostly young people, wore uniforms and received military instruction on weekends.

Year after year, on the anniversary of Theodor Herzl's death, they organized a memorial in the Jewish cemetery, at the tomb of the founder of Zionism. Their leader was Vladimir Zabotinsky, native of Odessa. His second in command was Menachem Begin, who later became Prime Minister of Israel.

Upon reading certain Viennese Betar publications, I learned of Zabotinsky's tireless lobby for the Jewish emigration from Europe. He even came to beg the European Jews to abandon their cities—surely, they'd succumb—and relocate to Palestine. Zabotinsky was one of the few who could clearly foresee what was going to happen. Scarcely anyone listened, and those who did survived.

My life in Brussels continued without significant interruption. I was happy. Little by little, I learned French with the help of school and my friend Maurice. At the end of 1939, I was able to express myself and engage in simple conversation. Every day I grew to know the city better. In Brussels, you could travel by tram with a single ticket. Maurice explained everything. He was two years older than I, and already versed in some history; his explanations felt to me like a history class.

I went to Waterloo with Maurice, and learned what had happened there: the defeat of Napoleon, a man who failed to measure the extent of his power, unable to understand the enthusiasm he'd brought about in Europe, in the end disappointing followers like Ludwig Van Beethoven, who, realizing the true intentions of his consul, retracted his "Heroic" Symphony dedication.

Buci drove Yolanka and me to Bois de la Cambre, a beautiful forest, where we went camping. We also went to Foret de Soigne, another forest farther from the city, and more rustic.

I didn't have much contact with my family from Vienna who lived in Brussels at the time, though sometimes they'd invite me over to eat. My cousin Hilde, and her husband Richard Leder, their sons Herbert and Jack, as well as her mother, my aunt Zilly. They lived in Scharbeek. Sigi, Louis, and their mother, my aunt Julie. Heinrich Wolfthal, Uncle Tibbik, and his wife, my aunt Ana, all were able to emigrate.

The Leders were able to reach Brussels in May of 1938, after illegally crossing Aix-la-Chapelle, the border between Germany and Belgium. Sigi Stark who had been in Brussels since March, sent them a *Sheliach* who met them in the Cathedral of Cologne. From there, they traveled by car to a house three kilometers from the border, crossing through a forest, and some fields. First Herbert crossed, and the *Sheliach* posed him as his "nephew from Koln." Hilde and Richard Leder were smuggled in the shipping container of a truck. The three were reunited at a farm ten kilometers into Belgium. Sigi Stark was there to receive them.

It's well known that my cousin Hilde became pregnant shortly afterwards, in spite of the prevailing situation in Europe. *"Aus Dafke,"* in protest to what was happening, an expression of profound desire to continue living as usual. And so Jack was born in January 1939, a rare event among the immigrants, a valiant act on the part of my cousin Hilde.

In May 1940, Richard Leder was arrested for being "German" by the Belgian authorities. The "J" on his passport was useless, and like so many others he was deported to the Gurs internment camp in the French Pyrenees. In 1942, he attempted to escape to Spain with some other prisoners. He was arrested by the French Surete, who handed him over to the Germans in October of 1942. From Drancy he was sent to Auschwitz in convoy number 42, November 6 of that same year. I found this information in "Memorial to the Jews Deported from France" by Serge Klarsfeld in Paris in 1946.

Aunt Zilly arrived in Brussels later, also illegally and with the help of a *Sheliach*. She had been married in Vienna in August 1899, to Samuel Isaac Biber, also from Brody. Samuel Biber started a tannery in Vienna, which many years later became the most important in the country.

It's interesting that at that time a marriage certificate issued by the Viennese Jewish community was accepted by the country's authorities. So apparently there was no *ketubah* issued by the rabbinate for the marriage of Aunt Zilly with Mr. Biber. The pair had four children: Louis, Ernest, Hilde and Else. Samuel Biber died of natural causes in Vienna in 1934.

Hilde married Richard Leder in Vienna. Else married Max Fridman. She was arrested in March 1938, and spent eight months in Buchenwald. Once free, she was able to escape to England, and she arrived in Australia in 1941. Louis was already in Australia, but decided to return to England, where there was a branch of his family's tannery. This turned out to be an unfortunate decision; his ship, bound for Southampton, was hit by a German U-Boat. He died with the vast majority of the passengers.

Ernest married Marianne, a Viennese Jewish woman, who had immigrated to Australia. There, Jaqueline was born, who lives in Melbourne and is married to Russell Korn.

Max Friedman changed his name to Fraser upon enlisting in the army in 1940. He and Else had a daughter, Ruth, who also lives in Melbourne, married to Henry Green. They have three children: Susan, Jeffrey, and Janet.

Herbert, one of Hilde's sons, is married to Viva Sharp. They have three children: Debbie, married to Nathan Koppel, Julie, and Marylin. Jack, her other son, married Gilah Vanderhoek, from a very religious Dutch-Jewish family. They have two sons, Richard and Karin.

In Australia, Hilde and Else Biber, now deceased, formed what could be considered a tribe of twenty members. During my visit there in 1990, I stayed with them, the descendents of Uncle Samuel and Aunt Zilly Biber.

It was not easy for Aunt Anna, my father's sister, to join her husband, my uncle Tibbik, in Belgium. Two times she tried to cross the border, and was detained. Fortunately, she was not sent to a concentration camp, and after two months of waiting, she was finally able to arrive on the Belgian side, where a *Sheliach* awaited her. Once she was settled in Brussels, she invited me over for lunch. She had a luxurious home. She was the youngest of the five Katz children, and the most modern and sophisticated. I remember how she set the table: starched white tablecloth, always a floral centerpiece, good porcelain crockery, silverware on each side of the plates, large white napkins, a glass for water…she had a Belgian servant to serve us food. She loved me very much, and was always correcting me. "For your own good," she would say.

My cousin Sigi was always working. Occasionally he would invite me to a restaurant or out for coffee. His mother was with him, my aunt Julie, and his brother Louis, who was a violinist.

I spent most of my time in school and at home with the Lanksners, as well as visiting family in Brussels. So I met Ignatz Lanksner, who was a kosher butcher. He showed me around his facilities: four giant refrigerated rooms where carcasses of game animals, calves, and a number of chickens hung. In the store, salamis, smoked meats, pastrami, and corned beef hung in refrigerated counters on every side. His wife was a fat woman, and taller than he was. He had two beautiful sisters, one called Zilly and the other Ester. All of them came from Nagyvarad like Buci. Ignatz had two sons and a daughter.

Everything seemed quiet in Belgium, a country declared as neutral by its government. On the other hand, we were aware of the progress of the war through the radio.

The skies were clear. It was a summer like no other. But at about six in the morning on May 10, 1940, we were awakened by an intense humming, as though planes were flying at a very low altitude over the roofs of Brussels.

Without officially declaring war, Germany—with a front of 350 kilometers—simultaneously invaded Holland, Luxembourg, Belgium, and France with mechanized troops and tanks. Around midday, we heard explosions. Our only airport in Zaventem had been bombed, destroying the small Belgian air force on the ground. This was *blitzkrieg*, the lightning war. King Leopold III took the reigns of the army. The Belgians were well-armed, but facing the German army was too much of a challenge.

On May 12, the Germans were steadily advancing, slowed in part by the Belgian soldiers' heroic defense. Buci decided we would travel to France by train. We thought the Germans wouldn't make it all the way there. France was defended by the Maginot Line by a huge army, who had defeated the Germans during World War I. This seemed logical to us. Thousands of families—Jews and non-Jews alike—thought the same, and set out for France. *Lech, Lecha.*

I packed a few things in the suitcase I'd brought from Vienna. So did the Lanksners. Together, we walked towards the train station. Buci left his car in a garage. There were no taxis: the whole world, it seems, had enlisted in the military. Nor were there trams: a bomb had struck the transformers in the central transit hub. Tremendous disorder prevailed in the avenue leading to the Gare du Nord.

Groups of people with suitcases moved in every direction. Some traveled on wagons pulled by one or two horses. These wagons—*charettes*—had two or four wheels, depending. There were also horseless wagons pushed by the travelers. Many wandered blankly, having not yet decided where to go.

We arrived at the station, sweating. We were waiting for the Herckovicz, a couple, and the Jellineks,—friends of the Lanksners. These last two came with a fourteen-year old daughter. They had already bought tickets to Paris. We're going to Paris! Dad was there! I was ecstatic at the thought of such a fantastic reunion.

The train was to leave in a half hour. We went to the platform and boarded the train. We sat and settled in with our belongings. We were eight people settled in second-class seats. Everything seemed in order: the starting signal was made with a long whistle; the train began moving, slowly at first, but gaining velocity little by little.

The first stop was Charleroi, a coal mining town, with a large concentration of foreign workers: Turks, Greeks, Portuguese, Italians, and Yugoslavians. Among them, many political refugees of different ideologies, who'd fought alongside the Spanish Republic and could no longer return to their countries of origin, many of them communists of the International Brigades, who fought alongside the Republicans.

From Charleroi we would go to Valenciannes and from there to Cambray. Later on, to Campiegne, Creil, Saint Denis, and Paris, according to the map I consulted with Buci. I could already see myself hugging and kissing my father. This unexpected trip had me excited and happy.

The posters at the station indicated that we were in Charleroi. The train stopped, and almost no one got off. Nor was anyone allowed to board, as the train was already full. Many people were waiting for the train. Armed gendarmes wearing dark blue steel helmets—*la Gendarmie*—served as a barrier preventing the passengers from advancing towards the wagons that were already full.

The train departed again and began gaining speed. This time I didn't hear the whistle, probably due to the disorder at the station.

We'd been traveling for six or seven minutes when I heard the sound of planes over us. They hovered over us at low altitude, dropping bombs. They were bombing the station, and so we were saved. The noise of the planes shook the train wagons. Suddenly, the train stopped. Buci grabbed me and hugged me. He opened the door of the compartment, and we were the first to descend. We fell into an open field. The planes returned; their engines could be heard. In the distance, about three hundred meters away, we saw the train station in flames. Yolanka appeared with our other companions, and we crawled beneath the wagon, onto the rails, ignoring the oil stains.

The aircrafts were above us once again, with their infernal noise. Machine-gun fire flew around us in staccato.

Luckily, we were well-protected. We soon learned what happened. A squadron of *Stucka* planes had bombed the Charleroi station, reducing it to ashes. From there, they returned to bomb our train, destroying the locomotive in one shot.

Without moving or speaking, we remained under the wagon for ten more minutes. The planes retreated. We came out one by one. We found other survivors. The train had ignited; the fire from the locomotive had spread to the wagons. We quickly took our belongings and walked about three hundred meters back to the station. In other wagons were lifeless bodies: the victims. Little by little other survivors began to emerge. We heard sobs and cries of anguish.

The train station ruins were still burning. There were ambulances from the Red Cross and others from the military. Upon arriving at the plaza next to the station, we searched for a bench where we could sit and rest. Fire trucks arrived. Others had already been here, trying to put out the fire.

Buci, who was already dark in complexion, was covered in soot. I was, too, probably. He took me by the hand and we went in search of a cart. Meanwhile, the others, having left the train, waited for us in the plaza.

It was the first time I'd seen him bareheaded. Buci was religious by nature, and never took off his hat, whether it was hot or cold.

His hat had surely fallen off during our jump from the train. But he didn't realize that it was missing; he was too busy with the matters at hand to notice. He walked upright and happy, holding me by the hand. Luckily, we soon fulfilled our responsibility.

We found a cart made of unpainted wood, with two big wheels, and which appeared to be very sturdy. Buci bartered with the owner. Finally, they agreed upon a price, Buci paid the man, and we took the cart with us. He lifted me at the waist and set me inside it. And so we went back at the plaza where everyone was waiting for us.

We loaded our luggage. The women carried packages. Buci, who had purchased a leather belt, put it on his shoulder and began to pull the wagon as if he were a horse.

We wanted to leave this place as soon as possible. The plaza was black with smoke; our eyes were watery and stung when we rubbed them. We searched for the main highway, Route Nationale, leading towards the French border, which was not too far.

Reaching the road, we stopped to rest. It was growing dark, and soon it would be nightfall. The men began to deliberate. We had to act quickly; the Germans could reach us in two days, and we were close to the French border. We decided to continue walking until Maugeuge, the nearest village. Our path lit by a full moon, we took to the road..."*Lech, lecha*..."

After two hours of walking, we were exhausted by the day's events and decided to ask around for a place to stay. We came upon the farm of a Walloon, a good man who gave us a night's lodging in his haystacks. Three groups of people had arrived before us and were already asleep. I fell asleep in the blink of an eye. The next morning, before six in the morning, Buci woke me up, already washed and shaven. The others were also ready. They let me sleep for fifteen more minutes. Our host, the Walloon peasant, gave us four liters of milk and bread for breakfast. When the winds of war blew and the dangers could affect us all, people reacted and helped each other.

We walked back towards the road, in the direction of France. This time Jellineck pulled the cart. There were many refugees like us, on the road, with a common goal.

Jellineck was a Polish Jew who lived in Anderlecht, the Jewish neighborhood in Brussels. He made waterproof winter coats for women. He was one of Buci's partners. Buci invested some money in his atelier, and helped sell the merchandise to his clients in the provinces. Jellineck arrived in Brussels in 1934, like many other Jews in search of a brighter future.

Herskovicz was a Hungarian Jew, a close friend of the Lanksners. They met in 1930, upon arriving in Brussels. Herskovicz manufactured leather goods: wallets, comb holders, keychains. Coming from a major capital city like Budapest, he had a sophisticated sensibility. He was not provincial like Buci.

We walked for about five hours without a single setback. The frontier was in sight. There were Belgian gendarmes who ordered us to get in line. There appeared to be many other refugees in front of us, but really there were three lines, one for cars, one for horse-drawn carriages, and a third for those on foot, and this was the longest of the three.

I was hungry, and I asked Buci when we were going to eat. "When we get to France," he told me. That was the end of our conversation.

We were nearing the customs crossing. On one side there was a large Belgian flag with yellow, red, and black stripes. On the other side, the French flag: blue, white, and red, in honor of the first people's revolution in Europe. The taking of the Bastille in 1789, a hopeful date later sullied by Napoleon. I had learned all of this from my friend Maurice.

We had no problems with the French border guards. Buci showed our papers and photo identification cards. At that time I had a *Laissez-Passer* from the Brussels municipality instead of a passport.

This document established the fact that the minor Hans Peter Katz, originally from Vienna, Germany—at that time there was no Austria—was born on May 19, 1930. Having been sent there by the International Red Cross, I was legally residing as a stateless individual in the *Royaume de Belgique*. This document was a mere sheet of paper, contemptuously dubbed in Yiddish as a *"visch," with a photo of me*.

Then the crossing gates were opened, and we passed through with our wagon. We were now in France, and everyone hugged each other, our faces lit up.

Little by little the human condition was unraveling: on one side of the border there was anguish. Crossing it revived us. These life experiences taught me the essentials of human behavior.

Buci and Jellineck went to exchange our money. The Belgian refugees who brought no French money were in for the surprise of a lifetime, as the French had no interest in receiving Belgian currency. "*C'est la Guerre.*" But Belgium would not disappear as an independent nation. In effect, this is what happened: after May 28, the Belgian army surrendered.

The Jews, however, were leading experts in the art of migration. They brought with them *grine lokshen*, or U.S. dollars they'd bought in Brussels. We had no problems whatsoever exchanging them for francs.

We are the chosen people. Chosen for what? Merciful G-d, for what? Deep inside myself, I sensed a great truth: the Jewish people were chosen to suffer the everlasting anguish of migration. "*Lech, lecha....*" We will have served for five thousand years, since Abraham Ovinu. Enough! We have died many deaths with your name on our lips, and when we cried "*Eli, Eli, Lama Azavtoni.*" We were thrown to the beasts in coliseums. When we were burned alive, our heads covered in hoods, we prayed "*Al Kidush Hashem,*" blessed be thy name. In Medieval times, when we were stretched on the racks, a rabbi wrote: *"Unezane Tokef."* When the Cossacks murdered us with their sabers, we repeated *"Shema Israel, Adonai Elohenu Adonai Echad."* Hear O, Israel, you are our lord, our one and only lord. Is none of this enough? *Gotenyu!* Enough! *Shoyn Genung!* Please choose another people to torture.

In Maubeuge we went to a restaurant with a terrace and tables on the sidewalk, all filled with refugees. I'd never been to a place like this, bustling with so many people, so many waiters. I enjoyed it very much. Buci ordered me a delicious, fresh, crispy *baguette au jambon*.

Once it was placed in front of me, I gaped at it. Ham? We can't eat that! Buci waved his hand, as he sometimes did, and said *"Allez, c'est la guerre."* If he said so, I could. I had all the faith in the world in him.

In Maubeuge we were sent to a school adapted for the influx of refugees. We entered an enormous room full of cots. We slept there. The next morning, Buci woke me up; I quickly dressed, and we took the highway towards Valenciennes.

Buci prayed every day when he woke up. He put on his *Talit* and his *Tefilim*, unlike us, his companions and me. I hadn't yet completed my Bar-Mitzvah, and the Jellinek and Herckovics were non-practicing. Buci was a tolerant Jew, and would never have thought to draw attention to his practices, but simply went about his business according to his beliefs, never imposing them upon anyone else.

The roads were full of refugees. This was the reality of France in 1940. Even military convoys of high priority had difficulty getting through. Dead horses lay on both sides of the road, their bellies bloated, probably due to lack of food. The poor things gave off a terrible stench that permeated the air.

We continued walking and before dawn we arrived in Valenciennes. Its tree-lined streets looked beautiful. There we saw a huge banner telling people where to go. We were led to a center for refugees, which had been a school before the war. I was struck by how well-organized everything was. Here, we ate what we'd bought on the road, and afterwards we went to sleep. Walking outdoors for so many hours had exhausted us.

Despite the adventures and daily experiences we had on the French roads, I couldn't stop thinking of my father and the moment we would meet again. How was I going to introduce him to the Lanskners? What would they say? What would I say? I hadn't seen him in two years. My mother had no idea I would soon meet with him. It would be a great surprise for all. Each step I took brought me closer to him.

It had been months since my mother had written me. She was unable to. Buci explained to me that Germany and France were at war, and there was no postal service. End of story!

We started for Denain, then to Cambrai. According to the map, we were moving in the direction of Paris.

I felt very safe next to Buci, leader of our group. He knew everything. I also knew that he loved me, that he would always do his best for me. But his kindness was, to me, what was most attractive about him. For me, he was an example of a just man. I felt so selfish next to him. Since I left home two years before, he had taken special care to protect and defend me. But through Buci, I learned that one could be strong without hurting one's neighbor.

We arrived in Denain after a lengthy journey, dead tired, our feet aching and blistered. Before I went to sleep I soaked my feet in a bucket of hot water, a huge relief.

In Denain news arrived that Brussels had been occupied by the invading German army. King Leopold III and his staff had surrendered to the Germans and were being held prisoner. At the king's command, the Belgian army surrendered: *Belgae Finis.* Now there was one more country occupied on what was now a bloody map of Europe.

The news depressed us. We had to move quickly, as the Germans were encroaching upon us day by day. At dawn we started out for Cambrai. The highway was even more crowded, and our advancement was slow. Abandoned cars sat on either side of the road. There was no gasoline at the pumps. Luxury cars probably costing thousands of francs were abandoned, left untouched, as they were of no use to anyone.

More dead horses. Cows abandoned by their owners and weakened with hunger. Those already dead gave off a dreadful stench.

Suddenly we heard aircraft engines. Two minutes later the *Messerschmidt* were hovering overhead, plunging toward us. And once again we heard the staccato of machine guns. Running, running as fast as we could to hide ourselves in the leaves of a cabbage field. The planes returned twice, and each time more people fell victim to the barrage. The appearance of the road was unspeakably bleak: wagons, hundreds of immobilized wagons without drivers, helpless bodies everywhere. Cries of pain, crying children running aimlessly, without any place to go, some having lost their parents…

There were no doctors, no hospitals, no medicine. The wounded lay bleeding on the asphalt with no one to help. The survivors were paralyzed with shock, not knowing what to do or where to begin.

After ten minutes, we got up, collected our cart and our belongings, and continued walking. But we couldn't go anywhere. Some uniformed soldiers—I think they were French deserters—were given the task of removing bodies and throwing them into the trenches at the sides of the street.

Why attack a cluster of weak, unarmed refugees, merely to topple our carts? Did we pose a danger for them? Were we a strategic target for the powerful German army? Perhaps Goering longed to be filled with the glory of killing hapless, unarmed refugees?

To our surprise, some ten army trucks were driving through the open field. We recognized they were British by their flat military helmets. They saluted us from afar, waving their hands.

There appeared a second group of khaki-clad soldiers: thirty of them were without helmets or arms. They were French army deserters hurrying north, towards the ocean.

Our mood was at a low point. Was it worth it to keep running? It was not easy to break through the crowd of refugees that choked the roads.

Before dark, Buci discovered an abandoned property, a *ferme*, the owners had deserted. Various families had already installed themselves in the vast courtyard of this farm. We took turns pushing our cart inside. We spread our blankets. The women stretched themselves out, dead tired. The men went to look for something to eat.

We went into the cellar of the house, and there before us were hundreds of bottles of wine, impeccably arranged, if dusty. Large vessels full of eggs in brine. Others full of sour cream, *crème fraiche*, and butter. There was no shortage of food. We climbed the cellar stairs and went in search of a chicken. We found two. It appeared that the owners and their servants had fled somewhere quickly, as everything was in perfect order.

In the courtyard, several refugees were killing chickens. They had fires going. People were eating. Buci found the kitchen. No one was inside, so we settled ourselves there.

I went with Buci in search of more chickens. I'd never held a live chicken before with my bare hands. Buci taught me how. We returned carrying four chickens by the legs.

Yolanka and Mrs. Herscovics had begun boiling water. Buci motioned to me; I followed him to a corner of the courtyard, and there, wielding a knife, he taught me how to butcher a chicken in accordance with Mosaic Law. This ritual killing made me feel sick. Finally the four chickens were lying on a table. Yolanka and the other women plucked the feathers off and cooked each piece over the fire.

Meanwhile Mrs. Jellinek had begun cooking eggs. I left the kitchen to walk around the farm. There were no lights; everything was immersed in darkness.

Night had fallen. In the large courtyard, groups of refugees were sitting, or reclining by a bonfire. We heard cannons far away. Sometimes the sky was illuminated by search lights. But in spite of everything it was a beautiful night. The sky was full of stars, it had cooled off, and a pleasant breeze was blowing. If it hadn't been for the preceding days' events, everything would have been perfect.

I wondered what my mother was up to in Vienna. Did she know what had happened? I'm sure she was worried about me.

And my father? He did not know that I was in France, and that we'd soon be reunited. Surely he thought I was in German-occupied Brussels. I'm sure this worried him greatly.

Suddenly, a truck entered the yard with headlights blazing. In the absence of other light, it was blindingly visible. I approached it and saw that it was French military. I ran to the kitchen to alert Buci. We both rushed to the truck, where the rest of the refugees had already gathered. Wounded soldiers got out and headed towards the barn.

They were coming from the front. An officer warned us not to leave the farm, that the Germans were not far away. He asked if there was a doctor among the refugees who could care for the wounded. When he finished talking, he saluted, bringing his hand to his helmet. He got back into the truck and quickly drove away.

A somber aura hung in the air. What would happen tomorrow?

The people returned to the warmth of the bonfires; us, to the kitchen, which gave off a delicious smell. Yolanka had prepared chicken soup, *"yoich"* with giblets. It had been a long time since we'd eaten soup. Buci found a gas lamp, and we sat down to eat in its light. Yolanka was a great cook. Buci urged me to try the *smetene*, fresh sour cream. This was like a banquet for us. Buci declared that we could eat. This spread was, of course, not kosher.

The women went to sleep in the barn. The men stayed up to discuss what the French officer meant when he said that tomorrow the front would reach us. The battle would be fought here.

After some time Buci and I left the patio. Seen from above—the kitchen was on the second floor—the courtyard seemed like a gypsy camp, with no less than eight bonfires. Near one of them, a young man played a *"Java"* on the accordion. The tone was far from happy. Everyone looked worried.

We talked with some other Jews, who had also fled from Brussels. Questions were asked and answers were given in the manner of the Talmud scholars. Everyone thought he was a *"mevin,"* an expert in the field.

What would we do if the Germans were to arrive on the farm? What would they ask us? What would we tell them? Were they going to arrest us? Were they going to incarcerate us? Send us to Germany, to a concentration camp? With regard to Jews, the Germans didn't fool around, and made it clear they wouldn't dispute anything, either.

The *Goyim*, or gentiles, among us did not seem as worried. It was not easy being Jews. Namely *"Sis shver tzu zain a yid."*

Following the departure of the military truck, it was decided that the gates should remain closed. They would not be opened to anyone under any circumstances. We appointed a *Shomer*, or permanent guard.

We dragged ourselves slowly toward the barn. We could barely keep our eyes open, as it was two o'clock in the morning. There were probably thirty people sleeping in the barn, and many more had fallen asleep in the rooms in the house.

To Buci, this didn't seem right: it was a violation of the privacy of those who had to escape. Nonetheless, the bedrooms and living rooms were full of refugees, lying down wherever there was space.

The deafening noise of cannon fire felt closer and closer. It was like this until dawn and continued into the following morning.

Planes could be heard overhead. Two Belgian refugees climbed onto the roof. They had binoculars, so we had some awareness of what was going on from what they were able to observe. They reported the number of planes in each squadron, and whether the planes were *Stukas* or *Messerschmidt*. They also informed us of any movement on the road, which was non-existent that day.

The *Messerschmidt* were the preferred aircraft for the bombing of Spain. Seventy of them, gloriously blanketing Guernica with explosives—the beginning of "Carpet Bombing," a great German invention. What was once a peaceful Basque city was destroyed in only 23 minutes. Franco hated the proud separatist Basques, and the German pilots complied with his desires. Hitler, his ally, sent them to him so that he could "practice" killing the largest number of people in the shortest amount of time.

After breakfast, we gathered and waited. Here in the *ferme*, Buci conducted a *minyan* for prayers. I attended and listened.

Everything around us remained calm. The sky was blue, the sun was at the highest point in the sky. Our watchmen were on the roof, ready with their binoculars. And now we were all here on the patio; no one said a word. We preferred to remain silent in the face of such uncertainty.

Around ten in the morning, we heard cannon fire again, but this time it was more intense, and much closer. The streets were deserted. Around midday, we heard a dull, distant sound that grew gradually stronger. It was a column of around eight heavy armored German tanks. They passed in front of our gate in the direction of Arras. Behind them were infantry trucks, followed by open Jeep cars, ragtop Volkswagens, and German Jeeps, each one of them dragging a light infantry canon. This information was provided to us in shouts by our lookouts. Occasionally, they saw an open Mercedes car full of German officers.

But that was all that happened. Not a single German parked by our gate. Unlike the French, the Germans moved in a mechanized way. The French moved like the infantry during the First World War: on foot.

We waited, unsure what we were waiting for, perhaps a battle. But there wasn't one, at least not where we found ourselves. Night fell. Buci and Jellineck kept watch, and the rest of us went to sleep.

The next day, nothing had changed. However, the lookouts discovered a large fire that they believed had lasted all night. Arras, our next stop, was burning.

The third day, a convertible drove up and parked in front of the gate. The driver honked the horn. We rushed to take shelter in the kitchen. *"Ce sont les Allemands,"* we said to one another. The door opened and a German officer stepped out of the car, clean and handsome, according to our French informants. Accompanying the officer were three armed soldiers. In French, he ordered us not to leave the premises, and told us not to worry. They'd already "cleaned" the area. Before leaving, he asked if we had enough food.

He didn't even try to come in. Nor did he ask if there were any Jews. He was from the *Wehrmacht*, which belonged to the regular German army, not the S.S. When the car drove away, we left the kitchen and went to meet everyone else on the patio.

Buci looked relieved. We were at the mercy of the Germans. Jellineck told us that when the Germans occupied Zcabze, his native village in Poland, during World War I, they behaved affably and civilly towards the Jews. There were many Jews in the German army. During Rosh-Hashanah, they asked permission to go to the synagogue to pray. This was in 1916. According to Yellinek, the *Niemetzky* were not so bad. *"Je vous l'avait toujours dit, d'ailleus."* he said in French.

Eight days later, we heard on the radio that Marshal Petain, at the head of the French armed forces, had surrendered to the Germans. An armistice was signed, under which the Vichy seat would not be occupied. Thus began one of the most shameful and sinister passages in French history. Pro-Nazi Laval was nominated Prime Minister, choosing Fascist and pro-German politicians for his cabinet. DeGaulle escaped to England where he organized the entire French fleet, including those stationed in North Africa. After the fall of Paris, negotiations began between the traitors and the German general staff, who chose to sign their agreements in the exact same coach where, years before, they'd signed for Germany's surrender. Historical irony.

Hitler, the boss, did not feel the same joy everyone else did. He was waiting for an allied counteroffensive that never materialized.

Hitler made a triumphant entrance into Paris, passing beneath the Arc de Triomphe at the head of his troops. The Parisian people—some of them, at least—came to see him. No one applauded, many openly wept at the *"defaite,"* humiliation of the French. Everything had happened so suddenly. How was this possible? The Maginot Line had not deterred them! A portion of the army had deserted in the heat of the moment, throwing their weapons at the side of the road. They had no faith in their leaders, in the grand Third Republic—*La Troisiemme Republique*—its reputation tarnished after not having assisted the Spaniards in 1936.

This was actually the darkest era of French history, the years between 1939 and 1944. Much has been written about this period, and to this day the French are ashamed of what happened, including the late president Francois Mitterand, one of Petain's partners during that time of upheaval, no politician could be trusted.

"The English Expeditionary Force," or the British Division, which fought on the French side on May 12, 1940, tried to save itself from the debacle, retreating rapidly to Dunkirk, which bordered the English Channel, where they were going to gather—literally gather—in hundreds of English civilian vessels. A great people, the English! When the time called for it, they elected a great leader, Winston Churchill. And so the bulk of the troops were able to return to Dover. This was, in fact, the only army that the British had. If Hitler had only known…

Fortunately, he ignored it, and so did the German High Command. A failure in intelligence? Or was G-d protecting them in the thick haze of the British Isles?

Instead of attacking the English, Hitler dedicated himself to traveling through France and savoring his victory. Having succeeded in so few days, and with so few casualties, was for him demonstrative of German superiority.

We stayed eight more days in the *ferme*. We had eaten well, although there was no bread—but that was unimportant.

The streets were filled with cars once more, and refugees. But now they were going in the opposite direction, away from German-occupied territories. In the end we decided to return to Brussels. According to the news, the Belgian capital hadn't suffered major damage from the bombings, with the exception of Zaventem, the airport, and its surroundings, reduced to ashes.

We walked beside the Belgian Jews. We were almost happy to return. *Lech, Lecha…* To me, this was a crazy world. First we fled from the Germans, and now we went back to them. Truth be told, we had no other alternative. But this was not clear in the eyes of a boy who had just turned ten. My birthday had happened while we were staying at the farm. No one remembered it, for there were other *Tzores* that worried us.

We walked for six hours. At the side of the road was a large German army truck. I recognized it by its greenish color, and by the license plates, always with "W" for Wehrmacht. Beside the truck were two portable kitchens, *feldkuechen* as they were called. One soldier was in charge of serving food to the refugees. He spooned us something with a giant ladle and served it to us in *gamelle*, or aluminum army bowls. I learned what we were eating was *Eintopfgericht*, a puree of potato, ham, and vegetables. Delicious and nutritious. How ironic that the German soldiers were feeding us! What more could one ask for? *Baruch ha-shem!* Thanks to G-d.

We spent the night at another abandoned farm. The following day, we set out once more. Each time there were fewer wagons and more military trucks. Around six in the evening one of them was stopped in front of us. An officer got out and walked towards us. We had no idea what to do, so we stood there and waited.

The officer saluted, bringing his right hand to his gray kepi with the German eagle and said to us in German: *"Kommen Sie, Wir Fahren Bis Zur Grenze."* I understood everything, and translated it into French. The others remained quiet, not wanting to reveal that they understood. We were Jews and, therefore, should keep silent. We got into the truck, taking our wagon with us. After so many days of walking, it was heaven, *Gan Eden*, to sit down. Later that night, they left us in the main square of Valenciennes. We stayed in the same school we'd stayed in before. This time, everything was better organized. There were nurses from the Red Cross, who were friends to me, friends from whom I'd previously received so much assistance in Belgium.

I felt safe, traveling along familiar roads. I knew where I was, and since I'd been allowed to translate I felt very important. I was an interpreter like my father during the First World War. My father, if he was still in Paris, was farther away each day.

But I still felt sad: I knew nothing about what was happening to my parents. I'd heard about the fall of Paris. What would happen to him? I never received letters from my mother; she had no idea where her child was.

The following day, Buci and I went to downtown Valenciennes to see what we could do to get back to Brussels. The city center was crawling with German soldiers. They did not bother anyone. There were no longer any French authorities.

We went to the *Komandatur*, the headquarters of the occupying forces. The Germans had a vested interest in returning the refugees to their homelands as quickly as possible, so that things could go back to normal. They wished to govern with minimal difficulty, and the refugees in France posed a huge problem.

We arrived in the courtyard of the "Hotel de la Ville" in the municipality of Valenciennes. Several German soldiers were seated at some tables with rolls of paper, attending to the refugees. One of them asked Buci where we were from, how many people were in our group, and where we were coming from. Buci answered him in French. The soldier was not wearing a helmet, and his hair hung loose. He responded to Buci in French in a friendly tone: to cross the border, or rather what remains of it, as everything is *Besetzte Zone*, occupied territory. On the other side, you'll find military trucks that will take you to Brussels. *"Merci Monsieur,"* Buci replied. And that was the end of the conversation. They let us go, and no one asked to see our papers. Not a single soldier bothered us.

We slept at the school and early the next morning we pulled our cart across the border. There were no barriers, no tricolored flags, nor customs agents. Only a German officer posted, holding a red flag with a swastika in the middle. This gave me chills. I was now back at the beginning of my journey. Nothing mattered, not the goodness of the Red Cross nurses, the generosity of the Lanksners, choosing me and giving me a place to live. Not our escape from the bombing at Charleroi. It was all for nothing! Once again I found myself under the swastika, just as in Vienna.

The German army brought us back to Brussels. We arrived at a *Caserne*, or headquarters in *Ixelles*, a suburb of the capital. Carrying our belongings, we took the tram along the Boulevard Maurice Lemonier, to the station at the Rue des Vierges.

We'd arrived home, right back where we started, and our abortive adventure was similar to that of countless other Belgian, Dutch, and French families who in 1940 set out in vain for the roads of France, away from the German invaders. Everyone returned except for those who remained buried in French soil.

From the tram I saw how much the city had changed under the German occupation. Due to the gas shortage, there was very little traffic, and scarcely any cars aside from German army vehicles.

All the luxury hotels were occupied by German officers, as were many other buildings on Avenue Louise, the main avenue near the Palais Royal, former residence of the Belgian king. On the facades hung enormous red flags with swastikas. No one was out in the streets. The Germans moved from side to side in their cars, or in motorcycles with "side-cars" which seemed to be a favorite mode of transport for the Wehrmacht.

In June of 1940, the Gestapo installed their offices and torture chambers on the Avenue Louise. In the basements began the systematic torturing of Belgian patriots, of communists from various European countries, of German and Austrian Jews. Also tortured were people accused of being pedophiles, spies, basically anyone deemed a "social parasite." Every night, gray ambulances full of lifeless bodies headed for the morgue, where families came to retrieve their loved ones and bury them.

Everything remained calm in Brussels. The people quickly grew accustomed to the occupying presence. We were aware of the Gestapo torture chambers; we saw the officers in plainclothes, almost always wearing black leather coats and matching hats. They were sinister-looking in their cars, which were either gray or black, with license plates reading GP, *Geheim Sicherheits Polizei*, police force in charge of the security of the German Reich.

The cafes were full of people. If a German officer walked in—generally accompanied by a beautiful young Belgian girl—he was immediately given a table. The Belgians had to wait their turn. It was the same in restaurants and cabarets. The wealthy Germans had the pick of the litter. The young Belgians couldn't compete. There were, of course, exceptions: for instance, the collaborators had priority for a table.

There was a clandestine resistance movement being formed against the Germans. Being a part of this resistance was extremely dangerous, as being captured at the hands of the Gestapo would surely mean torture and death.

The schools, closed during the invasion, were set to reopen in September 1940. I would resume classes. Many of my classmates had left, some going to England, others to Spain, the luckiest, to Switzerland. With the goal of taking control over the minds of the students, the Germans forced everyone to re-enroll in the public schools they attended before the war.

I went to the Rue de Six Jetons school and stood in line. I waited my turn; a secretary seated behind a desk asked me: *"Hans Peter Katz...Vous n'etes pas belge, n'est ce pas?" "Je suis apatride,"* I answered, showing my papers. She looked at them, looked again, and set them aside on her desk. Meanwhile, I wrote my name on one of the lists, the one for the fifth grade. At that time, learned, literate people like our school secretary, a woman in her thirties, were taught perfect penmanship, and so I wrote my name as though it were a work of art. Looking at it she said: "I am going to register you, but the truth is I don't know if you'll be allowed to attend class. I need to consult with the Burgmaster representative." I kept silent and let the next person go ahead of me. I hadn't anticipated there being a problem as long as the woman wasn't from the Gestapo or the Belgian Fascists, the "rexistas." At any rate, I went to school as if nothing had happened, and I had no problems. My being "*apatride*" was not an obstacle.

Many Europeans in 1940 didn't understand the significance of the word "stateless." Those who were "stateless" received purple passports called *"Nansenpass,"* issued in Geneva. These were sensitive documents, somehow implying nonconformity, a discrepancy on the part of the carrier. In the Europe of that time, this could indicate you were an extremist, communist, a spy, a gypsy, or worse.

This non-nationality was created by the commissioner for refugees, Hans Nansen (Danish), from the *Societe des Nations* (1924). Asked how it was possible for a person to be without a homeland, his answer was simple. New countries, new nationalities, are often formed on a whim—for instance, in 1919 during the signing of the Treaty of Versailles. So these stateless individuals were summoned to a plebiscite (which comes from "plebe" in Greek, meaning "people") so that each could adopt the nationality of his choice: that of his birthplace, or a new citizenship. Those who didn't want either remained as stateless. A Sudeten family, who lived and worked in Karlsbad for countless generations—Karlsbad with its hot springs and porcelain factories in what was Bohemia, part of the Austro-Hungarian Empire, near where my maternal grandparents, the Gruenfelds, came from—were in 1920 suddenly forced to decide between these three options. Left stateless, they headed for Austria, which was more hospitable and less volatile. Much like the Swarovsky family, originally from Gablonz and famous for their crystal. I had the pleasure of meeting them in 1958, and they became business associates of mine, as well as friends. The Swarovsky's left Gablonz and established themselves in Wattens, Austria in 1924. They later experienced the intolerance, hatred, and violence that erupted in the area between 1934 and1938.

After Bela Kuhn (a Jew) seized power in Hungary and reigned for a year, after the short-lived rebellion of the Spartacists led by Liebknecht and Rosa Luxemburg (also Jewish), after the Dimitrov revolt in Bulgaria, the Spanish Civil War in 1936, all the evil in Europe was blamed on the communists, the anarchists, and the Jews.

The communists, sadly deluded, didn't know or didn't care to know what was happening in Russia. The death of Vladimir Lenin in 1924 was a watershed moment. Stalin came to power, continuing to propel the revolution, with its ideals of liberty and equality for every individual, group of people, and nation around the world. Immediately, Stalin got rid of the NEP (New Economic Policy) instituted by Lenin in 1920 in response to the famine, and the failure of forced collectivization.

Little by little, Stalin formed a team comprised of henchmen like Beria—the worst, by far—Molotov, Budyenny, Voroschilov, Kaganovich, dedicated supporters who assisted in deposing the founding members of the revolution, like Trotzky, creator of the Red Army; Zinoviev and Bucharin, ideologues—all of them Jews. Kirov, popular idol in Leningrad, was also eliminated. Later came the purge of those supposedly behind the old regime. In less than two years, Stalin had eliminated all of the Old Guard, from military brass to battalion commanders in the Red Army.

Russia paid dearly, with blood and tears, for the atrocities committed by Stalin in 1941. When the Germans attacked, in the absence of leadership, the debilitated army could not fend off the Germans, rapidly encroaching upon Moscow. Stalin grew depressed, and began instituting firing squads and gulags.

Several secret police forces were put in charge of the repression and control of the Russian people. First, the CHEKA, then the NKVD, the GPU, and finally the KGB.

But the European communists were idealists. The economic situation and rampant unemployment in Europe provided them with a space for acting and the ability to proselytize. Before Hitler, they were the second most powerful party in Germany. In France as well. In Spain they were the best-organized party, with the great *Pasionaria*, who screamed the famous "They Shall Not Pass" in Madrid against the rebel forces of Franco and his German and Italian henchmen. In Yugoslavia, they posted Josip Broz Tito on the front and also counted on excellent paramilitary committees, which were very effective during the Second World War. In Bulgaria, Maximo Dimitrov was the leader of a disciplined Communist Party.

A large percentage of communists participated in the International Brigades, and many of them were Jewish. They gave their lives and did their best to fight with the Spanish Republicans in the name of freedom for their country, which since the monarchy had been mired in poverty. But confronted by the superiority of the enemy's weapons, the Republic was forced to surrender in 1939.

Spain lost a million of its greatest sons. Many of its intellectuals, such as Federico García Lorca and Miguel de Unamuno. Others made their way into exile.

Since I was a boy, I've felt a predilection for Spain, an interest in all things Spanish that I retain to this day, and which has probably increased through multiple trips, along with my intimate knowledge of Spanish history. And I start to wonder how these feelings came about in a twelve-year old child from Vienna, Austria.

Maybe it began while I was on a train sealed by the Reich and bound for Belgium, unaware that other children—Spanish children—just as sad and distressed, were crossing Germany in sealed wagons, too, but their final destination was the Soviet Union, which gave them asylum. Listening to the radio I learned of the final epilogue of the Spanish Civil War, and perhaps felt I shared a fate with those who had to venture into an unaccepting world as refugees. Perhaps it was when I heard about the men who were going to fight in Spain during the war. Perhaps, at twelve, I learned of the Spanish roots of some Jews, the Sephardic, like the Renous, with whom I shared so much of my daily life. They spoke Ladino, Medieval Spanish with Jewish voices. They told me of the "*llave*," the house key their ancestors kept when they left Spain in 1492, hoping to return someday. Like what we say during Passover: *"L'Shana Haba'ah B'Yerushalayim"* ("Next year in Jerusalem") they say: "Next Year in Granada."

At the beginning of 1941, the German expansion was daunting. A large portion of Europe was under their yoke. The only mistake they made in 1940 was not invading England immediately after the capitulation of France. Because of their overwhelming aircraft superiority, this might have been a possibility at the time.

Although the decision not to attack the British Isles was Hitler's, the truth is that the German High Command was divided. Herman Goering, chief of the Luftwaffe, Karl Doenitz, admiral of the fleet, and Von Rundstaedt, of the Wehrmacht, were not able to reach an agreement. And thank G-d, otherwise the war would have taken a different turn.

But what Hitler had accomplished was impressive. From the north of the French coast to the Atlantic. Franco's Spain protected it at the west. Scandinavia, with the exception of Sweden, which remained neutral, and, incidentally, managed to save Jewish refugees. At the south, Yugoslavia, Albania, and Greece were occupied by the German army. To the east, Poland, Danzig, Memel, and Czechoslovakia. Hungary and Romania had Fascist regimes that were in Hitler's favor. Bulgaria was also pro-German. The siege was complete, with the Soviet Union linked to Germany by the *"Ribbentrop-Molotov"* pact and therefore not presenting a threat in 1940.

The United States, although neutral—and allied with Great Britain—had seen a surprising increase in the production of military materials. Huge convoys of merchant ships traveled day and night to England, although many were attacked by German submarines, the *U-Boote*, known for their fearsome accuracy. Many lives were lost, but more and more war materials were arriving in Liverpool and Manchester.

The English leader Winston Churchill was an inspiration for us all. There was no household in Belgium where the BBC and its broadcast signal—the first notes of Beethoven's Fifth Symphony— could not be heard every single day. It was believed that if Ludwig Van Beethoven were alive at the time, he probably would have been sent to a concentration camp. Just as he'd rebelled against Napoleon's desire for conquest over other nations, he surely would have rebelled against what the Nazis did to their homeland, not to mention the rest of Europe.

The BBC informed us of the truth about what was happening in the world. And the news was incredibly sad. The Germans were advancing triumphantly on all sides.

My cousin Hugo Mordkovich was able to leave Vienna for Paris in 1939. There, he enlisted voluntarily in the Foreign Legion. Although being part of this army corps was highly prestigious, back then the French asked very few questions. You had to be less than forty years old, in good physical health, measure at least six feet tall, have no contagious diseases, and, above all, be unafraid of dying.

When the war broke out in September 1939, he wore his uniform, with the rank of Second Corporal. I'm not sure where he fought, nor in how many battles he took part. But he was able to pass to the Vichy side in June of 1940.

After the armistice, the government of Petain ordered all of the Legion, or that which remained of it, to go to North Africa for *"Raisons de Securite Nationale."* Among the legionnaires were many German and Austrian Jews. Once they arrived in North Africa they worked on the construction of the Trans-Saharan Railroad alongside Spanish Republicans and Greeks, prisoners and forced laborers. Many died beneath the burning African sun.

My cousin was at the labor camp Ain El Ourak and survived, in large part thanks to care packages sent by Paulette, a courageous French woman, whom he met and lived with in Paris from 1939 to1940.

North Africa, although nominally a French colony, was essentially a no man's land. The adherents to Charles de Gaulle's *"France Libre"* were persecuted. The Jews were removed from their administrative positions. Listening to the BBC radio was prohibited. The movie *Casablanca* was filmed there, I imagine, starring Humphrey Bogart and Ingrid Bergman. The Germans stationed there were very comfortable in this temperate climate next to the Mediterranean Sea, surrounded by women…it was much better than being in Europe and having to fight.

There appeared in Brussels a new social class, the *"Profiteurs"* or those who negotiated with the Germans, making great fortunes and profiting from their negotiations with cars, coupons for gasoline. They dressed elegantly. Among these *"Profiteurs"* were also Jews.

Apparently, a Polish Jew had taken over the production of a kilogram size *Cote d'or* brand chocolate bars. These were coveted by the German soldiers, who sent them back to their families in Germany, where there was no chocolate due to war rationing.

I don't know how many thousands of bars were sold. The factory suddenly had to stop production due to lack of raw materials, which were no longer arriving from Africa and Central America. It was impossible to find chocolate anywhere in Belgium. My beloved vending machine on the Rue des Vierges remained empty for many years, until the end of the war.

Jews soon began selling chocolates on the boulevards near the hotel where the German officials lived. This was the *Marche Noir*, the black market. The price was agreed upon through bargaining. The Jews would put themselves at risk like this? Yes, they could be arrested for public illegal trafficking, but the necessity to earn a few francs or marcs was worth the risk.

Up to this point, hostile measures had not been taken against the Belgian Jewish community. However, the terrorization began suddenly. One hundred and fifty Jewish youths were arrested and sent to old Belgian army barracks in Malines. According to the news they were being detained by the Germans for the *Arbeits Dienst,* the Nazi unit in charge of recruiting young, strong people for forced labor in factories, shops, and construction sites throughout the German Reich and occupied territories.

Doctor Ley—*Reichsminister fur Arbeit*—was author of the phrase *"Arbeit macht Frei."* This "free labor" was responsible for millions of "slaves," Jews and non-Jews, who were required to perform forced labor for the giant labor organization *Deutsche Ausruestungswerke fuer das Tausendjaeriges Reich*. The thousand year empire, whose logo was *"Gott mit Uns"*: God is with us.

After Jews from Brussels, there followed three hundred more Jews from Antwerp, along with political prisoners, socialists, and communists, Spanish Republicans, miners with political problems, ex-combatants from the International Brigades trapped in Belgium. They were sent to Normandy and Bretagne to build reinforced concrete fortifications: a network of gigantic bunkers connected by lighted tunnels with "injected" air, the air conditioning of that era.

In these bunkers, large, long-range cannons were installed, able to bomb the English coast, although they were never utilized. Years later, these fortifications served to repel the Allied Invasion of Normandy in 1944, known as "D-Day." The bunkers and the soldiers inside were responsible for many allied forces deaths.

Sigi, who had remained in Brussels, also made his way to France as a refugee in May 1940 with his mother, my aunt Julie; aunt Zilly, and her daughter Hilde with her two sons Herbert and Jack. They spent a month or six weeks in France, but later returned to Brussels.

In Brussels, there was a jewelry atelier owned by an immigrant from Vienna, Mr. Schneider. Sigi eventually started working there. I remember the shop on the Rue D'Audeghem well: a large room with a picture window, which let in lots of natural light. Mrs. Schneider was a typical Viennese woman from Leopoldstadt, full of kindness, but also quite bossy. The Schneiders welcomed many Jewish jewelers who'd recently emigrated, always offering them work, and if there wasn't work they'd at least give them food. The Schneiders were the product of the enormous immigrant wave that influenced the growth of the Viennese Jewish community, which increased from sixteen thousand in 1857 to two hundred thousand in 1937. They were the prototype of Jews who'd arrived from Galicia, from Bukovina in the Austro-Hungarian Empire: their children had developed an athletic prowess in the *"Thurnhallen"* or gymnasiums, like the rest of their peers. They also played soccer: there were teams in first, second, and third divisions. The *Schwimmbaeder*, or pools, were always full of Jewish youths. The Hakoach was the largest Jewish sports club in Europe, with five thousand members.

From one generation to the next, a surprising metamorphosis occurred. The children already had Viennese names, like Bubi and Hansi; the girls Fritzi and Mitzi. They spoke Wienerisch in addition to German, and probably Yiddish. They felt Viennese, part of a cultured society. They went to the opera, the theater, concerts, conferences, *Festspiele,* or festivals, *Vernissages*, or gallery openings. They also belonged to youth organizations like the Hakoach, the Macabi and the Zionist organizations Mizrachi, Betar, and Ha-shomer Hatzair.

This Austrian culture was in turn enriched by Jews. Social contributions between 1910 and 1938 were made primarily by Jews. The young Jew born in Vienna, having gone to college, or the Gymnasium, having received a masters or baccalaureate degree, was conscious of anti-Semitism years before the Anschluss. Years before the First World War they heard insults like *"Jude Verrecke"* or *"Saujude,"* dirty Jewish pig, quite often.

The reality was that in Vienna, anti-Semitism formed part of the political atmosphere, and was very much a part of the idiosyncrasies of its inhabitants. Governmental candidates like Karl Lueger, elected Mayor of Vienna (1895-1905) under Emperor Franz Josef, said *"Wer Jude Ist Das Bestimme Ich,"* which is to say, "I decide who is and who is not a Jew." At the end of the day, there were also Jewish and liberal voters.

In 1924, when the soccer team Hakoach had returned to Vienna from an international game, with the coveted victory cup, they were stoned in the railway station, by a mob of Nazi youths.

Nazi militants paraded freely throughout Vienna, singing *"Horst Wessel Lied,"* a German tune, without any police interference. Their leader, Seyessinquart, also conducted himself freely, visiting Chancellor Schuschnigg and Cardinal Innitzer. This was the prevailing democracy before the Anschluss.

I loved to visit Mrs. Schneider; she greeted me with a kiss and gave me a *Liptauerbrat* and *Himbersaft* or *Sauermilch* bread with Viennese paprika cheese and a raspberry soda. Sigi, whom I saw when I visited the Schneiders, told me he was getting married, and asked that I attend on Saturday at ten in the morning, in the Hotel de la Ville or City Hall in the Grande Place. This news surprised me. Why would you get married in such trying and uncertain times? When no one knew what would happen tomorrow? When I saw his fiancé, I understood why he wanted to get married then myself: she was beautiful.

Lilly Lenz was Viennese, born to Russian parents. She was active in the Viennese Betar, and probably would have immigrated to Palestine in March of 1937, but she was prevented from doing so by her older brother, in an effort to protect her, his only sister. Both went to Brussels. Her brother was killed in the basement torture chambers of the Gestapo, on Avenue Louise, when he came to defend his spouse, a gentile detained for *Rassenschande,* or racial crimes. This was a major offense during the Hitler regime.

Some of the family based in Brussels came to the wedding. Of course, Sigi's mother, the Schneiders, the Wolfthals, Aunt Zilly, and other people I didn't know. It was a brief civil ceremony, after which everyone quickly returned home. It wasn't safe for a group of Jews to be seen publically in Brussels in 1941.

In June of 1941, Germany invaded the Soviet Union on a front of 3000 km. The Germans began the offensive by pushing hard, at first meeting with little resistance. It was summer, and the rains had passed. The German motorized cars ran on dry ground. The tanks were able to maneuver. The German air force the master of the skies, they had absolute control.

The Russians, commanded by the few generals who remained after the Revolution and the Civil War that broke out after the invasion of the "white" armies, like Timoshenko and Budyoni, did their best to organize a heroic defense. Stalin had eliminated many of them during the purges. (1936-1939)

If the German invasion was a disgrace for the Russians, for us—the Jews—it was a national catastrophe. Polish Jews who had sought refuge in the Russian-occupied territories fell into the hands of the Germans. Ukraine, Belarus, Moldavia, Bessarabia, Lithuania and Latvia were all regions densely populated by Jews. In fact these territories contained 60% of the Jewish population of the Soviet Union.

This part of Russia, including Crimea, was overtaken in less than three months. The *Shtetlach*, or agricultural villages, were located in this part of Russia. The old *Pale of Settlement*, or Jewish settlement zone. It was the Russia of *Sholem Aleichem*, the precious cradle of our Jewish European civilization: Bialystok, Belz, Drohovich, Vilna Yerushalaim, D'Lite, Kiev, Kovno, Odessa, Czernowitz, Grodno, Baranovich. Kichnivev, Lublin, Riga, Vitebsk, Berdichev, Minsk, Tarnopol, Zhitomar, Borisov. I mention them for their Jewish population. For us, their loss lay not only in the sum of massacred victims, which was, doubtless, very high. But also in the complete annihilation of a culture, a way of life, a rich and irrecoverable literature, which would no longer be written, of a language that would no longer be spoken, of songs that would never be sung again...

The Germans advanced rapidly. The Russians retreated in disarray. Entire divisions fell at the hands of the Germans. Columns of prisoners of war were marched to Poland, Romania, and Germany. Kiev and Minsk fell, Smolensk, Odessa and Nikolayev. Here the Germans were detained. It was October, on the brink of winter, and they could not advance because of inclement weather.

Having learned from their experience in Poland, Eichmann, Heydrich, and Brunner installed the *Einsatzkommandos* and the *Sonderabteilungen*, command units dedicated to the massive elimination of Jews living in Russia.

They recreated scenes they'd enacted in Poland: the burning of synagogues with Jews inside. They functioned as such after an obligatory Communist indoctrination lasting more than twenty years. This in itself was a miracle in a Socialist state.

When the guns were silenced in Kiev, 36,000 Jews in the city were marched by force in rows of five to the edge of a deep gully in a place called Babiyar. They were systematically gunned down. Those who didn't die from the gunshots spent hours beneath piles of corpses before dying of asphyxiation. In comparison with those in Poland, the genocides in Russia took place on a larger scale. The gentile population helped the *Einsatzkommandos* locate the Jews and kill them in the places they were found. The killing lasted three days.

In general, Jews and communists functionaries were on some level treated as equals, both killed on the spot. The Germans, who sought to uproot the Soviet secretaries, the *Politruks* or commissars, denounced the local populations, whether they were Ukrainians, Lithuanians, or Belarusians.

Despite initial success, Adolf Hitler, like Napoleon in 1810, committed the grave error of invading Russian soil. The "Winter General" would be defeated in the year 1943. The German soldiers were exhausted by temperatures of less than 20 degrees Celsius and winds that blew at 140 km per hour. Napoleon retired after his arrival at the gates of Moscow, after finding the Russians had set fire to the wooden houses of the city in order to thwart his advance.

School ended in June; I waited to return in September. But, along with the start of the war against Bolshevism, there were issued a series of new edicts against the Jews.

Number one: Jews of both sexes, aged six years and older, were required to wear a yellow Star of David sewn onto their clothes.

Number two: a curfew was instituted. Jews could not remain out on the streets after ten at night.

Number three: Jewish children were prohibited from attending public school.

Number four: ration cards granted by the Belgian authorities, which had previously allowed Jews to obtain food, were cancelled. Jews could no longer get cards.

The famous *Etoiles Juives or Stars of David* were made of textile. At the beginning, this was a novelty, and I asked Yolanka to sew one to my only coat. The first day, I wore it proudly in the streets, so that the people could see me. For me, it was like wearing a medal. Of course, this feeling didn't last long, and I quit wearing it after two days. The raids by the Gestapo began in September 1941. The Gestapo were interested in recruiting healthy, strong men for forced labor. The mass deportations, part of the "Final Solution," or *Endloesung*, had not yet begun. Nevertheless, the Jewish quarters were closed until the Gestapo finished arresting all the Jews.

In Russia, mass murders were increasing. As in Poland in 1939, the *Sonderabteilungen* had received orders from Heydrich and Eichman to wipe the Jews from the face of the earth.

There were constant mass killings of Soviet Prisoners of War. There were simply too many of them, and the Germans, not knowing what to do with them, found them to be a hindrance. And the Geneva Convention? "With regard to this, we were given no orders," said the Wehrmacht soldiers, whose buckles bore the phrase *"Got Mitt Uns,"* which apparently gave them license to kill.

At that time, Stalin's son Yacov was taken prisoner. He was the product of Stalin's first marriage, and was married to a Jewish woman, Yulia Meltzer, from Odessa. Initially, the Germans protected his life because they could, perhaps, use him for an exchange. We never knew what happened to him. In 1943, during the Battle of Stalingrad, the Ministry of Foreign Relations in Berlin issued a brief statement that Yacov Yossefovich Dszugashvilli had died during the bombing of a prison camp in Germany.

On December 7, 1941, Japan—Empire of the Rising Sun, who had allied themselves with Germany and Italy in the infamous Axis tripartite in 1939—which until now had occupied itself with killing the Chinese, bombing the civil population of the Middle Kingdom and constructing arms factories in Manchuria, launched a surprise attack on the North American base at Pearl Harbor, in Hawaii.

We heard about this through the BBC. The entry of the United States into the war was our first ray of light after a long, dark night. We were encouraged and strengthened by these news. We heard about the destruction of so many ships and the death of thousands of marines. The Americans were surprised and hurt.

America was the strongest power in the world, and also the richest, and they expected their involvement would make the Germans hesitate. The fight would now be more evenly matched. England had remained alone up to this point, supporting all the weight of the war.

In June, Hitler attacked the Soviet Union. For him, the Soviets were easy prey, a weak country. But in reality they were a large nation only weakened by "collectivization" and afterwards by Stalinist purges. The Germans had advanced rapidly and without any organized resistance. Now, the fight would be more equal, at least that's what everyone was saying. Buci was happy, and said that now the war was about to change in favor of the Allies.

For me, America was a far-away dream. A country I knew only through photographs of tall high-rise buildings. They had built a Statue of Liberty, in reality a gift from France, as they believed freedom should be for everyone. It was a nation of immigrants from around the world.

1942 began with the German advance, the apotheosis of their military successes. The Russian campaign was going well. In September, the German troops had reached Stalingrad, on the central front 40 kilometers from Moscow. They failed to take Leningrad to the north, but they had besieged the city. In the south they'd taken all of Crimea, and were advancing toward the oil fields in Tiflis and Baku.

In North Africa, the Afrika Korps, at the command of Erwin Rommel, advanced toward Cairo. In Palestine, everyone worried about the German advance. Things did not look good for the Allies.

In Berlin, in January 1942, Adolf Eichmann, who was now in charge of the *Judenfrage* or "Jewish Question," convened a conference in a villa in Wannsee, which was attended by Heinrich Himmler, Heydrich, Hans Brunner and other high-ranking S.S. officials. One of Hitler's representatives also attended the conference, as did representatives of the armed forces, the Reichsbahn Railways, and the commandants of the recently reconditioned concentration camps of Auschwitz-Birkenau, Belzec, Maidanek, Chelmno, and Treblinka and Sobibor. These would now become the death camps.

They revised what had been determined thus far through detailed statistics. They concluded that they needed to proceed with more severity.

They asked the people attending this conference to make an extra effort to swiftly execute the *"Endloesung."* In other words, that they take more effective methods to perform this operation. The German technology would assist them in doing so.

Eichmann was assisted by two technicians from Bayer, who explained to him the effects of the new gas Zyklon B, manufactured in Lererkusen. Other technicians explained in detail how to efficiently work the crematoriums.

With the help of maps, they made plans to transport by rail the millions of Jews they planned to exterminate. This was the tragic start of the infamous *"Endloesurg"* or Final Solution.

In this conference they determined which should be the death factories. The other concentration camps, the K.Z., would continue functioning as before.

The following day, the mass deportations to these converted camps began. The raids began in France. Jews were hunted, arrested and sent to the large velodrome *"Vel d'Hiver,"* near the Baum la Rolande train station. From the Drancy camp, they were transported to Auschwitz-Birkenau.

The trains could transport nearly a thousand people; there were one hundred in each wagon. Each train had ten wagons, and all of them were empty, animal conveyors, containing only an old barrel full of stagnant water, and another empty one for excrement. The floors were strewn with straw.

In Belgium the Jews were arrested by the Gestapo and loaded into Wehrmacht trucks. One suitcase was allowed per person. Men, women, the elderly, and children, all deported without distinction. The only explanation they gave us: *"Umstellung Nach Osten,"* an evacuation to the west.

Anderlecht, the Jewish neighborhood in Brussels, was fenced in to prevent any escape. The S.S. posted armed guards with submachine guns. Those who tried to flee were shot. The trucks drove everyone to the fortress in Malines, Centre de Rassenblement, or point of reunion. From there the convoy left directly for Auschwitz-Birkenau, in Poland. The Jews in Antwerp were also brought here, first to Malines, and later sent to Auschwitz.

Holland was home to Jews expelled from Spain and Portugal, and these Jews had coexisted with the Protestant communities in Amsterdam, The Hague, Leiden and Harlem for centuries. Rembrandt found his favorite models in the Joodenstraat. Here in this tolerant climate, lens grinder Baruj Spinoza wrote philosophical treatises, which were widely read as textbooks in universities up north, such as Uppsala, in Sweden.

The Jews who were arrested were sent to Westerbork, an former Dutch army barrack, and from there boarded trains bound for Auschwitz-Birkenau.

Despite massacres, starvation, sickness, and epidemics, many still remained alive in the Polish ghettos. This "problem" was brought into consideration at the conference in Wannsee. These Jews were to go directly to the extermination camps.

Every day, transports left from the ghettos in Warsaw, Lodz, Bialystok, and Vilna to Treblinka. From the ghettos of Krakow, Czestochowa, and Sokolov towards Auschwitz-Birkenau. From the ghettos of Lublin, Brody, Reszov towards Belzec. Death factories operated day and night. Zyklon gas was pumped from the showerheads in what appeared to be shower rooms. Death by asphyxiation happened in mere minutes. The doors to these gas chambers were opened after a prudent twenty-minute wait. They had to be sure that the victims were dead.

Afterwards, the inert bodies, violet-colored from the effects of the gas, were brought to gigantic crematory ovens, pride of the German industry Deutsche Technik. These facilities were designed to operate 24 hours a day. Tall columns of smoke could be seen for miles around. Poland had been converted into one enormous death camp, a cemetery for our people and many other peoples from all over Europe.

Entire populations were reduced to smoke and ashes, and no one—no one—said a thing. To this day, there are still some who question the validity of these facts.

I was in Auschwitz-Birkenau with my sons after the war. And I cried. I cried for my mother, I cried for my father, but how many tears can one cry for an entire people?

There aren't enough tears for a tragedy of these proportions. I could only feel courage, helplessness, sadness. Not a lust for revenge, or for vengeance...this would be impossible, anyways. The crime was far too profound.

My father was in Paris when I trudged on foot on the road between Amiens and Arras with the Lanksners, the Yellineks, and the Slomovicz.

He was, of course, unaware that I was walking toward him, to hug him, shower him with kisses, to have a father again and to have his son return to him. He couldn't have possibly known my whereabouts...he thought I was in Brussels with the Lanksners.

When my father arrived in Paris in 1939, he headed straight for a small hotel in front of the Gare du Nord—the train station—called the Hotel du Nord, which still exists today.

Later on, he contacted his friends and silk suppliers in Lyon. He traveled there by train to ask them if they could help him obtain temporary visas, *visas de sejour*, for his wife and nine-year old son.

In France in 1939, it was dangerous to even speak with a refugee residing there illegally, theoretically being sought by the police. At least, this was the point of view held by one of the manufacturers. Besides—and here the human condition comes into play—this was not the same Monsieur Leo Katz, *notre client de Vienne*, who came to buy from them. This was Monsieur Leo Katz, *le refugié juif, le pauvre,* who came to ask for our help to bring his family into the country. They'd already had enough with the Spanish Republicans, with the German Jews from Saar—who had opted for France in 1936—with Communists from Germany, Austria, Italy... "There is no longer room in France even for the French."

In Paris, my father met with my cousin Hugo Mordkovitch, who wore the Foreign Legion uniform. Hugo lived with Paulette, a French woman who was not Jewish, with whom he'd fallen in love. She had a nine-year old girl from a previous marriage.

After the war, I learned that my father served as a translator for a military dispatch in Paris, and that's how he earned a living. Before the fall of Paris, he was able to escape to Clermond-Ferrand, in the Pyrenees within the Zone of Demarcation, or *Vichy* zone. I never knew he'd lived there at all, in spite of the letters I received from him from that location. They were delivered through the Red Cross in Geneva. I still have them.

In January of 1942, he was sent—together with other Austrian and German Jews,—then *Sujets Ennemís*, or "undesirable subjects"—to an internment camp at the foot of the Pyrenees, called Rivesaltes. Here, there were already Spaniards, Russians, and Bulgarians, all of whom were veterans of the Civil War.

In Gurs, Levernet, Ageles, and Rivesaltes were more than 42,000 Jews, in addition to Spaniards declared "dangerous"—read: Communists—and people of other nationalities. All of them were handed over by the French to the Germans in 1942.

The French authorities, the *Sûreté*, were not obligated to do this, but nonetheless acted under direct orders from Laval and Bousquet, both ministers of the Petain Government, a government looked back upon as shameful and embarrassing by the French to this very day.

In Brussels, Jews were disappearing. Raids were happening every day. Malines was overcrowded. Immediately, the number of trains to Auschwitz increased. Eichmann directed everything from Vienna. He enjoyed the Viennese environment. A lover of classical music, he often went to concerts. Besides, several of his childhood friends were in the S.S. and some were his collaborators in Vienna.

One interesting statistic: 42% of S.S. soldiers were Austrian, yet the overall percentage of Austrians in the German Reich was just 9% (1938-1945).

Buci had a friend for many years, a Belgian man named Jerome Carton. He was a client of Buci's, but also a good friend. I went with Buci to visit him many times. He lived in the *Place Rouppe*, a few blocks from the Rue Des Vierges. He was about sixty years old, very friendly, upright, always read to help.

When the Raids began, Buci went to see him and ask for advice. He offered to hide us in his house, but this would have been too dangerous. He lived in a very central location, with Gestapo constantly driving by in search of Jews. However, he told Buci he'd speak with one of his friends, a comrade in arms in the *Defense de Ypres* during the First World War (1914-18).

He promised to give us an immediate response. At eight o'clock that night, Buci and I went back to his house. The response was positive. We were given the address of his friend, where we could stay.

That same night—there was no time to lose—Yolanka, Buci, and I took two valises and moved to the home of Mr. Vanderbrook in Schaarebek. He led us to a room in the *grenier,* the attic on the third floor of the house. The door to the attic was a mirror in Art Nouveau style that closed from the outside, and that you couldn't see from the stairwell. The room was quite large and had a window overlooking the courtyard.

Mr. Vanderbrook begged us never to open the window during the day, only at night, whith the lights off. This was our hiding place! The Lanskners stayed there two years without ever leaving. I left after three months because I couldn't take being cooped up.

Many Jewish families hid in Brussels. It wasn't easy to find someone willing to hide Jews—this was an arrangement that cost a great deal. In turn, the price paid for hiding a Jew was extremely high: deportation to a forced labor camp, or at very least an interrogation by Gestapo officers. Nonetheless, there were those willing to do it.

There were those who denounced the Jews in hiding. Sometimes the very households that hid them would turn them over to the Gestapo in exchange for a substantial reward. This was, of course, before negotiating for their own freedom. In other instances, the "landlord" would throw them out or report them to the Gestapo for not paying rent on time.

Denouncing a Jew was always rewarded, and it paid well. Children the same price as adults.

I chose not to sleep in the hiding place to avoid attracting the neighbors' attention with so much coming and going. The Lanksners never left.

There were two places I could go to. Eszti Lanksner, Buci's cousin, had an Argentinian passport: she'd been married to an Argentinian Jew since 1939. He was able to return to his home country before the war. She let me sleep in her house without any problems and, above all, without asking any questions. Hers was a safe house.

My cousin Heinrich Wolfthal was married to an Austrian non-Jewish woman named Stefi. The apartment was in his name, and she had a German passport. That was my second safe option. Anything was better than returning to the hiding place.

At that time I began earning money. My cousin Hilde's son, Herbert, was three years older than I, and he was a photographer. He worked in a laboratory, as well as in a camera shop. He told me that on Sundays he went to the *Marche Au Puces*—the flea market—to look for used cameras that he later repaired and cleaned in order to resell them. He preferred to consign them in the shop where he worked. He invited me to do business with him, which is to say he invited me to do the same work he did, and have my own account.

I asked Buci for a loan of 200 francs, and on Sunday I bought my first two cameras, the Brownie from Eastman Kodak. They worked well, though they looked awful: the leather was worn away, and had turned from black to grey. With Hubert's guidance, I used a few drops of oil to fix the shutters, making sure they worked properly. Afterwards, with black paint and shoe polish, I polished the exteriors until they gleamed like new.

On Monday morning, I went to the camera shop. Hubert introduced me to the owner, who accepted my two gleamingly polished cameras on consignment. They'd cost me 110 francs, and they'd be resold at 95 francs each, with a 25 percent commission for the owner. My profit would be 42 francs, which was a great deal of money for me. Provided, of course, that they sold.

I also built crystal radios, relatively primitive radios without bulbs. Simple but fail-proof. You listened in with headphones. The trick lay in finding a station worth listening to in the crystal set. I earned a few francs this way. I bought the parts second hand at the flea market, assembled the radios, and sold them. This turned out to be a fruitful endeavor.

In May I met young people in the Resistance through Mr. Carton, a great patriot who had belonged to the Resistance since 1940. His work was discreet but effective. They asked me if I could be a mail runner for them. I was to deliver three times each week, but on different days—so as not to draw attention—an envelope, sometimes a package, from the Gare du Midi to the Gare du Nord, train stations on opposite ends of the city.

I accepted, as this would not be difficult for me. I was a school-aged child with light hair, and thus wouldn't catch the attention of the German guards, who were everywhere. They gave me two "Tin Tin" comic books in which to hide the letter or packet. In return, they "made" for me an *Arbeitsausweis* or work permit—they were experts at doing this—with a picture, under the name of Jean Vandervelde.

I began working at a photo laboratory called Photo M.G. on the Boulevard Maurice Lemonnier. The owner, Monsieur Guillaume, was very friendly, but he demanded hard work and punctuality, and he didn't pay much. Given the circumstances, I felt secure I wouldn't be discovered. At night, I would go to any of my alternate bedrooms. Occasionally I would sleep in the hiding place with the Lanksners.

I imagine M. Guillaume suspected I was a foreigner and a Jew, that my name was not Jean Vandervelde. But he never said a thing. He gave me the job, and I never objected to the low salary. We both needed each other. I felt happy: after all, I was working.

Monsieur Guillaume was an industrial photographer. He photographed machine parts, cogs, pans for hospitals, and so forth. At first, I served as his assistant. I carried the camera and tripod. The camera was made of wood, with bellows and large lenses, for glass plates 18 by 24 centimeters. Everything was kept in a large leather case and was incredibly heavy. The tripod was also made of wood, and also extremely heavy.

When we met with a customer, usually at a workshop or factory, I had to mount the camera onto the tripod, put the lens on the camera, and get a kind of black mantle that M. Guillaume would later put over his head like a *Talit*, to block light from entering while he observed the object he was photographing on unpolished glass. Afterwards, I would give him a flat wooden case with a sensitized plate and he would take the photo. I learned quickly, and soon I became a good assistant.

During the war, the industrial photography business went from bad to worse. Pictures of machines were unnecessary, as machines were only valuable to the German military effort.

The M.G. Laboratory was forced to develop negatives for the Germans. Who else was taking pictures during the war?

So we ended up inadvertently working for the German army. It made sense, because there were no other customers. Belgians had no money, and it was dangerous to have a camera. Taking photographs in public looked suspicious.

We also developed film in the laboratory. These various feature films were usually 35 millimeters. After processing a film, the photographs were printed: pictures of groups of soldiers in martial positions; joking around with their Belgian women friends, usually in the nude.

I was promoted to be a printer, a job requiring more care and skill, but of course earning me the same weekly salary.

With my *Arbeitsausweis* in hand I could get around. The Germans were checking more and more frequently due to the growing activity of the Resistance; they planted bombs in the German commissaries and often snuck into the barracks and murdered German soldiers off their guard.

I traveled every day by tram. Frequently I saw soldiers with submachine guns along the way. The tram would stop, and we were forced to get off and align ourselves against the façade. The inspection began: first the papers, then my aluminum lunchbox. Once opened, a soldier went through it with a bayonet from his belt. This was to make sure there wasn't a grenade or gun beneath the food. Finally, we were allowed back on the train, which continued its journey.

These inspections were practiced by the Wehrmacht or German army and were less dangerous than those done by the Gestapo, who would meticulously examine each paper to detect any possible forgery or falsification. Sometimes they ordered men to lower their pants, and those who were circumcised were arrested immediately.

Sometimes I asked myself, where was G-d? Where was he when all of this was happening? How could he permit such cruelty, such injustice, such misery? How could he have forgotten his people? How could he have allowed them to be exterminated in the gas chambers, and burned in the crematoriums?

Paradoxically, the Germans had *"Gott mit uns"* engraved on their belt buckles, which promised divine protection for the wearer. Also paradoxically, the Pope spoke in the name of G-d and kept silent in the face of the extermination of the Jews. Was G-d the same for everyone?

At twelve years old, I realized G-d was not physically present anywhere, that there existed something in man called faith. Faith in what? Faith in divine justice, human justice, faith that one day justice would prevail in this world.

These thoughts came to me in a more or less nebulous form. I had no one to ask, no one to turn to. Buci, an Orthodox Jew, never questioned the presence of G-d although, truth be told at times he had doubts. He would say *Yo Ishtenem hol vagysz?* My G-d, where are you?

One time, on my way home from work, I had a face to face encounter with a man around sixty years old who wouldn't stop staring at me, and smiling sweetly. When I got off the tram, this man—with his beret, his cane, and his old, worn coat—yelled at me to catch my attention, to get me to stop. He caught up with me and said: *"Jeunne home, attendez mois."* I had no idea how to respond. He continued talking to me: "Don't be afraid, I'm your friend."

He told me he'd like to see me again; we should go to the park for *une glace*, an ice cream, and we could chat...

We made plans to meet on Saturday at the same tram stop. I worked from Monday through Saturday, but on Saturdays I got off at noon. *Semaine Anglaise*, although now no one said so for fear of the Germans and the Rexists. Any use of English was prohibited.

On the day we'd agreed to meet, I arrived at the station, and there he was in his beret. On Saturdays I never brought food because I only worked until noon. We went walking in the Josaphat Park, which was nearby. First he brought me to the park restaurant to eat. Eating was relative in that time of shortage. There was no meat. Bread was rationed, and was not served in restaurants, only in bakeries, and you needed a ration coupon to buy it. There were deserts like *tarte au fuits* that were very expensive, there was *petit lait*, or milk diluted with water—water we had in abundance... We ate the *tarte* and washed it down with a glass of milk. All of this a luxury at that time!

Afterwards we walked through the park. He gave me a chocolate *cote d'or fondant*. Where had he gotten it from? Who knew! There hadn't been chocolate in Brussels for ages... We saw each other again the following Saturday at the same time. He recounted historical anecdotes. I loved history. I trusted him; he was an elderly man with a pleasant and gentle, erudite way of speaking. Surely he'd read a great deal, and was incredibly cultured.

After a walk around the park, he invited me to his house near the Porte de Namurs. We took the tram there. The car arriving was full; there were no free seats. I stood against the metal tube on the rear platform. My companion stood beside me, one hand on his cane, the other grasping the chrome tube.

The tram moved quickly and stopped only at the obligatory stations. If anyone wanted to get off between one stop and the next, he had to press a green button. I pressed it quickly when I felt the old man's persistent caresses. Flustered and confused, I got off the tram, an as soon as I'd made sure the old man was still on board, I began running. I felt a mixture of disgust and embarrassment.

What had the old man wanted? Thankfully, I never saw him again. That night I went to sleep at Eszti's house. I didn't want to see Buci and Yolanka after what had happened.

In comparison with other camps, the conditions in the Riversaltes were tolerable. It was a *camp d'internement* in the France of Petain. The prisoners wore civilian clothing. They were able to wash their clothes. At each call, the inmates gathered to wait for hours for roll call. Those who'd died of starvation were carried away and buried. There was a *Lazaret*, or military hospital, where drugs were administered—aspirin and sleeping pills.

When Hermann Von Beyer, German Jew and Nobel Prize winner, was able to successfully mix certain chemical ingredients in his laboratory in the Kaiser Wilhelm Institut fur Wissenschaft in Charlottenburg, launched on the market as Aspirin, he never thought that one day his invention would be distributed to his brethren in a concentration camp in the Pyrenees.

My father, together with ninety-nine other Jewish prisoners—making one hundred altogether—was shoved into a boxcar and sent to Drancy, where the car was hitched to a locomotive that would bring them to Auschwitz. They were given soap and a basket of bread for the two-day journey. The locomotive with its ten wagons set out eastward.

Convoy Number 24 contained a thousand deportees in total. Nearly half—four hundred, to be exact—were children from the Pithiviers Camp. They'd been apprehended during a raid in Paris, after being hunted like animals, running to save themselves.

Convoy 24 set out on August 26, 1942 at 8:55 A.M. This was according to the routine telex sent by Erich Heinrichsohn to Eichmann in Berlin, with copies sent to the general inspector of the K.Z. in Orianenburg and to the commandant at Auschwitz.

The Germans were painstaking. After the war, lists of names and characteristics—origin, gender, age—of all the deportees were uncovered.

I learned about the lists through Serge and Beate Klarsfeld in Paris, who after years of work were able to collect and publish the lists of Jews deported from France between 1942 and 1944. They dedicated their lives to investigating the Holocaust. Beate, a German gentile, dedicated herself to hunting Nazis, and was instrumental in the arrest of Barbi, chief of the Gestapo in France, found living peacefully in Paraguay.

The convoy arrived in Auschwitz on August 28, 1942. It was night. S.S. guards awaited them with their *Wolfshunde*. Light from giant *Scheinwerfer*, high-powered headlights made by Osram, dazzled the prisoners who'd just spent 72 hours in a dark boxcar.

The guards, aided by their dogs, grouped them five by five. These lines progressed amid pushing and shouting: *Vorwerts, Schnell, Marsch.*

An officer with a whip used at will received the captives. Twenty-seven young, strong men were selected for the work camp as well as thirty-six women. The first were tattooed with the numbers 62093 through 62119 and the others from 18609 through 18644. I don't know the mechanics behind the numeration. To this day, the few survivors of the camp retain these numbers on their right forearms.

Children, men, and women who were old or sick were sent to bathrooms, and later to the "showers" from which the gas emerged. That same night, smoke escaped from the crematorium smokestacks, the remains of my father and his companions in Convoy 24.

Where were their souls? The *Neshamot* remained with us, the survivors. Elie Wiesel said after Auschwitz: "I know that G-d is merciful. Please G-d have mercy on those who created this place."

In Auschwitz-Birkenau, one million, one hundred thousand Jews were killed, along with four hundred thousand non-Jews, Polish, Russians, and Gypsies. In this camp, killing was easy.

I have nowhere to say *Kaddish* for my father, aside from in that horrible place, a scourge on this planet. Like me, there are thousands in the same situation. This is what was handed down to us in the twentieth century, now drawing to a close. Will the coming centuries be better? I sincerely hope so for my children and their children's children.

In Vienna there were increasingly fewer Jews. Germany, to feed its population and its large army, brought food into the occupied countries. There was nothing to eat in Denmark, but there was Danish butter in Viennese stores. The same was happening with many other products.

Eichmann went to Vienna in person, although his offices—designed by the architect Spree, builder of the Reich Millennial Capital—were in Berlin. In Vienna, he met with Baldur Von Schirach, who demanded that the city be cleaned of its Jews. *Judenrein.* He was given a deadline: Christmas of 1942.

My mother had been able to stay in the apartment on Dominikanerbastei 10. I don't know how, I'll never know. She wrote to me from there. Her letters arrived as usual, if censored, to Belgium. She stayed at home; it was dangerous for Jews to be out in the streets.

In November of 1942, my mother received a court summons: she had to present herself at 8 in the morning in the Sperlgasse, now a *sammelstelle*, or gathering place for the deportees. She was summoned, not even arrested. She was sent in a convoy to Opole, a concentration camp near Lublin, in Poland. I received letters from her from there, don't ask me how! The letters bore stamps from the *General Gouvernement,* a future settlement for Aryans. The return address said "Opole Kreis Pulawy, General Gouvernement." The letters arrived in Brussels by mail. The last was dated February, 1943, and in it she described the conditions of the camp, told me that many people were dying of typhoid.

She wrote to me with so much anguish, and so much love. She probably handed the letters to a Polish guard, whom she paid with what little money she was able to keep. And he would send them in the mail. This is what I imagine, but I don't know for certain.

My poor mother, once a proud woman—a Viennese woman steeped in the culture of her birth city—was now reduced to a number tattooed on her arm. She was no longer Margarethe Grete Katz. In the camps no one remained the same as they were before: mere shadows, ephemeral apparitions with sunken eyes, shaved heads, wearing striped uniforms. Men and women alike, with their tattoos. Standing in the snow for hours during repeated roll calls, the *Appels.*

She must have been dead soon after that last letter. Perhaps in March of 1943. G-d rest her soul!

I was in Lublin with my son after the war. In Opole there was no trace of a K.Z. camp amid a wooded area near what is now the Russian border. In fact, only Auschwitz-Birkenau is preserved as a monument for all of humanity.

Even today, the Polish have failed to reconcile with their past. Lech Walesa doubted whether or not to allow the recitation of *Kaddish*—a prayer for the dead—during an official ceremony on the anniversary of the liberation of Auschwitz.

The laboratory where I worked in Brussels was always busy. As I mentioned, the Germans took many photographs and ordered a great deal of copies and amplifications. Business was good for Monsieur Guillaume.

Through a mistake I made, my boss discovered that I spoke German: he asked me, then, to stop working in the basement and instead help out with customers in the store. I refused because I thought it would be too dangerous. He didn't press me any further.

Day by day, the Allies were gaining ground on the battlefields. 1943 began. In Stalingrad, the Russians resisted; there was almost nothing left in the city, the old Volgograd. The Russians remained at their posts; the Sixth German Army at the command of Marshall Von Paulus had surrendered. The Red Army had surrounded the Germans like a tight steel belt. The Russian radio stations encouraged the heroic fighters, defenders of Mother Russia, of the *Mat Rodina*.

This was new. There was no longer talk of communism, of *Comintern*; now there was talk of Holy Motherland. Help flowed in from North America. Giant Liberty boats arrived from the Pacific at the Vladivostok port, and day and night was spent unloading supplies for the Russians: heavy artillery, tanks, and, above all, Dodge trucks, which were already common in the Soviet Union.

Although Hitler spoke on the phone with Von Paulus ordering that no one surrender—*"Keineneintzigen meter zuruek"*—the army was forced to surrender anyway. The soldiers were freezing to death in the cold. The BBC played the Russian National Anthem in honor of the courageous and enduring Russian people.

Stalin fell into a profound depression and sequestered himself in his offices in the Kremlin. It was almost impossible for him to imagine that half of the Russian empire had been conquered by the Germans. He couldn't believe that the Russian army, which he had weakened during his purges, had retreated in disarray before the Niemetzky, now only 38 km from Moscow.

Stalin was pulled from his depression by his close friends, Vorochilov, Molotov, and Beria, the last of whom held the reigns of authority. He was in charge of promotions and sent the *refusniks*, the protestors and nonconformists, to the firing squad. *Ras, Dva, Tri.* Three times, ending with the opposition.

Stalin, now back in place, delivered a speech that was transmitted to all of the Soviet Union, calling the Russian people to join the military effort, not only to liberate their mother country, but to march into Berlin and behead the Nazi beast in his own home.

In December of 1942, Baldur Von Schriach was cleaning Vienna of its last Jews. They came for my grandmother Carolina in her house in Wollzeile. She was 71 years old. She was healthy, but had difficulty walking because of her weight. Nonetheless, she stood on her own two feet and with her head held high; she refused to sit in a wheelchair. Her neighbors shut their doors when the Gestapo arrived. Like the Germans, the Austrians didn't want to face what was happening. When a Jew was arrested, they'd say: *"Noch Immer Sind Juden Bei Uns."* Which is to say: "There are still Jews in our midst?"

My grandmother was sent to Sonderlager in Theresienstadt, in Czechoslovakia. What a coincidence! This was the land of her parents, the Gruenfelds. As I've mentioned, she was only in this camp for a few months. She was later deported in a convoy of elderly Viennese Jews, bound for the pits at Mali Trostenec, near Minsk, in Belarus, where they were gunned down in April of 1943.

In the camp, food was scarce. Many died from starvation or from the typhoid epidemics sweeping through the prisoners. I was very close to my grandmother; in fact, she was the only grandmother I knew, and she showered me with love and tenderness. She was born in Vienna, and was an altogether a "Self-Made Woman" who subsisted on her memories of the Austrian Empire. She never accepted the Republic, nor the racial and political hatred and discrimination. She remembered her good emperor *Der Gute Kaiser* Franz Josef, and *Die Gute Alte Zeit*, the good times of yesteryear. May G-d bless such a wonderful woman! Amen.

I'll continue with a song transcribed from the poet Ruben Lifschitz, one of the few survivors from the Warsaw ghetto, living today in Tel-Mordejai, Israel. This little-known song, based on a traditional Jewish melody, was published in New York after the war by the Arbeter Ring within a collection of Holocaust songs entitled *"Mir Zenen do."* Here I use the phonetic accepted by the YIVO.

A Gut Morgn, Libe Mentshn people,	Good morning, dear
Warft Uns A Shtikele Broit bread	let us raise a piece of

Derfar Wet Got Aich Bentshn	G-d will bless you
Nisht Visn Vet Ir fun Kain Noit hunger.	and you will not know

Gehat a Tate-Mame	I had a father and mother,
Un Sheininke Shwesterlach Drei	three beautiful sisters.
Awek Mitn Roich un Flamen	They went up in flames and smoke
Geblibn Bin Ich Yetzt Alein	and I am here, alone.

Ich Drey Di Katarinke	I play my hurdy-gurdy;
Un Shpil Hynt Far Aich Mit Courash	today I play for you.
Wail Morgn, Ken Zayn in Treblinka	Tomorrow I might be in Treblinka
Wet Fun Uns Wern a Barg Ash	where all that's left of us is a pile of ashes.
Fun Hertzer Broist a Fayer	In our hearts burns a flame.
Genug Uns Gerkoilet Wi Shof	nough of slaughtering us like sheep.
Oy, Yidn, Nemt Di Naganes	Jews, take up arms!

Un Kumt, Lomir Machn a Sof	Come, let us end it.
Ich Drei Di Katarinke	I play my hurdy-gurdy
Farshpil Unsere Laidn un Noit	I sing our sorrows and anguish
Wil Eider Tzu Geyn Ken Treblinke	Better than Treblinka
Is Besser in Kamf Faln Toit	is to fall and die in battle.

In the different ghettos, songs were composed that accompanied the Jews through their darkest moments. The most well-known is *"Zog nit kein mol az du gueist dem letzn veg"* or "Never say it's your last trip," written by Hersh Glick and adopted as a hymn by partisans since 1942.

In 1942, Heydrich was killed—Eichmann's boss—in his convertible, a Mercedes, while turning on a small road near Prague. In retaliation the Germans killed every man in a populous village in Lidice, Czechoslovakia. Their homes were destroyed.

Two hundred and forty-eight innocent men were gunned down. This is how the occupiers dispensed justice. The Czechs never forgave them for this massacre.

The situation in the Warsaw ghetto was tragic. There was almost nothing to eat; Jews were dying of starvation at the rate of one hundred to three hundred per week. The ghetto was riddled with infectious disease. The Judenrat didn't know how to meet the deportation quotas established by the Germans: one thousand Jews per day.

Mordejai Anielewicz, 24 years old, was born in Warsaw in 1919. He was one of the many young men living in the ghetto. Against all odds, political life continued to thrive. There was *Sichot*: they studied Hebrew, prepared the *chalutzim,* or pioneers, for the *Aliyah* to Palestine. They all knew of the deportations to Treblinka but it did not deter them. The Germans were not able to crush their spirit. Jews now and in the future will always be proud of these young combatants in the ghetto.

Among the political organizations, the Bund was the strongest. Afterwards, the Communists. After that the Hashomer Hatzair, to which belonged Anielewicz, Poale Zion; Dror; Gordonia and Betar. Since November of 1942, they had already formed a committee united for an uprising. In December, after many long negotiations, the first batch of weapons arrived from the Polish resistance for the defenders of the Warsaw ghetto.

A staff was formed, directed by Mordejai Anielewicz, seconded by Michael Klepfisz and Josef Lewartovski, a former combatant in the International Brigades in Spain who had a great deal of military experience. Regina Funde and Mira Fucherer were at the head of the women. Ephraim Sagan was an ex-commander of the Polish army.

Also among the leaders were Andrés Schmidt, ex-brigadier; Edward Fondaminsky, Arieh Vilner, León Fainer, Jersy Neuding, and finally Dr. Adolf Berman, chief of the Polish Jewish committee Zegota, who served as dean of the Warsaw ghetto staff.

In January of 1943, Himmler, chief of the S.S., paid a visit to Warsaw, to inspect. His objective was to implement a more expedited system for exterminating Polish Jews. *Also, Schluss Machen Damit*: So that it will be finished, once and for all!

When the German soldiers arrived in the ghetto on the morning of January 18, 1943, they were greeted with gunfire. Behind the barricades and on the street corners, well-equipped Jewish combatants Mila and Zamenhof and Gezia and Niska killed the first uniformed German officers in a formal battle. This was unprecedented, *unglaublich*. The Germans retreated, and the Jews closed the front entrance to the ghetto. This first victory surprised everyone, including the Jews.

They could fight! Death was always a reality, but at least they could die fighting. Many volunteers—young and old, women and men—wanted arms for combat. The number of weapons was limited, but every time a German soldier fell, there were more to dispense. From January to April, resistance was sporadic but steady. The Germans no longer entered the ghetto, and deportations to Treblinka were suspended. But food was not brought in.

The first week of April, the Polish were able to send in additional weapons before Passover. On April 19, the Germans brought a military expert, S.S. Polizeifuhrer, General Jürgen Stroop, from Lemberg. He was in charge of the operations necessary for finishing off the insurgents. They prepared for what would be the final battle.

The Germans had field artillery; they built machine-gun emplacements. Three tanks were stationed in front of the main entrance to the ghetto, ready to enter. The ghetto's headquarters were in Mila No. 18. The defenders must surely have identified themselves with their ancestors in Masada, confronted by the Romans, commanded by Vespasian.

Flags appeared in the windows: red and white for Poland, blue and white for *Tivka,* and red on behalf of the arms suppliers, the Polish Communist partisans KPP.

The defenders countered with machine guns, grenades, and Molotov bombs, but they had no cannons and very little heavy artillery. The combatants concentrated themselves near the ghetto entrance in Nalewki and Zamenhof, in Gesia and in Muranov Plaza. Before nightfall, the Germans had retreated. They had lost twelve men. Himmler asked to be informed of the events every three hours.

The first confrontation lasted four days. The Germans couldn't manage to finish off the rebels, and they were suffering daily casualties.

On April 22, they received orders to set fire to the ghetto. The defenders retired to their bunkers and drainage channels, through which arms had been delivered from outside. The Jewish combatants were determined to fight, right down to the last man. *Mir Veln Kemfn Bis Zum Letztn Man, Bis Zum Letztn Otem.*

The Germans fought street by street, searching for rebels. They took no prisoners. Those captured with their hands in the air were killed immediately. On May 8, 1943, after a battle lasting two hours, the Germans overtook the ghetto headquarters. Felled by machine gun were Mordejai Anielewicz, his wife, Edward Fondamenski, Arieh Vilner, and Lev Grobsalz. This was the end of the fight. The ghetto burned for four more days. The Germans moved cautiously among the burning ruins, wood fragments, and fallen cement. On May 16, 1943, S.S. General

Jürgen Stroop reported to Himmler: *"Es Gibt Keinen Judischen Wohnbezirk in Warschau Mehr."* There are no more Jews living in Warsaw.

Until the liberation by the Soviets, the ruins were left intact, silent witnesses to a cruel battle.

There were other uprisings, but of smaller proportions. The Bialystok ghetto took up arms. From August 16 through the 23, 1943. Three hundred and sixty Jews led by Mordejai Tenenbaum and Danielle Moskovic were able to escape into the forest. They killed close to two hundred German soldiers. Alfred Galevsky and Salo Bloch also served as commanders in this epic feat in Bialystok. After the rebellion, forty thousand Jews were deported to Treblinka. The Bialystok ghetto was liquidated.

On October 14, 1943, a rebellion began in the Sobibor Camp. In September a group of Soviet war prisoners had arrived in the camp, among them Alexander Pechersky, a Jewish official who headed and planned the rebellion. Twenty-four S.S. guards were killed. Of the six hundred Jews who were able to escape, two hundred were killed; the rest escaped to the nearby forests, where they were annexed to the Soviet partisan units. Together the Jews and Soviets fought until liberation.

In Vilna, the city that contributed greatly to Jewish culture, there were only twenty thousand Jews in the ghetto. On September 14, a group of two hundred and forty young men and women escaped into the Narocz forests, where they united with the partisans.

In retaliation, six hundred and eighty Jews were taken to Ponar, where they were gunned down and buried in mass graves. The rest of the Jews left in Vilna were deported to Treblinka.

Below I have transcribed a song with lyrics by A. Rosenthal, sung in Vilna before the liquidation of the ghetto. It was published in 1948 in Paris by Yidisher Folksfarband Editions in *"Yirushalaim d'Lite in kamf un umkum."*

Pak Sich Ain, Pak Sich Ain.	Get ready, get ready
Svet Fun Uns Shoin Gorni	They will take nothing from us
Haint Herstu Noch a Sinfonie	Today you hear a symphony
Morgn Bistu Shoin in Estonie	Tomorrow you'll be in Estonia
To Pak Sich Ain, Pack Sich Ain	So get ready....

Haint Senen Mir Noche Hige	Today we're still here.
Morgn Forn Mir Kain Rige	Tomorrow we go to Riga
Svet Der Sof Sain Besser things	It would be better to end
Dosml Vet Sai Nit Gelingn win	This time they will not
Mir'n Sai dos Liedl Singen	We sing this song
Pak Sich Ain, Pak Sich Ain	So get ready....

Yechiel Sheinboim was leader of the resistance movement. His lieutenant was the brave young Jewish woman Asia Bik.

On September 14, the day of Yom Kippur, two hundred and forty young people organized themselves in preparation to escape into the nearby forest to unite with the partisans. They were able to accomplish this with only twenty-two youths killed in the process by the Germans. They in turn killed eight Germans and six Lithuanians.

The Kovno ghetto was liquidated in late September of 1943. The last residents were deported to the extermination camp Kloga, near Riga, in Estonia. Lithuanian John Damyuk worked there as a guard. He was extradited to Israel by the United States in 1990. Judged as "Ivan the Bully," he was pardoned by the Supreme Court for lack of evidence. He is currently living in the United States.

In 1944, two hundred and twenty thousand Jews passed through the ghettos in Vilna, Kovno, and the camp Ponar; less than five hundred eighty people survived; all of them as partisans. Mark Dvorszetzki writes: "No one will say Kaddish for these human beings who were massacred." *"Keiner Vet Nit Kenen Shive Sitzn Noch Sei."* "No one is in mourning for them, no one will sit shiva in their memory."

The final solution to exterminate the Jews from the face of the earth was not always easy for the Germans. How can it be done as coldly, widely, and rapidly as possible according to the Nazis' plan?

Below I've transcribed a speech by S.S. Reichsfuhrer Heinrich Himmer in Posen, East Germany on October 4, 1943, in which he invites his brethren to quickly and effectively take action. This was taken from the Bundesarchiv in Bonn.

"I would like to speak to you about an extremely important matter. Between us we can discuss this frankly, but we cannot do it in public. I speak of the evacuation, *Abschiebung*, of the Jews, the extermination of the Jewish people. It's something that's easy to talk about: 'The Jewish people will be exterminated,' says the

Fuehrer, and for every party member this is clear, it's in our program: let us carry out the liquidation and extermination of the Jews.

Then, of course, some eighty million Germans chime in, each one with his 'respectable Jew.' Of course, all of the other Jews are '*Saujuden*,' but the Jew that I've known for many years is respectable.

None of the Germans that speak this way have seen the cadavers, none of them have been in the K.Z. The majority of you know what it feels like to see crowds of a hundred, five hundred, or a thousand bodies, having seen, having lived *Miterlebt*—have endured in spite of human weaknesses—*Menschliche Schwaeche*—and have remained unharmed. This is what has hardened us, *Gehaertet*. It's a glorious page in the history of the German people, which has never been written. That will never be written about..."

In Brussels, we knew a bit about what was happening to the Jews being sent by the Germans to Poland. Not because anyone had returned alive to tell us, but rather by the BBC transmissions. Poland had managed to send *shlichim* to London with help from the Polish Resistance, who had reported the facts. The London radio stations reported this information, although the reporting was fragmented.

Life in Brussels continued its course. I worked every day, from Monday to Saturday. I did my "mail runs" for the Resistance, fulfilling my commitment. This was known only to Monsieur Carton, Buci's friend, who had helped me find my hiding place, as well as my working papers, my *Arbeitsausweis*.

During the Occupation, I never met anyone else in the Resistance. Avoiding contact was a necessary precaution, for if one was arrested, he or she could easily denounce someone else. In these times, almost no one knew more than one person from the movement, which was well-fortified.

Yolanka and Buci spent a year in hiding, without leaving, not even to venture onto the street. This was the only way to avoid the fatal consequences of being denounced.

It was interesting for me to see how I had transformed. I was no longer Hans Peter Katz. I never spoke German—I took good care to avoid doing so. I was Jean, and the whole world knew me this way. This is what my *Arbeitsausweis* said. Now I was Jean Vandervelde, born in Brussels on May 19, 1930. Hans Peter Katz no longer existed.

In that time, you lived from one day to the next. When I'd return to the hiding place from work and my "other" job, I would say to myself: "I came. I'm here. Today, I passed the test. Nothing happened. Tomorrow will be another day." This was the entire horizon I could possibly contemplate. I couldn't see further. How could we see any further without any control over our surroundings, our lives? The Germans controlled everything. And this is why I say we lived from one day to the next.

By the end of 1943, the Germans had lost the war. But no one in Germany—or very few, at least—wanted to recognize it.

In London, one of the *shlichim* arriving from Poland was accompanied by an emissary from the Jewish World Congress and by the secretary of Chaim Weizmann, and requested a hearing with the Allied Supreme Command. They were received by several high-ranking military officials.

They exposed the ruthless killing of Jews in the extermination camps in Poland, showing detailed maps of the locations of the five most important camps: Auschwitz-Birkenau, Belzec, Maidanek, Chelmno, and Treblinka.

They asked the Allies for British and North American planes, which were now routinely bombing German military targets and civilians, to destroy the railways and crematory ovens, located precisely on the maps.

The Allied officials listened to the Jews and promised them that within three days, they'd send a response to Dr. Chaim Weizmann. The response arrived. It said: "we are very sorry" but they had not planned to bomb Poland from the air. I suppose they didn't grasp the message. Or they had no interest in reacting.

Meanwhile, our people were being murdered and burned. Day and night, the Polish skies were full of smoke and human ashes.

In 1942, American amphibious troops disembarked in North Africa. After squelching the small resistance from French troops, loyal to Vichy, they advanced toward Libya to unite with the British troops, encountering some serious problems with the tenacious resistance of the Afrika Korps at the hand of Rommel.

The French troops didn't resist. De Gaulle had already proselytized among those who ended up ignoring their leaders. Admiral Darlan, French traitor, was taken prisoner. General Charles de Gaulle was proclaimed head of the armies of "Free France" and dissolved the work camps in Algeria. My cousin Hugo Mordkovich was liberated, and reintegrated into the French legion.

The sun of liberty was beginning to shine; it shined its first rays of light on Europe, which had been plunged so long into darkness.

Also in North Africa, the British Army, initially battered by the Afrika Korps led by General Erwin Rommel, as well as two Italian armies, achieved surprising victories in El Alamain. The Germans were defeated by "Monty", the English General Bernard Montgomery. The rest of the Afrika Korps returned to Europe. The Italians surrendered en masse. Their leader, Mariscal Graziani, escaped in a boat.

I've always considered the Italians a very civilized people. From centuries' worth of history, they have learned that wars are hatched by politicians, by the Machiavellians; by statesmen like Mussolini, but not by the people. That in any war, no one wins, and everyone loses.

They've learned that flags, parades, demonstrations, speeches in the Piazza Venezia, and calls to fight to the death—*Forza Italia, la Storia, la facciamo noi*—are nothing more than this: a call to die for the glory of Mussolini. A call to disgrace Italy…the Italians are not heroes, nor do they wish to be. They wish to live in peace with their fellow man, enjoying their lives.

The Italian army stationed in North Africa surrendered at the first opportunity. Il Duce was furious, but he wasn't surprised: he knew his people.

In Africa, the Jewish Brigade, a respectable armed force, also surrendered. They were trained in Palestine under British command, and, to date, had 1,500 men. With another 5,000 men, they later fought in Italy, elbow to elbow with the Polish Brigade, with many Jews in active duty under the command of General Anders—a Pole, not a Jew—and under the supreme command of General Alexander. They fought bravely, and many fell in battle. At least they died with their rifles in their hands.

In February of 1943, the Allies disembarked in Sicily. It was their first landing on European soil.

One could say that the Battle of Stalingrad, the invasion of Sicily, and later on the invasion of Normandy, were decisive contributing factors to the beginning of the end of the Germans. If this had been a game of chess, they would have had to acknowledge their defeat.

But they were far from admitting it. As far as the Jews were concerned, they not only continued with the massacres; they intensified them. There was hardly a corner in Occupied Europe where Jews still living were not vigorously pursued, and in an efficient, systematic form.

In just one night, the Jews of Rhodes were hunted and arrested. They were a Sephardic congregation that had lived in peace with their neighbors since

1492. They were taken onto three small Italian Army ships and, from Thessaloniki, were sent directly to Auschwitz by train. The same happened on the island of Kos, and also in Crete.

60% of the population of Thessaloniki was comprised of Sephardic Jews, who were very much appreciated in Greece. Creative and hardworking, they never had a problem with the gentile population. After the German Occupation, many of the young Jews from Salonika, Thessaloniki, united with the Greek partisans. More than fifteen hundred Jews had served in the former Greek Army. Partisan groups from the Trikala region and Larisa were at the command of General Moshe Pesaj, a young Sephardic Jewish rabbi.

From Greece, sixty-five thousand Jews were deported. Remnants of old Spanish Judaism, they had "the key," and dreamed that one day they'd return to Sephardic Spain, their former home.

In comparison with Ashkenazi Jews of German or European origin, the Sephardic Jews from Greece and Turkey had suffered less. They hadn't suffered through Pogroms, massacres, or as much, or as relentless, a persecution. During the Turkish domination, they were tolerated. The Orthodox Church never interfered with them.

Now, suddenly, the Teutons had arrived from the North, and the inhabitants of Thessaloniki, Athens, Yanina, Kastoria, Pireo, and Patras became nothing but ash and smoke in Poland, a country none of them knew. Why? Why such misery? Why such killing? Where was merciful G-d?

Kurt Waldheim, former United Nations Secretary, skirted by. He'd served as lieutenant of the German Special Forces in charge of communication. For me, there is not a shadow of a doubt that Waldheim was involved in the deportation of the Jews and most likely in the execution of Greek and Yugoslavian partisans. He denies it. Yet in spite of everything, he was elected Austrian president by an overwhelming majority.

When the Jewish World Congress provided evidence of his past in Greece and Yugoslavia, they delivered them to the Austrian newspapers and had them published.

The voters said: *"Jetzt erst recht, wird er Gewaelt."* Now, more than ever, we must vote for Dr. Kurt Waldheim. As though nothing had happened.

There were also positive developments, flashes of light in the long night that had descended over Europe, events that uplift humanity.

Denmark was occupied by the Germans in 1940. The Jews in this Scandinavian country were concentrated principally in Copenhagen, the capital. They amounted to 7,200 souls.

For the most part, they were not disturbed by the Germans; or, at least, not their physical integrity. When they were required to wear their "distinguisher," a Star of David, on a yellow background with the word "*Jude*," the king emerged from his palace on his gray horse, wearing on his chest the same star as a gesture of solidarity with the Danish-Jewish people. Nonetheless, this prevailing tranquility was deceptive, and lasted only a short time.

In August of 1943, the Germans declared martial law. The motive: find and arrest the members of the Resistance. Luckily, an employee who worked at the police radio station in Copenhagen intercepted this radiophone order. He immediately advised the Central Committee of the Resistance, who alerted the Jews. That same night, the Danish, with the utmost secrecy and the selfless help of sailors and captains of small boats, took several trips in their little fleet, carrying 5,920 Jews to Malmo and Helsingborg, in neutral Sweden. They helped without any hesitation.

When the Germans arrived to arrest them, they found only four hundred and eighty Jews, most of whom were old and infirm, that could not be evacuated, except to be immediately deported to Theresienstadt.

Here we have an unforgettable example of humanity, the brotherhood among men. How different from the Ukrainians, who voluntarily provided help to the Germans in Babiyar!

And why not mention how different from Franklin Delano Roosevelt, who remained disengaged when with just one signature he could have saved the Jewish passengers aboard the Saint Louis in 1938, but instead returned them to their homeland to be exterminated.

Fifty thousand Jews were living in Bulgaria. The majority were Sephardic, their ancestors from Spain. Bulgaria did not defend itself militarily in 1941; they merely made an arrangement with the Germans and the Italians, which permitted both armies the right to pass freely in Bulgarian territory. Under pressure from the Germans—who'd sent delegations from the S.S. and the Gestapo near the German Embassy in Sofia—the Bulgarians, to protect their nation, passed a law in 1941 that forced Jews to abandon jobs in public administration. This law also forbade the exercising of liberal professions—doctors, lawyers, notaries, professors of higher education, journalists and musicians. In Sofia the community was very cultured and well-educated. There were many Jewish intellectuals and public officials.

In March of 1942, in accordance with Eichmann's instructions, the S.S. demanded that the Bulgarians deliver their Jews so that they could be deported to Poland. Bulgarian society—including the king and Parliament—faced the Germans head on, and refused. An unprecedented case!

In Sofia, Monsignor Angelo Roncalli, the papal nuncio in Turkey—the future Pope John XXIII—together with the head of the Russian Orthodox Church openly backed up the Bulgarian government. The Germans were dumbfounded in the face of this exceptional and unexpected affront. This act was magnificently successful: not a single Bulgarian Jew was sent to the gas chambers. "We will not let you touch our Jews," said the Bulgarians.

Behold another shining example in the dark night:

Vichy France, the France of Petain, could have done the same. But they didn't have the valor to confront the Germans, like the Bulgarians did.

Xante is a small Greek island on one side of the Peloponnesus in the Ionic Sea, to the south of Corfu. It boasted a small Jewish community since time immemorial. Perhaps Paul—Saul of Tarsus—preached there, on his first voyage to Corinth.

Greece and its many islands were occupied jointly by the Italians and Germans. The Germans were, of course, ultimately in charge.

The mayor of Xante, Ludos Karrisikis, received an order to gather the island's two hundred and fifty-seven Jews on the pier.

The mayor, not knowing what to do, went to the Orthodox Archimandrite Kristostomos. It was eight in the morning and the Gestapo motor boat would arrive for the detainees three hours later.

Kristostomos, a young priest barely thirty-two years old, who had ties to the Greek Resistance and hated what was happening, went down to the main square and said to the islanders gathered there: "In the event that the deportation order of our Jewish citizens is carried out, I will unite with them and share in their fate."

With the participation of all the islanders, one hundred and ninety-five Jews were hidden—men, women, adolescents, and all of the children—in the far-away corners of the island. Only the elderly and invalids—sixty in total—remained at the mercy of the Gestapo, to be taken to Corfu, and later to Auschwitz. However, the vessel full of deportees did not stop on the island.

The Germans annihilated the elderly with machine guns, in front of the horrified villagers. They left immediately afterwards. But thanks to the courage, decency, and humanity of Kristostomos, one hundred and ninety-five Jewish souls were spared.

I only speak of some of the just and righteous. There were many others in this lacerated and tormented Europe during the years between 1933 and 1945.

The Allies had already taken Sicily and were advancing north on the Italian boot. The Italian resistance was weak. It ended in 1943, a terrible year for us, a year in which more Jews were annihilated.

The Red army continued their advance, delivering one blow after another to the Germans. Millions of youths, German and Russian, were buried beneath the snow.

On September 14, 1943, Marshall Pietro Badoglio announced to the Allies the capitulation of the Italian armed forces in Cassibile. The Germans, feeling betrayed, invaded on September 16, occupying the rest of Italy to the south of Rome, forming a new defensive line. It was a sad day for Italy. The Italians, an ancient people, had never in their history witnessed such savageness.

On March 20, 1944, three hundred thirty-five Italians were taken prisoner in retaliation for six Germans murdered during an ambush in Rome. Among the Italians there were fifty-seven Jews, all persons of great renown, well-known in Roman society. On March 24, they were executed and thrown into the Ardeatine ditches, outside Rome.

Josef Priebke, the officer who commanded the S.S. platoons, was able to escape after the war and lived peacefully in Bariloche, Argentina, Alpine city, nest of Nazis. He was later extradited to Italy, where he was put on trial. On one of my visits to Italy I visited these ditches, now adorned with solemn granite stars.

Italy was now a country occupied by the Germans. The raids , and the "hunt" for Jewish people, began. Like those in Rome, there were many Jewish communities in Italy formed before the Christian era: Livorno received those expelled from Spain and Portugal with open arms. Ferrara, Florence, Venice, Foscoli, Bologna, Verona, Pisa, Alessandria, and so many other cities had Jewish communities. The Jews were arrested, loaded into trains now driven by German conductors from the Reichsbahn, as the Germans had no confidence in Italian conductors. The Jews were deported via Villach, Vienna, and Ostrava to Auschwitz.

On November 9, 1943, almost a thousand Jews were captured and assembled in the Piazza di Santa Maria Novella in Florence. Then S.S. officers with machine guns herded them to platforms five and six of the Stazione Centrale Di Firenze. Of these Florentine Jews—artisans, lawyers, doctors, jewelers, and small business owners—only thirteen had survived by 1945.

At the beginning of 1944, the Germans had essentially lost the war. Italy, their strongest European ally, had abandoned them. Their armies had suffered irreparable defeats on the Eastern Front. The Allies were advancing on Rome. They'd already liberated Naples and Termoli. England had converted itself into a gigantic military camp, where the largest army known to man was being trained. English, Americans, French, Polish, Austrians, New Zealanders, and ghurkas from India were preparing to invade Europe and free it from barbarism.

Meanwhile, Hitler had not given up his dream of exterminating the Jews, and found time to ask Himmler: *"Wie steht es mit den Juden?"* What's happening with the Jews?

Himmler, in turn, asked Eichmann: *"Wie steht es mit der Endloesung? Der Fuerer ist undeguldig, und verlangt einen sofortigen Rapport."* That is, "How is the Final Solution progressing? The "Fuhrer" is impatient, and is asking me for an immediate report."

Thus, Himmler ordered Eichmann: *"Los, machen sie schluss damit."* Eichmann, get moving. Put an end to the Jewish situation.

In fact, the Eastern Front was collapsing, but the annihilation of Jews remained a priority. There were even heated discussions between the S.S. and the Military High Command, now led by Marshall Von Keitel and the generals Guderian and Gustav Jodl.

They argued over the use of railway transportation: the army needed trains to transport the troops to the Eastern Front; the S.S., on their part, were preoccupied with using them to transport Jews to extermination camps. It's very possible that Eichmann could have gotten away with it. I do not know, but the pace of the crematoria in Poland never ceased.

In Barrack Number 4 in Auschwitz, Dr. Josef Mengele, S.S. Captain, had a hospital where he experimented with inmates, whom he'd selected personally, assisted by Dr. Clauberg and Dr. Kremer, both S.S. doctors. They performed genetic testing: prisoners were injected with phenol and chloroform so that they could observe the reaction. They were assisted by nurses, Jewish doctors temporarily exempt from the gas chambers.

Above all, Mengele took an interest in twins. He awaited the arrival of the convoys and their passengers and directed any sets of twins out of line and towards the hospital. In his barrack adjacent to No. 4, he amassed a collection of thirty-seven pairs of twins. He performed his "medical research" and sent the results to various universities in the Reich. The object of the experiments, among other things, was to demonstrate his theory: that the Jewish race was inferior, and in the process of degeneration.

The exact numbers are not known, but it's estimated that between 1942 and 1945, no less than 36,000 victims passed through the hands of the "Angel of Death."

The infirmary was set up in Barrack No. 15. There, Dr. Klein reigned, chief doctor in the S.S. He was a *Schvab,* a Hungarian of German ethnicity, born in Kolosvar in Transylvania. There was also a pharmacy, a drug reservoir supplied and supervised by a resident physician from Bayerwerke. Prisoners infected with scarlet fever, typhus, and other infectious diseases were brought here. Prisoners beaten by the S.S. but not finished off completely.

The nurses were prisoners of Auschwitz-Birkenau. Their boss was an "S.S.," Irma Griese. Jews served as doctors, nurses, and midwives. They worked as assistants to the *Stubendienst*, and thanks to this work, some of them managed to make it out alive.

In Auschwitz there was a building constructed by prisoners called "Canada," where valises, clothing shoes, and eye glasses of the deportees were stored. Jewelry, cash, watches, and gold teeth, extracted from the prisoners before they were sent to the gas chambers, went directly to Germany, to the *Reichschatz*, the nation's coffers. The Ministry of Finance, led by Halmar Schacht, was in charge of converting the jewelry and gold teeth into lingots.

The flow of the transports was never interrupted. Jews were arriving at the gas chambers from France, Norway, Italy, Greece, Croatia, Bosnia, Serbia, Montenegro and Dalmatia. The victims were from all over the world, but with one common denominator: they were Jewish.

And so began 1944. The war seemed to have gone on forever. "Now our liberators will arrive, and we are not dead yet!" we thought.

Food was scarce, and everyone had to wait in long lines. There was no whole milk or white bread, only dark. Legumes were scarce; we had only those imported from the north. There were no tomatoes—these were reserved for the Germans.

Of course, there were also no bananas or oranges, but there were pears, apples, and rhubarb to jam. There was no sugar, but saccharin.

I continued working; work didn't cease its flow. The quantity of photos taken by the German soldiers was impressive. Monsieur Guillaume's business was doing well, and he made good money. Sometimes at midday, after closing the doors for security reasons, we'd share food purchased on the black market. For us, this was delightful: cookies, salami, paté, brie. Foods that, for years, we couldn't find in stores in Brussels. The *Marche Noir* had all of this and much more. Of course, it was incredibly expensive.

Yolanka and Buci continued hiding. Buci lost a tremendous amount of weight; he couldn't eat. Not because there was little food, but so as not to spend money. He was extremely worried about the lack of money he had left. No one knew how much longer the war would last.

One Sunday there was a great commotion. I was in the hiding place with the Lanksners. Suddenly, we heard a deafening noise, like a truck stopping in its tracks. We didn't move. Monsieur Vanderbrook had already informed us how to act in such cases. Minutes passed, and nothing. Absolute silence. After five minutes, there were three knocks on the mirror, our only door, our only link to the exterior world. It was a signal for us not to move, that there was danger. Yolanka began sobbing. Buci was sweating, but remained calm. I did whatever he did. What was happening? Was it the Gestapo? Had they come for us? Had someone denounced us? Had someone followed me from the tram stop?

Then we heard the sound of car breaks very clearly, and then knocks on the front door. We were on the third floor. The knocks grew stronger: they were actually kicks. There was no doubt in our minds: it was the Germans.

Then noise on the stairs. The sound of boots. Orders in German: *Aufmachen Staatspolizei Gestapo.*

Now there was no doubt: we'd been discovered. In a few seconds, they'd find the door…And I, who tried never to be in the hiding place…now I had to face my fate. They would deport us to Poland, just like the rest. We would share the fate of all the Jews. I had to form a common front with Yolanka and Buci; strengthen them, help them. I pulled out my *Arbeitsausweis*, my documents, and hid them underneath a one of the marble slabs in the chimney.

The minutes passed. There noise of footsteps climbing up and down the stairs. The noise was definitely one of boots. The deafening sound of a door being kicked in on the second floor, beneath us.

Time continued to pass. It was odd, this noise was happening downstairs, not where we were. Not on the third floor.

We didn't move, tried not to make a single sound; we tried not to breathe. The window was closed and covered by a thick curtain. Buci was hugging me to calm me down. But really, I was calming him down. Yolanka was tranquil. She'd stopped crying; she'd put a handkerchief in her mouth to silence her crying, her sobs, her breathing. The noises became increasingly sporadic.

More than an hour had passed, which for us was like an eternity. First the car left, then the truck started its engine, allowing it to warm up. Finally, the truck was gone, too. We then heard two taps on the door, the signal that the danger had passed.

Buci was crying, and put on his Talit. He began to pray. He didn't speak to anyone, didn't say a word. He spoke with G-d, praying. In Hungarian first, he gave praise to God, giving thanks for saving us.

The Jewish people had different prayers for praising God: *Yisgadal* is one of them. The *Shema* is another. Buci prayed for an hour. Then he carefully folded his mantle and put it away. He closed the *Sidur*, the book of prayers, kissed it, and put it away. Then he extended his arm and placed his hand over my head, giving me the Hebrew blessing dedicated to children, the *Yevarechecha*:

> May G-d bless you and keep you.
> May G-d enlighten you and grace you with his presence.
> May G-d watch over you and give you peace.

We hugged and began to cry from happiness. *"On l'a echapee belle."* We've escaped from danger, a French expression widely used in Belgium: *"Men Darf goiml Bentshn,"* "We must give thanks to G-d for having saved us," said Buci.

It happened that Monsieur Vanderbrook had rented a room on the second floor to a youth in the Resistance who, from there, had sent messages from the Belgian Command to London. We were, of course, not aware of this.

The Germans had circulated day and night in their trucks with electronic equipment—rotating antennae—to try and detect any radiophonic transmission.

This was the truck we'd first heard, that then called for reinforcements and soldiers, sealed all the exits, including the roofs of the neighboring houses. Later on, a car arrived, breaking loudly, in which came the Gestapo officials. Luckily, we escaped this time. They had not come for us.

The spy was arrested by the Gestapo, along with Monsieur Vanderbrook, who was sentenced to hard labor in Germany for giving asylum to an enemy of the Reich.

The soldiers dismantled the radio transmitter and confiscated it. Then they got into the second truck, whose motor we heard from the hiding place.

I saw Maurice, purely by chance, two years after I'd last seen him. The Renous had remained in the Rue des Vierges. They had nowhere to go. Hiding was expensive.

The owner of the building on the Rue des Vierges also owned the building to the rear, overlooking the Rue des Mouettes. The basements, used to store coal, were connected by means of a heavy iron gate. It was an excellent hiding place. When the Gestapo searched for Jews on the Rue des Vierges, they would escape to the Rue des Mouettes, and vice versa.

Maurice had changed a great deal; he was more mature. I imagine that he found me to be equally different. I was fourteen years old. We embraced. He cried from happiness; he was very emotional, very Espagnole. We agreed to meet again the following Saturday. At the appointed hour in the afternoon, we met on the Boulevard du Midi, near the Abattoirs.

Two old friends reunited once again! He invited me to the movies. He knew of a theater that showed old American movies that played continuously—which is to say, one could enter and leave whenever he wanted to.

We went to the movies. They were showing *Gunga-Din*, a movie about India and its fabulous maharajas. In black and white, of course, because color films had not yet been invented.

Before we got there Maurice explained that the theater was frequented by young people, and that hopefully we'd meet some pretty girls; *"Ici mon vieux, il y a des Jolies Filles."*

This was new for me. I'd already begun puberty. I was proud of my moustache, the hair on my upper lip. I did not, for any reason, let the barber touch it when I went to get my hair cut.

I'd also gotten hair on my genitals. These, in my view, were very few, and came in too slowly. At night, I'd begun getting erections and woke up in wet sheets. This was very embarrassing for me. I was most embarrassed about it in front of my second parents. Everything related to sex embarrassed me. I blushed when sex was talked about at work. If anyone asked me why, I'd get even redder still. It was horrible.

Maurice told me that the girls who wanted company sat separately, that they left a free seat beside them. He later found a free seat and sat down with a girl. I stood in the aisle and tried to find one, but I couldn't see anything, the theater was so dark. After a few minutes, my eyes grew accustomed to the darkness, and I could see better.

Next to Maurice there was another girl, and at her side, a free seat. I sat there. The girl was around fifteen or sixteen years old. I wasn't sure. I couldn't distinguish much in the darkness of the movie theater. I tried to see her. She had pretty red hair. At least, it seemed to be red. I was worried she would discover that I was only fourteen. That she'd think I deceived her.

In the darkness I felt her gently place her hand on my knee. I liked it. I felt a slight tremor, a *frisson.* Obviously the girl wanted me to know that she was happy I was sitting at her side.

She put her head on my shoulder. Her hair smelled wonderful. I'd never smelled anything like it. I had no idea what to do, if it was the right thing to do in that moment, but I stroked her face and her precious hair. Now I was worried about my hand; the palm of my hand was wet, sweaty...this was nothing new. In awkward situations, I would start sweating. Imagine my surprise when she went to caress me and her hand was sweaty, too.

She glanced at me sideways—her head was still on my shoulder. With a hushed voice, almost raspy, she said *"Embrasse moi,"* kiss me. I'd never kissed a girl on the mouth. I tried to do what I'd seen in the movies, begging G-d I wouldn't fail with this girl. Especially when she found out she was with a fourteen-year old boy. It seemed to be going well. The kisses followed one after the other, as though she couldn't get enough, she wanted more. Truly, she helped me out of my trance. I began to open my mouth. After awhile, I had her tongue in my mouth. What a strange sensation! But lovely. I was in seventh heaven. We obviously didn't see any of the movie.

Then she took my hand, no longer wet, and brought it to her blouse, which was open. My hand touched one of her breasts. The touch of her skin was so smooth! I touched her hard, pointed nipple.

I thought, I'm now a man, like the lovers in the movies. I thought of whom I could tell about my adventure. Who would believe me! I would tell Estzi, Buci's cousin. She was understanding and good to me. She would believe me. I could chat with her and she'd never laugh at me.

Now it was time for the other breast, with more and more kissing. I felt warm, all over my body. It was a beautiful sensation, completely new to me.

My hand moved freely over her chest. She wore a slip underneath her blouse. She slid back into her seat, in the *Fauteuil*, I imagine to give me the go-ahead. My hand moved to new places. I felt a smooth surface, then a navel, and then something very smooth, her silky pubic hair. Much softer than mine, much thicker. I'd never touched anything so smooth. I touched her, and then I retired my hand. She returned her head to my shoulder. With that, the lights came on in the theater. Maurice stood up, and straightaway we invited—well, Maurice was the one talking—the two girls to the Promenade, to walk around.

Though I was only fourteen years old, and Maurice was sixteen, I was taller. The two girls, one blonde, the other a redhead—I'd seen it right—were not very tall. They were smaller, like Maurice. We headed toward the Boulevard de Midi; we walked in the pleasant shade beneath the trees. We bought a cone at an ice cream shop. We sat on a bench to enjoy it and chat.

Then we brought them to the train station. We made plans to see them outside the cinema the following Saturday at one in the afternoon. She told me her name was Danielle: *"Je m'appelle Danielle, et toi."* "Jean," I answered. She gave me a kiss on the cheek and both of them boarded the tram.

Maurice and I said goodbye. He patted me on the shoulder. *"Tres bien, tres bien,"* he told me. Very good, as though he were proud of me, his little friend Vus-Vus.

I was walking on clouds. I'd never felt this way before. It was getting dark; I headed toward Eszti's apartment, near the Boulevard du-Midi.

I told her what had happened. She listened attentively and without interrupting, while giving me supper. She smiled. I even had a feeling she approved of what I'd done. Interestingly, I didn't blush. I wasn't embarrassed, as I usually was. On the contrary; I felt relaxed.

After dinner, we tried to listen to the radio. That night the interference was so strong we couldn't hear anything from London. Of course this was the work of the Germans, who'd done everything possible to block foreign radio stations.

So we went to bed. Normally I undressed in the bedroom and slept in shorts. Eszti always undressed in the dining room and came out wearing pajamas. There was only one big marital bed. We had to sleep side by side, me on the left.

That night, Eszti, wearing green silky pajamas with black stripes, lay down in the bed, on her back. She opened her pajama top and, without joking, said to me: "I'm going to teach you how it's done with a woman." Because I needed to know about these things. I was old enough now.

I couldn't believe what I saw with my own eyes. She raised herself slightly, throwing her pajama top on the floor. She took my hand and brought it to her chest. When she was lying down, her chest was almost flat, like mine, but when she got up, her breasts took the form of precious ripe fruits. She was wearing only pajama pants. She approached me, and with the tenderness of a mother, took my shorts off, sliding them down my legs. For me, watching her movements was something I'd never seen before or experienced, and I felt pure delight.

She stared at my genitals, what little hair they had. She kissed them. From this, my penis was erect and of decent size. She caressed me with love, touching me until I ejaculated, abundantly. Then she got up, brought a small wet towel and with lukewarm water, carefully washed me off. As though I were her son. A great woman and a great friend.

She brought the towel back to the bathroom and returned naked, wearing nothing but slippers. She was majestic with her enigmatic smile. She came to bed and lay on her back again. She took my hand, this time bringing it to her belly. She explained: "Babies grow inside here, and leave from here." Then brought my hand to her clitoris; she let me feel her labia. Her pubic hair was abundant, and much thicker than Danielle's. It was almost as black as her hair. She was an absolutely beautiful woman, and the only one I'd ever seen naked. I had no one to compare her with.

She beckoned me to her side in French: *"Maintenant je vais faire un home de toi."* I'm going to make a man of you, she said with infinite tenderness.

All at once, with unimaginable gentleness and care, she taught me everything I'd need to do. With typical patience, she shared her experience in the matters of sex with me.

After that day, and, more importantly, that night, I was no longer a boy; I became an adolescent. I could not have thanked that woman enough. What I learned served me for the rest of my life.

The next morning, she said to me: "You must promise me you will never say a word to anyone about what happened, much less to Buci. You promise?" I answered affirmatively. It only made sense. Then, with an enigmatic smile, she confessed: *"Mois, je suis contente, et toi?"* I'm happy, are you? I leaned in and kissed her passionately on the cheek, but dared not go further. *"Merci,"* I replied.

The Soviet Army's advance was quite impressive. The tanks came in like waves, enclosing around the Germans, who surrendered or were decimated.

The Soviet generals Zhukov, Koniev, and Malinovsky were excellent strategists. Everyone in Brussels remarked on the success of the Soviets, as well as the English and the Americans in Italy. The Allies were nearing us, but here, the occupation dragged on.

With the help of the British, Moshé Dayán and Moshé Sne—with elements trained by the Haganá and the Palmaj—organized the Jewish Brigade in Palestine. Beforehand, during the First World War, the Mule Corps existed for a very short time. They fought against the Turks with General Allenby. It was the first time since Bar Kojba (140 A.D.) that the Jews had fought beneath their own flag. The Brigade at that time had five thousand men, stationed in Italy under the order of General Alexander.

Two thousand, six hundred forty-two Jewish volunteers, men and women, were admitted into the Royal Air Force and the Women's Auxiliary Air Force. They fought between 1940 and 1945. Among the volunteers were Lilly Berci, sister of Kurt Berci, who was my partner at Iluminacion Tecnica in Mexico, along with Ezer Weizmann, future commander in chief of the Israeli Air Force and later president of the State of Israel.

Now, with British authorization—at the end of the day, the British Protectorate of Palestine was the supreme authority—the Palmaj recruited a small number of volunteers to be dropped by parachute behind enemy lines; their mission was to attack German targets after establishing contact with groups of Jewish partisans and recruiting more Jewish youths to the ranks of combatants.

Aviva Reich helped to organize an uprising in a women's work camp in Kremnicka, near Auschwitz. She was assassinated by the Germans.

Jana Szenes was able to get as far as Nagykanizsa with the help of Yugoslavian partisans who helped her to pass into Hungary; her mission was to get to Budapest. But she was imprisoned by the Germans, who tortured and killed her in the basement offices of the Gestapo.

Enzo Seren established contact with Jewish groups in Milan, in occupied Italy. He was captured and sent to Dachau, where he was executed.

The Germans' stronghold was disintegrating throughout Europe. More and more German territories were being liberated; the inhabitants, the survivors, could now breathe freely.

During the time when deportations were happening en masse in Florence, a young Florentine Jew, David Caro, joined the active partisans operating in the Apennine Mountains near Bologna. His family had emigrated in 1494 from Lisbon to Livorno, a major port town where Jews were welcomed for their expertise in maritime transportation and international commerce.

With a command of partisans, he was able to cross enemy lines near Anzio and joined the Brigade, into which he was accepted thanks to an Order of the Day from Brigadier Samuelson, their leader. Caro returned to Florence with the liberators, proudly wearing his British uniform, with the blue and white flag on his right arm.

However, many, many stories of heroism and the courage to survive, of deliverance, or even simple acts of humanity, will never be recounted.

Despite the military setbacks the Germans suffered, they continued to "clean" Europe of its Jews. They began organized raids in Alsace, annexed to Germany in 1870 and then again in 1940.

Alsace was the cradle of Ashkenazi Judaism. When the first Jews arrived with the Roman legions, they settled on both banks of the Rhine. In Worms, Oppenheim, Mannheim on the German side and Colmar, Strasbourg, Neuviller, and Bergheim on the French side. They prospered until the Crusades began (1110-1280). In 1944, fifteen hundred Jews were arrested and sent to Drancy. Among the women, there was a young girl hardly sixteen years old, Simone Weill (née Jacob), one of the ninety-five who survived (1945). She became the French Minister of Health, and in 1979 she became President of the European Parliament.

I will speak of other anonymous heroes, men and women, many women—the men were in uniform or on the battlefronts in Italy or the South Pacific—who produced arms, tanks, and planes, which aided not only the American Army, but also the British and Soviet armies. The North American arms factories ran in three shifts, twenty- four hours a day.

In the United States, great changes had occurred after Pearl Harbor. A once self-absorbed nation refusing to care about or notice the problems in Europe was now, thanks to Roosevelt, involved in the war as a world power. They couldn't sit with their arms crossed in front of Hitler and his political expansion. In 1940 the United States had an army of only four hundred and eighty thousand men, with few fighter planes, no bombers, although they had a decent navy.

In 1940, Germany had an army of six million fully mobilized soldiers, state of the art tanks and combat planes; their navy had more submarines than any in the world. They'd been secretly producing war submarines since 1934, and these vessels patrolled every sea in the world.

The United States went from a neutral nation to an "arsenal of democracy," with more than a million and a half men in England alone, preparing to invade the European stronghold, combining forces with the other Allies, ultimately totaling two and a half million soldiers. A large army had been trained to fight in the Pacific. Planes, tanks, boats, cannons, jeeps, and army planes were being built each day in preparation for liberation.

At work, the news spread by word of mouth: the Allies had disembarked in Normandy. It was incredible. We cried from joy. The news had still not been confirmed. It still hadn't appeared in the papers, for two reasons. One was time—the newspapers, censored by the Germans, printed at four in the morning. The other was political: the Germans and their collaborators suppressed any encouraging news. The BBC, for strategic reasons, also didn't transmit information that could be valuable to the Germans.

During the occupation, other, more powerful means were developed for communication: transmission by voice.

The long-awaited invasion had arrived. Soon, our liberators would appear. The famous "second front" solicited by the Soviets was a reality—after landing in Italy—that they were willing to accept. In the laboratory we hugged and made the V sign for Victory, like Churchill.

I went home to listen to the BBC. I casually bought Gouda cheese on the black market, which I jubilantly brought back to the hiding place.

Yolanka and Buci were not even aware of what was happening: they only turned on the radio at night so as not to make noise and not to call attention to themselves, and because at night there was less interference and they could listen in better.

When I shared the news with them, Yolanka and Buci began to cry. They couldn't believe it. The Allies in France! So close! Then Buci gave me a big kiss, thanking me for the cheese. It had been a long time since we'd eaten like this. Mrs. Vanderbrook brought us bread, and we sat to eat dinner.

When the sun set, we turned off the lights and opened the window. It was hot outside, and a pleasant, fresh breeze was blowing. We stayed awhile in the dark, without saying a world.

Yolanka and Buci had spent two years in the hiding place. Although it might seem otherwise, this was not easy to endure. I, at least, left every day for the outside world. For them, the hiding place was like a prison. But Buci gave thanks to G-d for being alive. Many of his friends and relatives were no longer in this world.

We closed the window and shut the thick curtains, turned on the lights and turned on the radio. We heard the typical modulations and high-pitched sounds, like whistling, until we were able to tune in with London.

The news was very vague. There was no mention of specific places. Only the names of beaches: Omaha Beach, Juno Beach, and names like this. We weren't familiar with these locations. The BBC hid all valuable information from the enemy, who did not know the true extent of the invasion.

Nonetheless, it was confirmed that the points of invasion that on June 6, 1944 were under Allied control. The operation had been a complete success and became known as D-Day.

On the radio, we listened to the program directed towards the Resistance, which were mostly messages in French like "Julio will leave two pairs of boots in the house with the chimney" or "four pigs and six chickens tomorrow morning at nine." Only members of the Resistance understood the significance.

We went to sleep with high hopes. Our liberators were coming. But really, in Brussels, we had no idea whatsoever about the true magnitude of the invasion, the "Overlord" operation.

It was the largest fleet ever seen. American, English, Canadian, New Zealander, Australian, and French troops, in a little over a year, had been trained under the supreme command of Dwight Eisenhower. It was the largest amphibious operation in all of history.

Other Allied generals like Bradley, de Lattre de Tassigny, Montgomery, andPatton also participated in the invasion. It was the first invasion of French territory since the "Debacle" of 1940.

From the beach headquarters, established in Caen, Normandy—which came at a high cost in lives (p. 145)—the Allied armies began their advance on Paris.

Fortunately, the Germans, commanded by Von Rundstaedt and Guderian, were, completely misguided in their strategy. First, they relied on bad weather: they didn't expect a landing under these conditions. Secondly, they waited for the invasion in Calais, further towards the East, where the distance between Dover and the continent was lesser. They concentrated most of their troops here. The Germans were very quiet that 6th of June, 1944, so much so that their commander in chief, Erwin Rommel, went to his home in Colonia to celebrate his wedding anniversary.

The advance of the Soviet Troops, *Krasnaya Armiya,* was irrepressible. After liberating the territory initially conquered by the Germans between 1941 and 1943, they seized the Baltic States, Poland, and Romania.

Hitler, the Fuhrer, was furious: he claimed his generals had betrayed him; that the military chiefs who'd surrendered could no longer be considered Germans, in his eyes. Obviously, he preferred the prisoners of the Untermenschen dead. They were inferior beings, the *Ekelhafte Slaven*, the foul Slavic people.

Hungary was governed by Admiral Horty, an admiral without a fleet—since 1919, Hungary had no outlet to the sea—who was of the old school, the Austro-Hungarian Empire, and started as a maritime ensign in Fiume.

At first he flatly refused to hand over Jews. Later on, he was obligated to do so when in 1943 the Germans solicited fifty-five thousand men for "forced labor" in the Russian front in the name of the fight against Bolshevism. Until then the Hungarian-Jewish community had suffered no casualties.

There was a large Jewish community in Hungary. More numerous than that of Germany and Austria together, and also very old. The first Jews arrived in the land of the Pannonian Magyars with the Roman legions, around 670 A.D. They numbered 850,000, or 10% of the population, which was very impressive. 120,000 lived in Budapest, but there were 560 communities in the country, in the Carpathians, in Marmoros Sziget in Transylvania, and in Voldovinia. During the reign of Emperor Franz Josef the number of Jews increased, thanks to his tolerance. The Jews were represented in the military, in liberal professions, in universities, banking, and commerce. In 1939, 45% of doctors and 43% of lawyers were Jewish. With this increase in Jewish professional presence came increased anti-Semitism.

There was a marked division in the community. On one side were the very Orthodox, and on the other, the Neologists, often assimilated into Hungarian society. Since 1860, many altered their names to be Hungarian: Aranyos (Goldman); Biro (Richter); Feher (Weiss); Fekete (Schwartz); Szold (Gruen); Gombos (Knoepfler), etc.

An important seminary educated rabbis, who went to various countries in Central Europe. By 1860, 346 Jewish families in the high bourgeoisie obtained nobility titles. But at the same time, the Jews of Marmoros Sziget spoke only Yiddish and attended Seder and Yeshivot.

Theodore Herzl was born in Budapest although he lived his life in Vienna. I might mention he was not very popular in his home country. Opera composers Imre Kalman and Ferenc Lehar, famous in Vienna, were also from Hungary.

In Budapest, the capital city, there still exists a gorgeous synagogue on the Dohány Utca, built in the Eastern style, with a capacity for 1,800 people. On that same street is a magnificent Jewish Museum.

In 1937, there were eighteen Beneit Berit lodges in the country, and a Maccabee club that organized national competitions among the Jewish youth. While in one part of the country the Hasidic Chabad movement was being formed, in Budapest the Neologists proclaimed assimilation from their temple pulpits.

In March of 1944 the Germans informally occupied Hungary. Horty the dictator had to accept this *fait accompli*.

Eichmann installed himself in Budapest and, along with the S.S., took charge of deportations. In 1944, the war was all but lost. The Soviets were within 300 km. The Allies were in Rome and advancing towards the Alps.

After the assassination of Heydrich in Lidice, the S.S. high commanders headed by Himmler—Eichmann, Alois Brunner, and Kaltenbrunne—were promoted. The massacres continued.

They immediately began the deportations. Their system was similar to that in Poland. In just a few weeks, tens of thousands of Hungarian Jews were forced to abandon their homes, apartments, and ranches and were crammed into ghettos. Some were extremely religious, like the Marmorossziget, Munkacs, Nagyarad and Miskolc. In April, the first transports left for Auschwitz. Some communities—like Szombathely and Dunaszerdahely—were completely liquidated.

The 120,000 Jews who lived in Budapest were arrested and concentrated in schools. Later they were brought to a military camp outside the city, in the Martonvasar Station, there the transports were readied, destined for Auschwitz-Birkenau.

Raoul Wallenberg served as Commercial Attaché of the Swedish Embassy in Budapest. Animated by deep humanitarian sentiment, completely disinterred, furious, and disgusted by the German occupation of Hungary, he devoted himself to saving Jews. They called him the "Angel of Life." He issued certificates of protection for many, and visas for others. He rented "extra-territorial" houses, where he sheltered them under the Swedish flag. Once he travelled to the Martonvasar Station, and with Swedish documents in hand was able to free 2,000 Jews already in the train cars bound for Poland. In 1944, he saved a total of 4,200 Jews.

Wallenberg's heroism is one of the most outstanding acts of the "righteous" non-Jews during the Second World War.

In Budapest, there was another "angel," Carl Lutz, whose story I'll recount below. From 1942 on, Carl Lutz served as chief of the "Foreign Protection Division" of the Swiss Embassy, which, as its name indicates, protected those foreigners trapped in Hungary during the world conflict. Carl Lutz, a great humanitarian, also protected many Hungarian Jews, providing letters of protection recognized by Adolf Eichmann. What he accomplished was indescribable. He was able to save so many Jewish lives, in spite of not only the Gestapo, but also the Nyilas, the Arrow Cross Party, a Hungarian anti-Semitic, Fascist organization, who claimed not to recognize any type of document issued by foreign embassies. They were worse than the Germans in their actions against the Jews.

There was also an apostolic Nuncio in the Vatican, Monsignor Angelo Rotta, who later became Cardinal of the Roman Curia. He helped Jewish families, providing them asylum in the Nunciature in Budapest.

By July of 1944, 430,000 Hungarian Jews had been deported, the majority of them directly to Auschwitz-Birkenau.

The tragedy that struck the Hungarian Jews was in some sense ironic, since the occupation happened so late in the war. Until February of 1944, Admiral Miklos Horty, chief of state and German ally, had protected them.

The Hungarians, mostly a Catholic population, began suffering the effects of the occupation. The Germans seized Hungary and were suddenly everywhere. News arrived from Kolosvar, Transylvania of soldiers raping schoolgirls and young women coming from Mass.

The Hungarian Fascists, on their part, with Ferenz Szalasy as their leader and with police chief Gabor Vaina, surrounded 42,000 Jews in Budapest. They divided them into groups of fifty and, in chains, they were forced to march on the shores of the Danube, in the freezing rain and snow, under the vigilance of the Nyilas but also the Honveds, the Hungarian army. Thousands died, and their corpses were left in the road; the last fifteen thousand were finished off on the banks of the Danube; their bodies were dumped in the river.

Jo Ishtenem hol Vagyszd? Nem Vagysz Magyrorszagban! G-d, where are you? You're not in Hungary!

Four days before the landing at Normandy, an S.S. commandant was assassinated by the Resistance in the north of France. In retaliation, the Germans massacred 620 people from Oradour-Sur-Glane. The men were finished off with machine guns, the women and children burned alive in the village church.

In the German Reich, mainly in Poland, Russia, Czechoslovakia, and Austria, three types of camps existed: extermination camps, concentration camps, and forced labor camps, the last called *Arbeitslager*.

After 1939 the Germans formed armies of forced laborers, with recruits from conquered nations, for the production of weapons. Among them were the Dutch, Norwegians, French, Belgians, Hungarians, Czechs, Poles, Russians, Greeks, Serbians, Bosnians, and Jews.

Jews from concentration camps were selected according to their overall health, capacity for manual labor, their profession, and experience. They were then set apart from the others; they lived and slept in separate barracks.

The major German brands utilized—for free!—the working masses. Among them I.G. Farben, Heinkel Werke, Messerschmidt, Bayrische Motor Werke, Telefunken, Krupp, and many others.

Dr. Ley, Minister of Labor, drove to the *Arbeitsfront*, granting concessions for stakeholders. The "army" of forced laborers had reached 2,000,800 "recruits" and was moved from one location to another according to the necessities of the manufacturers and of the war, similar to those transported from the New Spain in the sixteenth century.

They were poorly fed; hardly enough food for optimal performance. The accommodation was similar to that of the concentration camps. The work camps were guarded by the S.S. In all the camps, there were towers with soldiers carrying machine guns. At night, powerful spotlights detected any abnormalities.

The work camps were located at strategic points, like Stutthof, near Danzig; Krasnik, near Lublin; Zichlin and Poniatova, near Warsaw; Kluga and Reval in Estonia; Riga in Lithuania; Sachsenhausen and Augsburg, near Berlin;

Gunskirchen and Ebensee in Austria; Sered in Hungary; and Gross Rosen near Breslau, to name only the most important.

Near one of these camps, in Bohemia, Czechoslovakia, Oskar Schindler—German industrialist, originally from the Sudetenland—had an ammunitions factory in Brunnlitz, where he employed Jews in order to protect them. One time he learned that a convoy of 1,200 Jews was departing for Auschwitz, all of them workers in his factory. He immediately had them transferred to the Zwittau station. After negotiating with the S.S. he was able to free them from death.

Oskar Schindler was another "righteous" non-Jew now honored in Israel.

When the arrival of the Allied troops was confirmed in Versailles, outside Paris, the Resistance, together with the *Forces Francaises Interieures*, took up arms to fight the German troops. On the morning of August 19, there were skirmishes in four parts of the city. First, an attack at the Komandatur, the German military headquarters. Afterwards, the Radiodiffusion Française was taken.

The Resistance didn't know that General Ditmar Von Choltitz had direct orders from Hitler to blow up the most important monuments and buildings in Paris, to reduce the "City of Lights" to ruins. Von Choltitz personally negotiated with the leaders of the Resistance and the FFI from whom, in exchange, he obtained a full guarantee for his life and that of his family. At 6 p.m. the French forces entered triumphantly at the command of General de Lattre de Tassigny. General Charles DeGaulle arrived the following morning, along with his staff. He marched triumphantly on the Champs Elysees, from the Arc de Triomphe to the Place de la Concorde, amid cheers and cries of joy from the partisans. The defeat, the humiliation of 1940, had been vindicated by Charles De Gaulle.

Paris was free and had been liberated by its own citizens; thousands of German soldiers were taken prisoner.

The Germans had different nicknames for each kind of soldier: *Boche* for the French and *Kraut* for the Italians. The Russians were called *Ivan*, the Americans, *Amy*, and the British, *Tommy*.

After the invasion at Normandy, more and more men joined the Belgian Resistance. The group of Belgian combatants intensified their actions to sabotage the occupiers. They struck against the German army with increasing recklessness. The Germans responded with more raids and summary executions, which provoked yet more resentment among the people towards the occupiers.

At this stage of the war, before the rapid advance of Allied forces towards Brussels, there were a greater number of air bombings. At work, when the alarm sounded, we stayed in the laboratory, as it was two meters below street level. This type of foundation was common in European homes. Those who didn't have a cellar, or found themselves in the street, had to go to an *Abri* or shelter until the sirens had sounded, indicating the aerial attack had ended.

Although the bombings in Brussesls were mostly directed at military targets and railway facilities, some bombs fell over civilian objectives, incurring a great deal of damage and claiming many victims. Each day I went to work on the train, we passed by houses and buildings that had been destroyed. Yet I kept telling myself: our freedom is nearing.

Meanwhile, the Soviet army was advancing on Poland under the command of General Rokossovsky, who'd united the partisans, many of whom were Jews, operating in the dense forests. A company of Jewish partisans under the command of Yejiel Grynspan took part in the liberation of the Maydenek extermination camp on July 23, 1944.

The Germans had already bombed the gas chambers and the crematory ovens, ordering the inmates to remove all traces of the killings perpetrated over the last four years. All the Soviets encountered were old wooden barracks, empty and in ruins. The surviving prisoners had already been evacuated by foot to Radom and Auschwitz on one of the many "Death Marches." This tactic would be repeated on numerous occasions. On the roads, the liberators found only Jewish cadavers—dead from exhaustion, or shot for having left the line or stopping to tie their shoes. Their bodies remained there, among the bodies of Polish partisans, Soviet soldiers, and Germans.

On July 20, 1944, an attempt was made on Hitler's life. In the Wolfsschanze barracks, Coronel Von Stauffenberg, from the old Prussian class, placed a briefcase with an activated bomb beneath the work table where Hitler and Generals Keitel, Jodl, Brandt, and Korten, along with their staff, were perusing maps of the Eastern Front. The bomb went off, killing a general, but none of the major ones. Hitler was unharmed. This was the first time something like this had happened, the first time anyone had attempted to destroy the regime from within. The implicated officials paid dearly, almost all the Wehrmacht and the old school, and some high functionaries from the old Weimar Republic. There were 243 executions and three suicides among the conspirators. Hitler, incredulous and furious, came down with the full weight of the law. This was a bloody, relentless repression. Erwin Rommel, a German hero who'd fought a year before in North Africa, was one of the suicides.

The Russian troops found themselves in Praga, a suburb of Warsaw, on the right bank of the Vistula River. This was the signal for the insurrection in Warsaw. Its inhabitants—commanded by former Polish army general Bor

Komarovsky—took up arms against the Germans. The struggle lasted for eight days. The Germans were forced to use their artillery in the Old City, reducing it to dust. The Russians, on the other side of the river separating the city from the eastern suburbs, didn't move.

This was all part of Stalin's strategy to drastically weaken the Polish patriots, loyal to the exiled government in London. "May the Germans finish them off; we didn't give orders for an insurrection," said the Russian high command.

The Polish endured their part of the suffering, death, and open animosity on the part of the "Ruskii," such as the mass murder of eight thousand Polish officials in Katyn in 1940. Stalin hated the Polish, never forgetting when in 1920 their army, under the command of Marshall Pilsudski, fought the nascent Red Army, inflicting severe casualties over the course of two years.

At the end of the Second World War, the deluded communist idealists—and there were many—could have concluded that both Comrade Stalin and the Soviet Union were moved by *Realpolitik*, a cold policy in their own interest and not for the good of humanity, as the Western Communist Party proclaimed. It was a well-organized and orchestrated farce.

Before the advance of the Soviet troops, the Germans continued the evacuation of the *Arbeitslager*, or work camps. Auschwitz-Birkenau was now close to the front, and the survivors were forced to begin a Death March to Sachsenhausen. The Allies were nearing Bergen-Belson, and some of the prisoners were evacuated to Ravensbruk.

The Auschwitz crematory ovens and gas chambers worked day and night: eight thousand Slovakian Jews were murdered in retaliation for the uprising in Banska-Bystrica, headed by Tobias Jacobovitz, a Jewish intellectual for Bratislava.

Encouraged by the encroaching Soviet Army, the partisans liberated Sered, Novaky, and Banska Bystrica.

Brussels was liberated by the Second British Army on September 3, 1944. It was incredible: the night beforehand, rows of trucks loaded with German soldiers were leaving the city in the direction of Aachen. Other smaller vehicles, like the Volkswagen jeeps, were crammed with furniture, pictures, and brass, bound for Germany.

Enter the Allies: the Resistance openly arrested those Germans not able to escape. They left their homes with their hands in the air, and surrendered. The

Resistance also arrested those who'd collaborated with the Germans, negotiating with them, or worse.

The women who'd served as the Germans' lovers were shaved and paraded through the streets, where they were insulted and spit on. The Resistance members protected them from being harmed by the crowd.

The British entered through the Bois de la Cambre, everyone cheering in their wake.

For my part, I ran to the hiding place. I'd been at work. There was no transit. With my lab coat on, I hitchhiked to Schaarebeck. It wasn't difficult, amid the din; I arrived there in only fifteen minutes.

Yolanka and Buci were sitting on the stairs to the front door. They'd heard the news from the good woman of the house, whose husband was deported to Germany after a spy had been caught in their home.

Buci put on his shoes for the first time in two years. Both of them were extremely pale; they weren't accustomed to daylight. *"Baruch Hashem,"* said Buci.

In the street, Buci held Yolanka and me by the hand, with his hat on—he always wore it. Thanks to a *Shehecheyanu*, he'd remained alive. We hugged, and Buci cried, but from happiness. Yolanka said nothing, did not stop sobbing. Buci ran up to Mrs. Vander
brook; we hugged and kissed her. She was also crying, and kept repeating: *"Mon mari, mon pauvre mari."* My husband, my poor, poor husband.

"Manayunk a Rue des Vierges," Buci ordered—as though two long years hadn't passed. He was always alert. He always knew what to do. We packed our meager belongings. Buci checked for his keys, and suddenly, as though it were 1942 again, we returned to our apartment.

There were neither trams nor taxis. The streets were choked with joyful people. The Resistance members sported tricolor bands of black, yellow, and red. The communists wore red bands. Everyone carried weapons. Some wore old helmets from various armies. They continued looking for cohorts. The few police in their white helmets tried to maintain order, but with little success.

The atmosphere was one of celebration, more than I'd ever seen before. We walked with our suitcases. When we arrived on the main street where the church was—with its bells ringing—we stopped in front of a parade of Tommies. The people cheered them on, and we were unable to pass. We waited a half hour, and were finally let through.

Buci searched for some means of transportation, someone who could do us the favor of taking us home. We found nothing. We continued walking in the direction of the city center. Our suitcases were heavy, but not enough to dampen the festive atmosphere that prevailed.

Suddenly a large open car approached us; the grey-green of the Wehrmacht. Driving it was a youth from the Resistance, at his side a young man in a khaki uniform. We motioned for them to stop, and asked if they could bring us to the Rue des Vierges. I told them I was a "mail runner" for Group IV in Brussels. At first they looked at us with suspicion. Then Buci showed them the *Cartes D'Identitees*, his and Yolanka's. I showed him all that I had, my *Arbeitsausweis*. Buci told them, *"Nous allons a la maison, après avoir etes caches deux ans, s'il vous plait."* "We are on our way home, after having hidden for two years." Finally they replied: *"Bon, ca va on va vous emener Vive la Belgique."* And they brought us home.

We climbed the stairs to our apartment, and everything was covered in dust; nothing had been touched. We opened the door. It smelled musty.

Yolanka and Buci began to clean. The superintendent and his son came and brought us two buckets and brooms. It was all kindness and adulation. Before, they'd never said a word to us. Such is humanity. Now we were like heroes. I went out in the street. I wanted to participate in what was happening. The festivities continued, especially in the boulevards. The military received applause and shouts of joy. Women came up to the cars and embraced the soldiers. The people were grateful to be free. It had been four long years…

Many were no longer here, and so we felt a mixture of happiness and sadness. I walked along the side streets far from the tumult. I meditated on the significance of the liberation. I no longer had to fear the Germans. They no longer had power. They'd returned to Germany, or surrendered, as I'd seen that morning.

The war would continue until the Germans and their Japanese allies had been completely defeated; but not here in Brussels. Despite the jubilance, I couldn't be entirely happy: my parents weren't here. Only G-d knew where they were. I dreamt of them. I saw myself in a jeep with a British soldier bringing me to a concentration camp where my mother was waiting for me, in rags, shaved, and very thin, but alive.

I couldn't be happy: so many of my friends and acquaintances were no longer alive.

We expected some of the deportees would return. We were unaware of the true situation at the camps. That night the cafées were all lit up, full of people.

The party continued, surely, until the wee hours of the morning. But I went to sleep.

The next morning I went to the laboratory, and Monsieur Guillaume was waiting for me. He told me he was satisfied with my work during these last two years, and from September 1st on, he would double my salary. I thanked him for what he'd taught me, and also for not asking questions about my *Arbeitsausweis*, and finally told him I'd used a false identity.

I told him my real name. He said he'd continue calling me Jean, and told me why he was giving me a raise: "I prefer to pay the person for the quality of their work, not for who they are." A funny explanation, after having paid me half of what my work was worth. Nonetheless, I thanked him for the raise and got to work.

I was happy. Now I was making decent money. I gave the first half of my paycheck to Buci. I wanted to pitch in with our living expenses. I wanted to help with some of their burden.

Little by little, Brussels returned to normal. The trains were running again; the public buildings once again hung the Belgian flag. But there was the occasional exception: there was no food. The Brutish were very generous, of course, and distributed small amounts of food to women and children from "C-Rations" trucks. They gave me chocolates, which I hadn't eaten for so long, and two cans of corned beef. Nothing could extinguish the spirit of the liberators. There was also no gasoline; there were no cars in the streets but military vehicles.

The building at the Place Rouppe 17, the Rexist—Belgian Fascist—headquarters during the occupation, was ceded to the Jews. Here they installed a *Comite Provisionel des Juifs Belges*. The few Jews who remained left their hiding places; others returned from the provinces. As well as children who'd been taken into Catholic convents. Everyone appeared like mushrooms after the rain.

I went to the Place Rouppe where I was told I could consult the list of survivors from Belgium, France, and Luxembourg, appearing daily on a long wall. I tried in vain to find my father's name.

Of course, the disclosure of such lists, and consulting them, became a ritual during the following months, until June 1945, when the last concentration camps were liberated. It was a type of modern "wailing wall."

In one of these many visits, a red-haired girl came up to me. She was my age. She invited me upstairs. On the first floor, in an amply-sized room, there was a large table, rows of chairs, like a classroom, and at the back, on the wall, behind the table, was a large red flag.

She told me her name was Moumous, Moumous Bunim, and she was organizing a movement of young Zionists. Soon there would be conferences, excursions, camping. The ultimate goal was Palestine, far from Europe and the "suffering in the concentration camps."

"We need boys like you," she said. "Why don't you come next Thursday at six in the evening to meet the others? There will be boys and girls: *Javerot* and *Javerim.*" I didn't quite understand the relationship between the red flag—a communist symbol—and Palestine, although I promised to come the following Thursday.

Meanwhile, the British fought in Holland, where they encountered a ferocious German resistance.

The Americans, at the command of General Patton, were getting closer to Germany each day. They were fighting in the Ardennes.

The Russians approached Auschwitz and Budapest, after liberating half of Poland. They approached from the north, later liberating the area from Vilna and Riga, to Konigsberg, in East Prussia. Further south, Rome had been liberated; the Anglo American forces waged a fierce battle in Montecassino, where the Germans kept ammunition in a convent.

The Germans continued the Death Marches, evacuating the concentration camps, and thousands of Jews were killed who'd had the "better" luck of remaining alive in the camps.

On Thursday, at the appointed hour I went to the Place Rouppe. Downstairs, there were many people in front of the "wall." I went to the first floor and into the salon. Thirty Jewish youths had gathered there, most of them women between thirteen and eighteen years old. Moumous left the group to welcome me. She introduced me to several of the attendees. Now, in addition to the red flag, there were maps of Eretz Israel on the wall, then called Palestine. There were also a hammer and sickle, black on a red background, and two blown-up photographs—I later learned they were of Ber Borojov and Leon Pinsker, Russian Jews. In 1882, Pinkser wrote a work called "Auto-Emancipation" advocating in this time of Bilium for the mass emigration of Russian Jews to Palestine.

The meeting was delayed for half an hour. Several speakers spoke, among them Moumous' sister Zahava. She explained to us the ideals of the future organization *Poale Zion Smola,* which is to say Zionist Laborers of the Left. They explained that socialism was the only system capable of resolving the world's inequalities and bring peace. That to immigrate to Eretz Israel was the only solution for the remains of the Jewish people, to return to their homeland.

We sang beautiful Jewish songs, which Zahava accompanied on accordion. I tried to follow the tunes. I was very pleased. Feelings were awakened in me I'd never felt before. I belonged to something: I was Jewish and I could shout it to the four winds. *Baruch Hashem*, Praise the Llord, I've found this group. My blessing in Hebrew, perhaps out of tune with the red communist flag. We bid farewell to our comrades with our fists in the air. We would meet again that coming Sunday.

Suddenly, there was news that the Germans under the command of Von Rundstaedt, had launched in Bastogne, in the Ardennes, a powerful and surprising counteroffensive against the Americans.

Several lines of Panzer tanks were advancing towards Brussels. It couldn't be—my coworkers and I said to each other in the laboratory—The Germans were fortifying themselves! They'd moved their best troops to the Eastern Front to defend themselves against the Bolsheviks. A counteroffensive? Impossible!

But it was true. The German staff thought they'd discovered a weak point in Bastogne. A heavy snow was falling in the Ardennes where the American General Patton was camped, the "Enfant Terrible," who was known to move at lightning speed in his jeep with his three-starred flag. He was called the "Three Star General" and defied his enemies. *"Patton fonce sur l'Allemagne."* "Patton will make his way to Germany," said Le Soir. In effect, two columns of Panzer planes were in Namurs, causing many casualties among the Americans, with the consequent panic of the civil population. The Panzers, which threated to be victorious, were halted—even with their snow chains—by lack of fuel. The Germans couldn't resupply them. There wasn't a drop of gasoline in Belgium.

After the liberation, the reconstituted Belgian army immediately called for a general mobilization. The permits to the English and Americans were cancelled. Preparations for war were made once more.

Anxiety prevailed in Brussels. The Germans were advancing; they could return in a matter of days. Later on, we learned of the reality: the immobilization of the German motor equipment.

All around, in the streets and on the trams, were military recruits; lines of military trucks circulated toward the front along the boulevards. American

141

soldiers were seen, and the people cheered them on. On each truck was a large, white, five-pointed star.

We didn't work in the laboratory. We all remained in the streets. Josef Moelemans, one of my coworkers, enlisted in the army.

That night I went to the Place Rouppe; eight American army trucks were stationed at the side of the building. Moumous wasn't there; I found myself with another member of the Paole Zion, Bernard Zhitomirsky. He told me the trucks had come to evacuate Jewish women and children from Brussels in case it was necessary.

The situation was incredibly confusing. Bernard was glued to the radio listening to the news. The Germans had launched a counteroffensive in Bastogne; the battle known later as the "Battle of the Bulge" was at its peak.

When the Germans asked him to surrender, American General Hodges answered them with "Nuts," which made him famous. Of course, the Germans didn't understand his flat refusal. On the radio, we listened for news of the bad weather preventing Allied aerial action. Meanwhile, the battle continued.

Bernard asked if I could help him evacuate the children the next morning. Fortunately, this turned out not to be necessary.

Zhitomirsky, or Berl, as everyone called him, was the oldest of the group. During the occupation, he'd hidden in an attic. He was tall, extremely skinny, and had a beard, which had grown during the final years of the war. He was very intelligent and well-educated, analyzing everything beneath the lens of historical materialism. "Lenin said...Lenin thought..." He sounded more like a communist than a Zionist; he helped me to properly understand the ideology of Poale Zion. *Le Mouvement Borochoviste*, the movement of Borochov, idealist from the 19th century.

My paternal grandparents Juer and Rifke, accompanied by several of their children.
My father is the second from the left, standing.
The woman seated at the right is Aunt Zilly with her husband, Uncle Salomon Bieber.
This photograph was taken in Vienna in 1900.

My father, Leo Katz, Vienna, 1938

My mother, Grete Katz, Vienna, 1938

My maternal grandmother, Caroline Bachruch Gruenfeld, Vienna, 1938

My uncle Julius Bachruch in lieutenant's uniform in the Austrian Army at the beginning of World War I. Photo taken in 1915.

Joshy Gruenfeld in Austrian Army uniform during World War I. Photo taken in Lemberg, 1916.

With my father in Burggarten at one year old. Photo taken in Vienna, 1931.

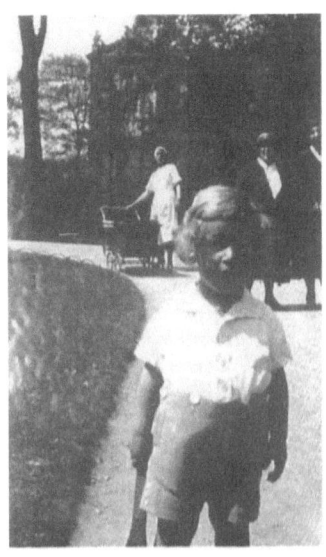

In the Burggarten at two years old. My nanny is in the background, next to the carriage. Photo taken in Vienna, 1932.

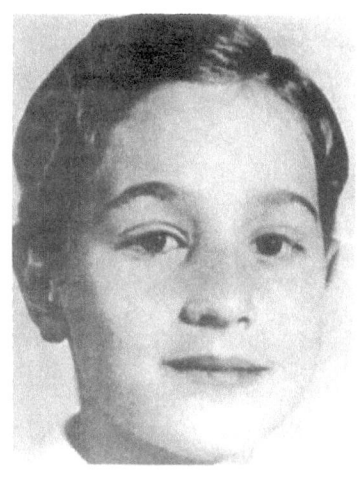

Me at eight years old. Photo was used for the issuing of my "Vish," or identification document, on my arrival in Brussels. Photo taken in Vienna, 1938.

The Gruenfeld family. Standing from left to right: my cousin Oscar, father of Joshy; Leopold and his children Gerda and Erich. Seated below, Aunt Sidonie, mother of Gerda, Aunt Rose, her daughter Yoshy, and behind her Gerty's mother, Emma.

Joshy Gruenfeld, with the Hakoach team captain in the soccer stadium in Vienna. Photo taken in 1923.

The Hakoach soccer team. In the center, Josef Stricker, President of the Austrian Zionist Federation. Joshy Gruenfeld is second from the left. Photo taken in Vienna, 1930.

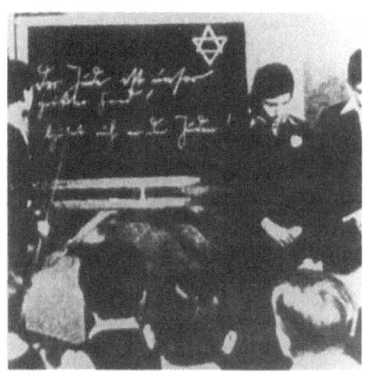

Classroom in Vienna, April, 1938. A student is forced to draw a Star of David and write an infamous legend of the Jews: "They are our enemies." Another student points to the writing and reads it aloud. "Dokumentations Archiv des Oesterreichischen Wiederstandes." Vienna.

Jewish immigrants in front of the commissary in Margarethenstrasse, the elderly to receive their "Auswanderungs Ausweis" in order to leave the Reich. Photo taken in May, 1938. "Dokumentations Archiv des Oesterreichischen Wiederstandes." Vienna.

The Shamash, or bedel, of Stadttempel on the Seitenstaettengasse, at the moment when the S.S. soldiers took him into the street and forced him to squat down and clean the sidewalk, for the delight of the passerby. April 1938. Photo from the "Dokumentations Archiv des Oesterrereichischen Wiederstandes." Vienna.

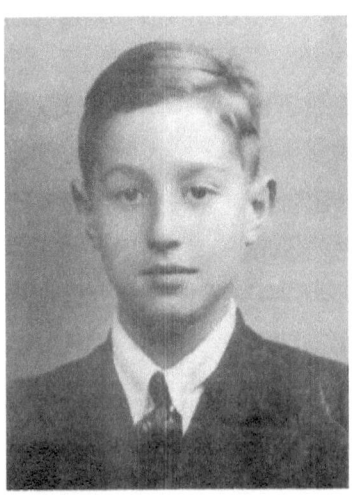

Me, right before I turned ten years old. Photo taken in Belgium in April, 1940.

Me at age twelve in the Boulevard. May, 1942.

Me at twelve years old with Tanti and Buci. Photo taken in Brussels, 1942.

Execution of Jewish partisans. The woman was seventeen years old, and the man nineteen, in Minsk, in Belarus, October, 1941. Photo from the "Bundesarchiv" Koblenz, Yad Vashem. Jerusalem.

In Brussels after the war, at fifteen years old. Photo taken in December, 1945.

Me at thirteen years old with Monsieur Guillaume's "work equipment." Photo taken in Brussels, 1943.

The Poale Zionist youth at a demonstration in the streets of Brussels, 1945. The placard reads: "Aliyah, Avodah, Haganah."

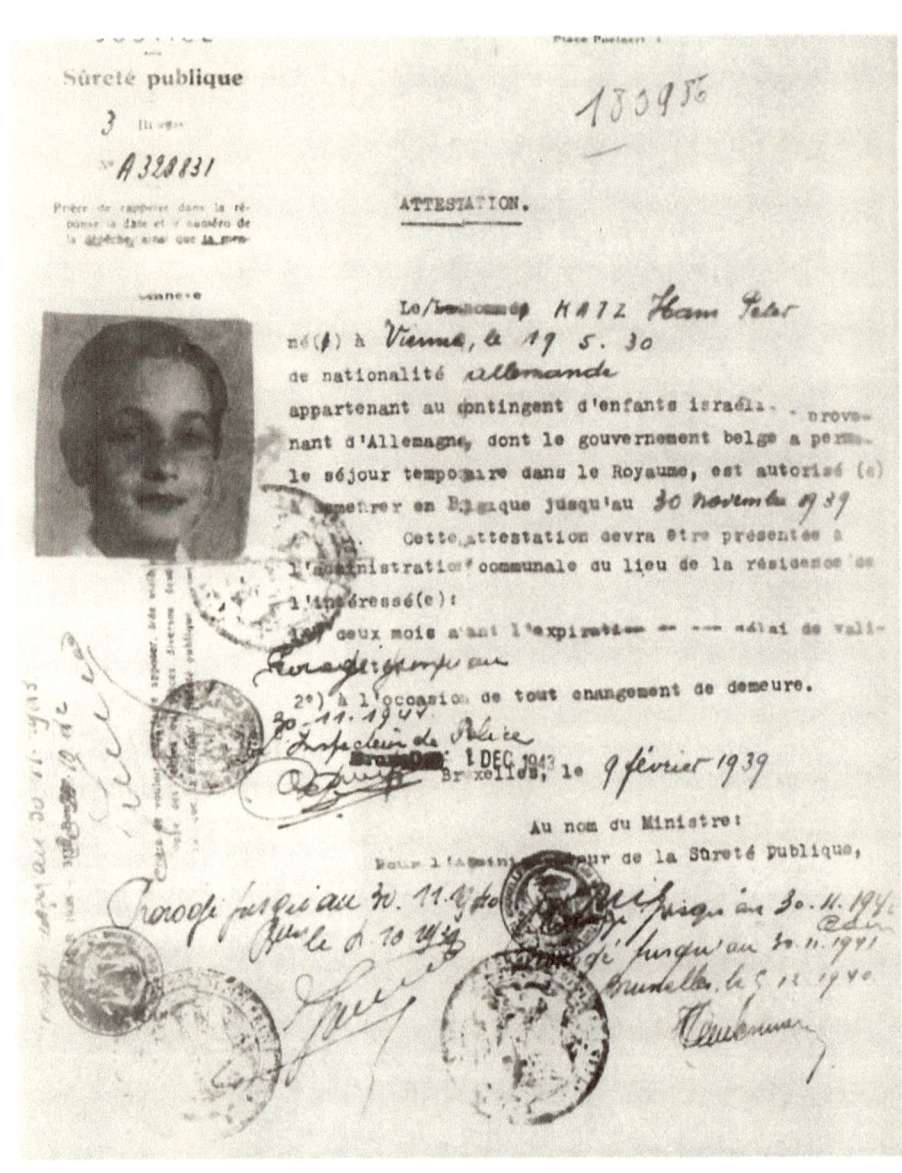

Document authorizing me to reside in the Belgian Kingdom that was issued to me on arrival in Brussels with the transport of children from the International Red Cross. This was my "Vish."

Uncle Otto Kleitnik, my grandmother Rifke's brother, born in Odessa, died in St. Petersburg. Photo taken around 1905.

About to board Mexicana de Aviacion to go to Mexico. From right to left: Sigi, me, Aunt Julie and the driver carrying Georgie Stark. Havana 1946

At eighteen years old, already "acclimated" to Mexico. Photo taken in Palmira, Morelos, in March, 1948.

We had a red flag, since the blue and white of the Zionists was, for them, a reactionary flag. Herzl, Zabotinisky, and Weitzmann were considered reactionaries. In the Poale Zion, we were progressives, socialists—the hope and future of the Jewish people. We had our own *Kibutzim* in Palestine where, of course, we flew the red flag. We fought for the rights of Jewish laborers.

In the days after liberation, I learned more about Jewish history and Zionism than I ever had before. I discovered that the Jews were a tribe, like the tribes of the past, that we were a nation with our own culture. The only thing we lacked was a territory. Palestine was occupied by the English. "The Jewish Homeland" was defined as such by Lord Balfour, and it was only a promise.

I knew little about Jewish culture: Bible stories, and some prayers. I knew nothing about the history of my people. At fifteen years old, I didn't know Yiddish or Hebrew. I'd never seen a map of Eretz Israel, but I learned rapidly and read voraciously, which surprised me. What was I? I was born in Vienna. Was I Austrian? No, they'd thrown me out in 1938. Was I Belgian? No, I was only tolerated there thanks to my *Vish*, a document that identified me as *"Resortissant, allemande, non ennemi, extent de tout controle"*: born in Germany—Austria did not exist back then—I was not an enemy, and free of any control. This was what I was. Stateless, like so many other Jews in this bloody, destroyed Europe, clambering for a country long-awaited by the Zionists.

I wanted my decision to join the Poale Zion to be the right one. I wanted to learn how to become well-versed in history, like Berl.

For several days, everyone lived in fear of the possibility the Germans would return.

I didn't go to work the next day. It was the first time I'd missed work. It wasn't a problem; I told myself that if there was an uproar in the city, very few people would show up at their jobs.

I walked to the Place Rouppe. It was full of Jews wanting to know what was happening: What time would the trucks leave with the children? And what about the adults? There was tremendous disorder.

In our meeting room were Zhitomirksy, Zahava, and her brother; Moumous; Armand Zaslavsky, Josef Tchernizky, Zipora Pomeranz, Phillipe Weinreb, Fanny Zysberg, Jeanne Rechtmann, and many others.

Waiting for orders to evacuate, we organized a *sichu*, a meeting, with those present. Berl introduced us to people who would form *"les cadres"* of young

Poale Zion leaders. They told us that he, Zahava, and Moumous—those who had the necessary knowledge—would instruct us on what to do. I couldn't believe what I was hearing. I, too, had been elected? I didn't have the knowledge, much less the experience. At fifteen, I was the youngest of the group, just slightly older than Fanny Zysberg, who was thirteen.

While we were waiting on the Americans, we took our first class in the history of Zionism. I felt important. Grateful, but fearful at the same time, for the responsibility of this charge.

The battle in Ardennes lasted eight days. Many American lives were lost, but ultimately the Germans were surrounded and defeated. On the fourth day, the skies cleared and Von Rundstaedt's counteroffensive was stopped short. From then on, the Allies gained air superiority.

Now on the offensive, the Americans continued unmatched towards the German border. Patton had penetrated through the Rhine in Ramagen, and the army of the Ardennes united with the English, who were advancing from Liege, taking Aachen after reducing it to ruins. The Allies also penetrated *"Die Festung Deutschland,"* considered the German fortress (fortitude? Fortaleza p. 178). However, the first to succeed in penetrating Germany on the Eastern Front were the Soviets.

As a last resort, Hitler organized the *Heimwehr*. He recruited young and old to defend the *Vaterland Den Deutschen Boden*, albeit at the cost of the combatants' lives, their last drops of blood. Just as in Stalingrad, before giving in to death. He would repeat this catastrophic event, but this time on German soil.

The Russians were advancing on the Eastern Front. Although the Germans concentrated their best efforts there, they were unable to maintain their counter-offensive in Ardennes. All of the attention of the Fuhrer and his staff was needlessly concentrated on keeping the Russians at bay. German aviation, pride of Goering, no longer existed. Hitler was continuing to give orders at his headquarters on the Messerschmidt output maps, but there were no longer enough planes for a squadron. But no one contradicted the Fuhrer; his orders were still his orders.

Many Germans were becoming convinced of their imminent defeat. Nonetheless, few desertions occurred. The advancing Allied troops did find bodies of unarmed soldiers hanging from poles or trees, accompanied by letters that said, in German, *Verraeter traidor.* But these were few and far between.

1945 began after an extremely cold winter; the bad weather continued. The Soviets were in their element, much better accustomed to cold than the Germans.

As I've already written, the first to arrive in the *"Festung Deutschland"* were the Soviets. They arrived on January 12, 1945 in East Prussia, near Konigsberg.

Vienna fell on April 13, with surprisingly little damage. Although, of course, there were buildings destroyed by Soviet artillery. All the bridges over the Danube were bombed by the Germans. St. Stephen's Cathedral and the Opera were burned.

The evacuation of the camps continued as the Soviet troops advanced; Chelmno was evacuated in January. The gas chambers and crematoriums were destroyed. At the end of January, the Soviets were very near to Auschwitz, and another "Death March" was begun to Gross Rosen, Ravensbruck, Sachsenhausen, and Bergen-Belsen. The prisoners—who could barely walk—fell dead in the streets. This was the S.S.'s last crime, completely unnecessary and foolish.

According to the Gestapo archives found after the war in Berlin, on January 22, 1945, Himmler ordered that operations in extermination camps be discontinued, and that gas chambers and crematoriums be destroyed. It's difficult to believe that this order was ignored. We will never know the truth.

Meanwhile, in Poale Zion, things were happening quickly. The courses were intense. I spent all my free time working for the organization. I began reading every book I could find about socialism and Zionism. I don't think I've ever read as much as I did during those six months.

I owe my voracious appetite for reading to my cousin Hilde. In 1942, before the deportations began in Brussels, she gave me two books about the adventures of Tarzan by Edgar Burroughs. Because it was accompanied by several illustrations of Tarzan and Jane, reading it was easy. Just half a block from our hiding place, the Schaarbeck Public Library served as my source for reading materials. My first authors were Romain Roland, Jules Verne, Jack London, Gustave Flaubert, Victor Hugo—I read his poetry. Once I checked out Baruch Spinoza's "Theological Political Treatise." I returned it after attempting to read five pages. It was too difficult for me; I didn't understand a thing. Obviously, during the occupation, many books were censored; there were no political books, or books by Jewish authors. Who knew how Baruch Spinoza managed to escape this filter?

In 1945, I became aware of the connection between Jewish people and worldwide liberal and revolutionary movements. Our prophets, the Neviim Amos,

Ezequiel, Jeremiah, and Isaiah from Biblical times, had also striven for jusice and equality among people.

In 1837, Moses Hess—an assimilated Jew who adopted Zionism enthusiastically—published the first communist treatise in Germany, "The Holy History of Mankind." He was a disciple of Spinoza.

In 1848, Karl Marx, alongside Friedrich Engels—a gentile—published the Communist Manifesto.

That same year, two Jewish doctors, Adolf Fishhof and Josef Goldmark were the architects of the first bourgeois revolution in Germany.

In 1863, Ferdinand Lasalle, German Jew, founded the first Labor Party in Europe, the *Deutscher Arbeiter Bund.*

In 1864, the First International was held in London, attended by several Jewish delegates. It was led by Karl Marx.

In Vilna in 1897, the Bund was founded as an organization of laborers from Russia, Poland, and Lithuania.

In 1905, during the first Russian Revolution, Lev Davidovich Bronstein Trotzky led the St. Petersburg Soviets. Later, during the second revolution in 1917, he was entrusted with forming the Red Army, *Krasnaya Armiya.* Collaborating with Vladimir Lenin in organizing the U.S.S.R. were no less than twelve Jews.

In 1918, Kurt Eisner and Gustav Landauer proclaimed the "*Raeterrepublick Bayern*" in Munich.

In 1919, Walter Rathenau and Eugen Preuss became ministers of Reconstruction and Finance, respectively, of the Weimar Republic.

In 1919, after World War I, Bela Kuhn took power in Hungary. He and many of his ministers were Jewish. That same year, Gustav Landauer and Rosa Luxemburg attempted to take power in Germany through the Spartakus Bund. Rosa Luxemburg and Karl Libknecht, who were not Jewish, failed in their attempt. They were assassinated.

After the advent of socialist nationalism, some Marxist Jewish philosophers like Herbert Marcuse and Ernest Bloch—to name just two—returned to their forced exile in Germany and continued to fight for their socialist ideals.

In 1936, Leon Blum, Jewish socialist, was designated Prime Minister of France.

The International Brigades, who fought alongside the Republicans during the Spanish Civil War, were organized by the Comitern—otherwise known as the Third International—to help the Republic. The Germans and Italians openly assisted Franco. It was a military body formed only by volunteers, like the German Taeleman Brigade and the North American Abraham Lincoln Brigade.

Within these communist-leaning ranks were French, Germans, Austrians, Polish, Russians, Bulgarians, North Americans, Belgians, and Dutch, among others. 35,000 men from these ranks fought in Spain, almost a fourth of whom were Jewish—7,000 men. Why?

In Europe, as well as in the United States of America, Jews felt like pariahs long before World War II. Tolerated, but not accepted. The Jews have always felt attracted to liberal, often utopian movements preaching brotherhood among men. Zionism maintained that the Jews were a nation among nations. The revolution in 1917 enjoyed great popularity among the Jews, precisely because of their desire for equality.

In the Soviet Union, equality was not only encouraged, it was enforced. Anti-Semitism lay "outside the law." Both concepts were embodied in the constitution.

The Russian Jew knew that he wouldn't be easily accepted by the Ukrainians, the Belarusians, and the Russians in general. Now, with the communists in power, everyone had to respect the law—at least, until Lenin died in 1924. After his death, anti-Semitism returned, and reigned until the death of Stalin in 1953.

I dedicated my free time to the organization, but I didn't work on Saturdays. Yolanka and Buci demanded my presence at home. I argued with them; that I wanted to live, that I hadn't lived in the four years during the occupation, that the organization needed me there. Finally, they had to begrudgingly—albeit respectfully—accept my decision and my weekend absences.

We already had a uniform: blue cotton shirt, red scarf, and pants of our choosing, or a skirt for the *chaverot,* the girls. We still didn't have funding for the uniforms. The *chaverim* greeted each other as comrades. We chose a shield, which we sewed onto our shirts.

The organization now had sixty-two members. It was structured like a *Kvutzot*, organized on the scouting principles of Baden Powell. Each *Kvutza* had its

Rosh, or leader. The *Roshim* formed the executive council. They made all the decisions. We had no superior.

On Sundays, we organized excursions, or *Tiyulim*, to the areas surrounding Brussels. During holidays, Jews went camping, *machane,* for three or four days. We received funding from Poale Zion in Brussels.

The Allies and Soviets penetrated deeper into Germany each day. The profound impact of the British troops was published in daily newspapers around the world.

Days later, Dachau was liberated by the Americans. It was documented on films, which were later exhibited in theaters around the world.

An American journalist said of Dachau: "We witnessed scenes that seemed like they were from another planet, beings covered with rags that didn't seem to belong to the human race." General Dwight D. Eisenhower, head of the Allied forces, was interviewed after a two-hour visit to Dachau, and couldn't speak from the shock he'd experienced and the rage he felt.

The subsequent events occurred rapidly. The Americans invaded Czechoslovakia, liberating Pilsen and Karlsbad. The Russians' main objective was to take Berlin, the lair of the Hitlerites.

Long lines of German refugees fleeing back from Poland and Czechoslovakia—*Volksdeutche*—tried to return to Germany. The ones in Poland came from places like Memel, Breslau, Neustadt and Danzig, which would become Polish territories after the Yalta Conference. Those from Czechoslovakia came from the Sudetenland, territories traditionally populated by the Germans and whose territory had been annexed by Germany in 1939. Since the eighteenth century, that region had been home to carving workshops in Gablonz, where Hochschiffglass, a type of crystal, was made. Gablonz, Polaun, Harrachsdorf, Antoniwald, Reichsberg were the most well-known production centers.

Among the refugees who had arrived in Karlsbad—already taken over by the Americans—where they felt protected from the Russians, was the family of Josef Riedel. They had been glaziers since 1756. When the Russians invaded Poland, they took Walter, the father, as a technical prisoner and brought him to Russia, where he stayed ten years, producing television screens for the Russians. He returned to Austria after his imprisonment.

The Russians recruited thirty-seven thousand, eight hundred German technicians. They were sent to Russia, not to be killed or be imprisoned in camps, but to work in Russian industries.

The Riedel family of refugees consisted of Claudia, her daughter Sabine, her son Johann, and her other son Claus, an official of the German army and prisoner in a camp in Civittavecchia, near Rome.

After spending three days in Karlsbad, rumor was spreading that the Americans were to evacuate and retreat. According to the Allied High Command, all of Czechoslovakia was about to be occupied by the Russians. Such were the political fluctuations during the occupation of Germany; obviously the German refugees did not wish to be under Russian control, from which they'd fled in the first place. And so the throngs of people marched once again, following the Americans into Bavaria.

Many years later, in 1958, I became good friends with Claus Riedel, who after leaving a prison camp in Italy married an Italian, Ada Parodi. After the wedding he built a crystal factory in Kufstein, Austria.

Born between us was a sincere friendship, full of mutual respect and caring, and we remain friends to this day. Once Claus told me: "We understand each other, because we've been through the same thing." *Wir Haben Dasselbe Mitgemacht.* I responded that this wasn't entirely true. One can't in any way compare expulsion to massacre, mass killing with dispossession.

He understood this immediately; in fact, his respect for me grew because of it. He had three sons; the eldest, George, married a Jewish woman, Eva Konig, native of Vienna, whose parents immigrated to Palestine in 1938.

We hosted Riedel at our home in Mexico; I visited him many times at his home in Kufstein. In 1972, my eldest son, wishing to learn the art of crystal-making, worked in his factory and lived with the Riedels for two months.

Claus was in Israel twice. I served as his host. He donated a large collection of pieces he designed to the Eretz Museum in Tel-Aviv.

On May 8, 1945, the Germans officially surrendered in Berlin. I say "officially" because two days beforehand, there was a partial surrender in Reims, France.

Shehecheyanu! We have survived, we are alive to see this day! Hitler was in power for twelve years, from 1933 to 1945, and now he was dead, by suicide. Germany was ruined, much more so than in 1918 at the end of the First World War. Entire cities were reduced to ashes. Nearly fifty million human beings, in total, had been exterminated.

The war in Europe had ended. All too late, for those who hadn't made it through alive. But this was the first sign of hope in a new life for those who had survived.

When the clouds of destruction had dissipated, the fires devouring entire cities had been extinguished, and the crematory ovens had ceased to function, we could scarcely comprehend the absolute loss, the misery, the millions displaced who were now homeless, and starving. Mothers without their children, children without their mothers. And the invalids…not to mention those who'd gone mad in the camps having born witness to such atrocities. Nothing would ever be the same.

So much of Europe—especially Poland, Russia, and Germany—was destroyed.

On May 8, the German High Command formed by Admiral Friedrichsburg, General Guderian, and Marshall Keitel surrendered unconditionally before Marshall Zhukov and Generals de Lattre de Tassigny and Pedder. In Italy, the Germans surrendered on May 2.

Mauthausen, in Austria, was the last camp to be liberated by American troops. Ten thousand cadavers were found in a mass grave that had been recently dug. The prisoners had likely been killed just hours before the arrival of American troops. This was one of the most inhumane camps in the entire system.

One interesting fact: in 1941, 3,280 Spanish prisoners were remitted to Mauthausen. Since 1938, these Spanish Republicans had been at Rivesaltes in a "camp" in the Pyrenees overseen by the Vichy government. It's worth noting that the Geneva Convention did not permit the remission of prisoners to third parties, nor returning them to their places of origin.

The Germans immediately sent them to Mauthausen, to work in the granite quarries. The hostages toiled from sunrise to sunset. They drank water and ate whatever they could once a day. On May 2, 1945, when the camp was liberated, only 256 remained alive. A bit more than three thousand Republican soldiers had been killed.

In Brussels, the festivities continued: military parades, the Belgian army marching with flags to patriotic music. High officials in gold-braided regalia watched the parade from a platform installed in the Place de Broukere.

Also parading were British riflemen, preceded by a platoon of bagpipers in tall black hats, something I'd never seen before. The Americans in their simple uniforms marched with their machine guns across their chest behind a long line of jeeps.

The Resistance marched as well, grouped according to political party. A few months after the liberation, divisions began reappearing among those who'd maintained a united front during the occupation. The Communists were most numerous, marching beneath a red flag. The Catholics marched beneath the tricolored Belgian flag.

The Communists were better organized, the most disciplined; in a short time they were able to attain command. And they deserved it; they were always willing to tackle dangerous missions, taking on the most difficult tasks.

The Communists were, of course, good politicians; one never knew whether they were fighting for the wellbeing of the working class or for the glory of the Soviet Union. In June of 1941, when the USSR was attacked, they united with the Resistance.

During the war the Communists in Belgium encountered a dilemma: unite with the Resistance or remain neutral under the Molotov-Ribbentrop agreement. The Germans hated the Communists. The Belgians considered them untrustworthy. But once the Germans invaded the Soviet Union, the problem was resolved.

I earned good money at the photo laboratory; work had already returned to normal. Monsieur Guillaume was offered a new Gevaert printing machine, impressively quick, and well-suited for times when a client requested multiple copies. I received instructions from the factory and learned how to use the printer. I learned so well that Guillaume gave me a 25% raise. I felt incredibly proud of myself. Although I had to be careful of my fingers, work became quicker and more efficient. I most enjoyed making amplifications: one could improve the effects of the camera. It was creative work.

One Friday night, a soldier from the Jewish Brigade arrived at the Place Rouppe. A *chayal*! The first Jewish soldier we'd seen! His khaki uniform identified him as English; on his left arm he wore a badge with a Star of David on a light blue background and gold letters that spelled out 'Jewish Brigade.' Above his badge was a fringe that said Palestine. His name was Uri Katzenelson. He was from a *kibbutz*, or collective farm, called Mishmar Haemek, in Meujad ha-Avoda. He belonged to our movement in Eretz Israel! He'd been sent to help us! He was a *madrich*, an instructor. We were thrilled to welcome him.

Berl spoke with him in Yiddish, as none of us spoke Hebrew. That night he taught us Hebrew songs, accompanied on accordion by Zahava.

Before then, we'd sung in Yiddish; revolutionary songs, like "The International," "*Bandiera Rossa*," "*Yunge, Gwardie*," "*Partisaner Lid*," and "*Sog Nit Keinmol, as du gueist dem letztn veg.*" He taught us: *"David Melech Israel,"* and "*Hora*," "*Hinei matov umanaim,* " and many others songs from Palestine. Uri helped us to create an atmosphere like Eretz Israel.

The first survivors from the concentration camps returned to Belgium, among them Mrs. Herskovicz, who'd first been in Ravensbruck, later in Bergenbelsen, where she was liberated by the English. Isaac Kelerstein also returned, native of Bychawa, Poland, whom I met in Mexico and who remains my friend. He was liberated from a camp called "Lager 4" near Munich, after spending time in various *Arbeitslager* camps. At sixteen years old, he was imprisoned. He toiled for three long years, subjected to subhuman conditions, for Heinkel, a factory that produced planes. First in Poland, and later in Germany. His youth, his faith in life, and his good health allowed him to survive.

The Americans sent survivors first to German hospitals, where they were attended to until they were able to regain their health and will to live. By and large, these were military hospitals, under strict control of the American military doctors, but staffed by German nurses. The sad irony is that many survivors, unaccustomed to this level of care, passed away.

It's estimated that from the camps and "death marches" almost 280,000 people survived. Once liberated, they had to figure out where to go and how to proceed with their lives. Many no longer wished to return to their homes, not wanting to coexist among a hostile population; almost everyone wanted to emigrate elsewhere. Shaare Hapleita dubbed the survivors D.P.: Displaced Persons.

The Palestinian Jews organized transit by sea from Italian ports to the Holy Land despite the British blockade and "White Paper" issued by British command, the same that prevented the legal entry of Jews into Great Britain. On the other hand, the British continued with their policy of dealing with Arabs and Jews under the slogan "divide and conquer."

England had already forgotten that the great Mufti Husseini had gone to Berlin in 1942 to pay homage to Adolf Hitler. They had forgotten that the Jewish Brigade had fought hand in hand with the British at Montecassino.

Winston Churchill, the British leader who'd led Great Britain to victory in 1945—with his maxim of "Blood, toil, tears and sweat"—lost the elections. Clement Attlee, a socialist, came into power. Ernest Bevin was in the Foreign Office. Ben Gurion was hopeful: a socialist government in England could help things. What a farse! Before long, he was disappointed.

Jewish veterans from Poland organized convoys across Czechoslovakia to the Italian ports and the transit bound for Palestine. All with the intention of rescuing the Jewish survivors and helping them towards a new life. Other survivors were brought to Romania and, from Constanza, embarked for Palestine.

Little by little, rescue centers were organized for the "Displaced Persons" in Germany, in Munich, Stuttgart, and near Frankfurt. *Chayalim* were appointed to teach Hebrew classes; conferences on Zionism were organized, all with the aim of guiding and comforting the survivors.

Most of the aid came from the United States. Specialists in rehabilitation; instructors in vocational training; doctors; nurses; medicines and food courtesy of JOINT. After visiting one of the rescue centers, Earl G. Harrison, a representative of Harry Truman, gave orders that they be administered with a system of self-government.

A small boat called the "Dalin" set sail from the Italian port city of Gaeta, with the first thirty-five *olim* youths, who arrived and established themselves in Eretz Israel.

Eight more ships arrived—mostly small vessels, so as to more easily mislead the British ships—with another 1,040 survivors. This was the resumption of illegal immigration Aliyah Bet, operated by the Mossad, or Yishuv secret police. The British were furious.

In October, David Ben Gurion visited the rescue centers in Germany and brought with him a message of encouragement. By then, he'd become a legendary figure.

Jewish survivors—most of them young—continued arriving at the rescue centers. Many had fought with the Russian and Lithuanian partisans, and were reluctant to return to their homelands. Poland, Lithuania, and Russia were drenched in blood and covered in ashes. There were also soldiers and Jewish officials from the demobilized Red army, anxious to leave the USSR.

Many years later, I was living in Mexico and met three of them: Adam Eliakimovich (Abrasha), Lev Buckrinsky, and Moise Shuster. They were ex-combatants from the *Krasnaya Armiya* and we became good friends.

The American military opened offices in the refugee centers in order to speed up the paperwork process for Jews immigrating to the United States and other countries in North America.

The American military government—preoccupied with "de-Nazification"—forced German civilians, especially those who wished to become future officers, postmasters, police chiefs, etc., to attend screenings of movies they'd filmed the moment the camps were liberated.

As the survivors returned and assessments were done of villages, counties, cities, and finally countries, we began to see the true dimensions, the breadth of the catastrophe suffered by the Jewish people, and all of humanity.

Seventy percent of the Jewish population living in Europe in 1938, not including those able to leave before the Holocaust, was annihilated. 1.5 million of those killed were children.

These were cold figures. In 1905, the word "genocide" began being used to describe the massacre perpetrated by the Turks of the Armenian Christians. A total of 700,000 men, women, and children were killed between Yerevan and Mount Ararat by the Turks.

In Europe, there were millions of deaths, hence the word "Holocaust" and its Hebrew equivalent, *Shoah*.

The personal tragedies of the survivors began to form a pattern. Otto Frank, father of the tragically famous Anne Frank, returned to Amsterdam to find no one in his family left alive. His wife, both of his daughters, and all of his friends had been killed in Auschwitz. Anne became known for her diary, written when she was just thirteen years old, discovered by her father in their hiding place and published in 1945.

Dr. Victor Frankl, a psychiatrist from Vienna, was branded with the number 119.104 in Auschwitz. After the liberation he discovered—based on his experiences in the camp—the theory of logotherapy. According to this theory, those who cling to life and continue making plans for the future are most likely to survive under subhuman conditions.

Halina Samet, originally from Warsaw, survived Auschwitz. Her parents were assimilated Jews, and she'd attended the Polish school *gimnazjum*; she later studied two years at the university. In 1941, her family was confined to the ghetto shortly before the uprising in 1943. Halina, already orphaned, was sent to Auschwitz, where she remained for two years. I met her many years later in Milan, and she was married to Paolo Samet. She gave birth to a son named Niccola, a veritable miracle for a survivor.

Her husband Samet, a friend of mine for many years, fought in Italy in the Anders division, formed by Polish volunteers. After the war, while consulting one of the many lists of survivors, he came across the name of a cousin he'd been looking for in Germany. They were married in 1946. Now they live in Milan.

Isaac Kelerstein lost his mother and his three sisters. At the end of the war he reunited with his brother in Germany, who'd also survived the concentration camps. He now lives in Mexico.

Throughout occupied Europe, Jews went into hiding, clinging to their lives in attics, in dormers, garrets, basements, in sewers and drainage systems. Some saved themselves this way, but suffered conditions nearly as inhumane as those in the camps.

I maintain that this was a relentless war against the Jews, as even those in hiding were always terrified that the enemy was lurking. If they didn't kill you on the spot, they'd take you prisoner and send you to the gas chambers. The final result was always death. Children survived by hiding in convents or with families in the country. Little ones left fatherless and motherless, remaining alone and helpless.

In April we learned of the death of American President Franklin Delano Roosevelt. Even at the Yalta conference a year beforehand he'd been sick. He was a great leader. Thanks to him, the United States entered into the conflict against the Axis powers, joining forces with the Allies after Pearl Harbor. Harry Truman, the new president, attended the conference at Potsdam, in Russian-occupied Germany. They discussed the war against Japan, as well as the future of the Soviet-occupied Eastern European countries. Although Stalin initially appeared to be a *Batyushka*, a good-natured paternal figure, little by little he began to unmask himself. The Soviet Union began conducting itself as an imperial power, openly favoring communists in the countries recently liberated from the German yoke, and attempting to eliminate all democratic opposition. The war had been fought for this? So many lives were lost for this? Czechoslovakia, Poland, Hungary, Romania, Bulgaria, Yugoslavia, and Albania were transformed into communist dictatorships. Churchill, who spared no words, said "An iron curtain has been dropped over Eastern Europe."

Meanwhile, Americans, Australians, and New Zealanders were advancing in the Pacific, fighting against the Japanese. This was a war that cost us many human lives.

The Japanese tenaciously defended themselves to the bitter end. This included organizing suicide squadrons, in which pilots, *Kamikaze*, launched themselves into American battleships. The fight against the last remaining Axis power was a bloody one.

The Zionist organizations grew as much in Brussels as in Antwerp. Young people sought a Jewish environment with which they could identify, and so these communities flourished. There were Ha-shomer Ha-tzair, Dror, Gordonia, Betar, and Benei Akiva, and, of course, ours at the far left, Poalei Zion. The organizations sometimes met at a theater with four hundred and fifty seats, numbers never seen before the war. There was intense interest in emigrating, more among the youth than among adults.

When the weather was nice, we danced for hours on the patio in front of the Place Rouppe, but above all, and for any reason, we organized excursions to the areas around the city. Uri, the *chayal*, took part in all of our activities. Phillipe Weinreb and I were responsible for the *Kvutza*. Peretz, named after Yitzjak Leibush Peretz, the Yiddish writer. We were *Roshim*, or fifteen-year old guides, the majority young women between thirteen and fifteen. For each board we had to prepare the theme for the *sicha*, or talk. It was assumed that the leaders should know everything; that was why they were leaders. But the younger members were much more mature than we were. They quickly found our weak spots and made us suffer.

To perform *aliyah* was to ascend, to ascend to something sublime, to abandon the past. Eretz Israel was an egalitarian society, the utopia of Russian Jewish thinkers in the nineteenth century. Our goal was to build a socialist Palestine, with *kibbutzim*, or agricultural communities.

Our organization rented a farm in the Wallon country near Namurs, designated for our *hakhshara*, or training. Before immigrating to Palestine, we would need to learn the basic skills and techniques of farming. We would begin in January of 1946. There was a list of twenty young people, including myself, to participate in this training.

I changed jobs for this. One of Monsieur Gauillaume's employees was called to a laboratory in Chaussee de Wavre. The pay was better, and by the hour. At her suggestion, I interviewed with the owner, and he gave me the job, essentially because I knew how to operate the new Gevaert printing machine. I notified Herbert Leder, who began working with me. So we were together. At sixteen years old, I was earning the salary of an adult. I felt accomplished and proud of my achievements. I was self-sufficient.

I felt like I already knew everything. Years later, when I read the Greek philosophers—especially Socrates, who said "I know one thing, that I know nothing"—I realized the error in my ways, my naiveté.

I had survived; I had a home, a job, I'd found a group of Jewish friends who'd accepted me with open arms. I had a goal: to immigrate as a *chalutz* in

Palestine, work in an agricultural commune. For me, as for many other young people, everything was clear: "What's white is white, what's black is black."

My sixteen-year-old logic—not yet fully formed—told me there was nothing to worry about. I long for that security in myself, which I don't believe I'll ever feel again.

War, destruction, concentration camps, and crematorium chimneys: we would leave all this behind. We were preparing ourselves for a clean, luminous future.

Yolanka and Buci were my family. They never imposed their views on me, nor their will. Ours was a relationship of mutual respect, untethered in such a way that when I announced my departure they grew sad, but never resented me for it. Buci would never be a Zionist, although he recognized, that had there been a larger migration to Eretz Israel before the war, many Jewish lives would have been spared. Moreover, the mindset of the Jewish community in Brussels had changed by the end of 1945. Immigrating to Palestine was the future of the Jewish youth. The presence of the Jewish Brigade helped, in its part, in this change in the community, or *Yishuv*. Many made *aliyah* between 1945 and 1947.

It was a great surprise to everyone when, on August 6th, a specially equipped American plane launched the first atomic bomb on Hiroshima. The resulting destruction was horrific. More than a hundred thousand people died from this first explosion.

The atomic bomb was a new kind of weapon; its victims died consumed by fire. Everything was destroyed in minutes. Three days later, the Americans launched a second bomb over Nagasaki.

The following day, August 12, 1945, the Japanese surrendered. They capitulated unconditionally, signing their surrender aboard the American aircraft carrier "Missouri" before Generals MacArthur, Lord Mountbatten, and Koniev, and on behalf of Emperor Hirohito, nine of his officials were present.

The Second World War had ended with two explosions stronger and deadlier than anyone could have possibly imagined.

Starting in 1943, the atomic bomb had been secretly developed in the Mojave Desert by a group of scientists headed by Robert Oppenheimer, a Jewish American. He was assisted by Enrico Fermi, an Italian Jew; Edward Teller and Laszlo Szilard, Judeo-Hungarian immigrants; Lilienthal, John von Neumann and Hans Bethe, German Jews, among others. In this desert location, they built and tested what was to become the deadliest weapon in all of history.

Among them was Joseph Rotblat, a Polish-Jewish scientist. He was fortunate enough to leave Warsaw in June of 1939, thanks to his friend, Swedish Jew Niels Bohr, who was able to obtain a Swedish visa for him. He was then invited to collaborate with the research team in the Mojave. In 1945, he became an acerbic critic of the atomic bomb, and was expelled from the United States. At the end of the war, he settled in England.

This "Manhattan Project" was based on studies of the theory of relativity as developed by Albert Einstein, German-Jewish scientist who immigrated to America from Switzerland in 1936, having been invited by Princeton University. The Germans, led by Nobel Prize-winning physicist Otto Han and his partner Von Weisszaker, were also working intensely on the same project at the Kaiser Wilhelm Institut in Berlin. They came very close to finishing.

At that time, news arrived of the murder—in Kielce, south of Warsaw—of forty Jews who'd survived the camps. A pogrom in Poland in 1945? How was this possible? A month beforehand, in Sokoly, north of Bialystok, seven Jews who'd returned from the camps were murdered. But the killing in Kielce was a mere drop in the bucket. There was, of course, an economic undercurrent: the Jewish survivors of concentration camps intended to reclaim their homes, which they were forced to abandon in 1941 when the Germans forced them to occupy the Warsaw ghetto. In the meantime, their homes had been occupied by the Polish.

This was nothing new; the Polish had always been anti-Semites. After the First World War, Poland's newly-drawn boundaries were comprised of Russian, German, and Austrian territories, and in 1920 Poland boasted a population of slightly more than three and a half million Jewish souls.

The Jews enjoyed autonomy in the Poland of Pilsudzki. There were forty-six Jewish representatives in the *Sejm*, or Polish Parliament. There were *shtetlach*—villages—populated entirely by Jewish inhabitants. In cities like Lodz, Bialystok, Brody, Kalish, Lublin, and Pinsk, nearly three quarters of the population was Jewish.

Warsaw had three hundred and fifty thousand Jews, or one third of the capital city's population. Perfectly organized in *Kehilot*, the Jews never had to turn to the Polish authorities, except in the case of war. They had their own hospitals, clinics, sanatoriums, and rabbinical court, the *Beth Din*. Not to mention schools, including the gymnasiums where students prepared for the *matura*, necessary exams for entering into the universities in the face of the dreaded "Numerus clausus", which limited the enrollment of Jewish students to ten percent in fields like medicine, law, and engineering.

There were Jewish community outreach centers, responsible for providing for brides without dowries, for widows, orphans, and the elderly. They owned schools, cemeteries, and also led teacher training seminars. Every *Kehilla* had a *chevra kadisha*, in charge of rigorously carrying out the Jewish funereal rite. In a way, they ran a state within a state.

They had their own language, Yiddish. Jewish children were not accepted into Russian schools until after the First World War. They attended the *cheder*, and then primary school, and were instructed in Yiddish. Polish, Russian, and German were second languages. They learned other languages once they attended the Gymnasium, which helped prepare them to enter university. Such was the *Status Loquendi* of the enormous Polish-Jewish community.

In the Russian empire under the tsars, Russian and only Russian was the official language. No one, at least in theory, was allowed to speak anything else. On one occasion a Hasidic rabbi in a village near Minsk in Belarus was called before the authorities. They asked him whether he spoke Russian. They brought him an interpreter. They asked him: *Ihr red kein Russisch?* The rabbi, so as not to lie to the authorities, resorted to the dialect spoken in the Yeshiva, and said: *Oib ich red Russisch? Ich red Russisch vi ij red Polnische.* I speak Russian as well as Polish.

Moreover, thanks to the universal use of Yiddish, a rich literature and extensive dramaturgy was allowed to be cultivated. Later on, Yiddish movies were filmed in Poland and Russia.

Many creative works were produced, and widely published. The great writer Shmiel Yosef Agnon, winner of the Nobel Prize in Literature; as well as famous poet Hayim Nachman Bialik, both immigrated to Israel, where they created the bulk of their work, written first in Yiddish, then in Hebrew. Bialik said: *"Ivrit redt men, ober yidish redt sij,"* a word game according to which Yiddish comes from the soul while Hebrew comes from the mind.

The Jews were productive citizens, paying taxes, contributing to the arts through artists, musicians, doctors, actors and writers in Polish.

Jewish theater was just as popular among Polish audiences as it was among Jewish ones. Klezmer music ensembles enlivened weddings just as the mariachi do in Mexico.

In an attempt to understand the Polish hatred towards the Jews in 1945, we must go back to the Jewish migrations in the sixteenth and seventeenth centuries.

Alsatian and German Jewish survivors of the Crusades were invited to Poland by Polish feudal nobles, still mired in medieval customs. They needed administrators and tax collectors who could read and write.

These were the first Jews to meet the Polish, who came to resent them for representing their oppressors, the nobles.

Unfortunately, the Catholic Church contributed to creating a negative image of the Jew: Jews were users, guilty of deicide and murdering Christian children—whose blood, according to certain accounts, was used for the baking of unleavened Easter bread.

In the wake of the events at Kielce, an emergency meeting was held in Brussels, in which a protest march was organized in front of the UNRRA offices, responsible for refugees in Europe. Another in front of the Polish Embassy, now representative of the "People's Socialist Republic." This meeting was attended by all the Jewish agencies, except for the communists: they criticized the Catholics for their dogmatism, but they were much the same.

Some Catholics even joined us with banners denouncing the closing of Polish churches, along with members of the resistance in favor of *"les droits de l'homme"* or human rights. They also called for free migration—which was then prohibited—for Jewish survivors in Poland. We numbered 220, a truly impressive group of protestors. At least, according to the newspaper "Le Soir." We felt very important, satisfied that we'd fulfilled our mission. Truth be told, the demonstration did virtually nothing, and yielded no concrete results.

Germany in 1945 was home to refugees of all sorts. The International Red Cross, the French, and the UNRRA worked to restore order and help these throngs of people.

The Allies were, in fact, the ruling power at this point; there was no longer a functional German government. The Americans, the French, the English, and the Russians did what they could to help these refugees.

Dachau, for example, was converted into a center for documentation where Jewish survivors could receive provisional paperwork to travel abroad. There were also many German refugees in Russian-occupied territories. Volksdeutsche from Czechoslovakia, Germans from Danzig, Konigsberg, Memel, and Baltic states now annexed by the USSR. The refugees numbered several hundred thousand, and were moving in search of food and shelter on the roads of the Old Reich.

Thousands of S.S. infiltrated the throngs of demoralized, starving people, along with their collaborators in the German-occupied territories.

Very few knew of the existence of Odessa, an organization devised by Himmler, unbeknownst to Hitler since 1943, for the rescue of S.S. leaders and the *Kamaradenwerk*. This organization was made up of contacts from abroad, mainly in Argentina and Chile, Switzerland and the Vatican, and individuals willing to help in exchange for money. Funds had been deposited in Swiss banks long before the German debacle.

The criminals, eager to get to safety, began by obtaining documents issued by the International Red Cross attesting that they were refugees from the east. They would then penetrate into Italy, head for the Vatican and be given false names and altered birthdates.

Pope Pious XII remained silent. The Roman Curia and some parishioners came forward to provide aid for Nazis who'd fled—according to them— from certain death, at the hands of the Bolsheviks.

Nazis joined the Catholic Church in a frenzy to save themselves. In the Vatican, priests expedited "legal" documents, visas for Argentina, Brazil, Chile, and Paraguay.

Aid for the Nazis was organized by the Kamaradenwerk. Bishop Alois Hudal, native of Graz, had lived in Rome for many years, and served as father confessor for communities of German-speaking Catholics. He was later promoted to Rector of the Pontificio Istituto Teutonico Santa Maria dell'Anima. He took part in the negotiations between the Vatican and Germany, signing the concordat in September of 1933. Franz von Papen negotiated on behalf of Germany, and on behalf of the Vatican, Secretary of State Eugenio Pacelli, who later became Pious XII. The candidates eligible to emigrate were assembled in Austria. Ample funding was available to send the Nazis to Rome, with ecclesiastical paperwork, to avoid problems that might arise along the way. They were received in Rome by Monsignor Giovanni Montini, later Pope Paolo VI, who was in charge of coordinating the rescue operation with Caritas, an international Catholic aid organization.

A cottage in Castelgandolfo—which served as a summer home for the popes—was used to provide temporary asylum for the Nazis, while they awaited ships to depart from Genoa and Napoli for their final destinations.

Thanks to this rescue operation, *Kriegsverbrecher*, war criminals like Franz Stengel, commandant from the extermination camp Treblinka, were able to escape to Syria. Martin Bormann, second-in-command to Hitler, and Alois

Brunner, Eichmann's lieutenant, who served for a time as commandant of Sobibor, were also able to escape to the Middle East. Dr. Josef Mengele, "Angel of Death," from Auschwitz, fled to Argentina, though later settled in Brazil. Eichmann himself traveled to Argentina with the help of this operation, although he was later captured by the Mossad. Walter Rauff was responsible for the operation to exterminate the occupants of Porsch trucks by administering exhaust gasses, causing the death of hundreds of thousands of Jews. He arrived in South America like the others.

Josef Priebke, responsible for the massacre of three hundred and sixty innocent Italians in the mass graves at Adreatina in Rome, was also sent to Argentina. We will never know the exact number of war criminals who escaped from Europe between 1945 and 1948. Among them were not only Germans, but henchmen in occupied countries, Croats, Lithuanians, Ukrainians, Norwegians, Slovakians, Hungarians, etc. Argentina alone, under the dictator Juan Perón—Eva Perón was a Nazi sympathizer—let in 72,000 between 1945 and 1947. The United States and Canada were also benefitting from these criminals during this time.

Yet these criminals had committed acts not just against the Jews, but against all of humanity.

General Patton of the US army earned a perfect score. When General Eisenhower asked him on the telephone how many Nazis he'd found in Nymphenburg, a suburb of Munich, he responded that he'd found none. Eisenhower then questioned Patton about the presence of prominent Nazis in the Munich civil government. To this, Patton responded: "I need people who are apt and professional to run this government, and I am not going to put it upon myself to investigate whether or not they are Nazis." The Americans were most naïve of all the Allies.

The first of January 1946, we arrived at the *Ferme* where we began our *hakhshara*. Uri, our *chayal*, and three other young men were already there, so we were all set up: the beds had been made, there was food in the kitchen, as well as a makeshift mast with a blue and white flag, not the red to which we were accustomed. Friends from the organization and several parents saw us off. At the end of our training, we were to embark for Palestine from the Rotterdam port. Twenty "Aleph" certificates had arrived, legal documents for our *aliyah*.

The first few days were dedicated more to military exercises than to agriculture. Uri taught us proper formation: "*Echad, shtayim, shalosh*" one, two, three; "*yemina, smola*," right, left, and we formed a line. We obtained three guns, and began to dismantle them and clean them several times in order to become accustomed to doing it quickly. Never with bullets, so as not to have problems with the authorities.

After a while we were taught how to use the plough, to make furrows for planting. We were also taught to use a sickle to cut down chestnuts from trees—it was January, after all. We were just about dead from exhaustion by the time we showered and ate dinner.

There were three impromptu wooden showers in the bathroom. The women bathed first, followed by the men. As there was only one doorway to and from the bathroom, the women wrapped themselves in towels that barely covered their bodies, and as we stood in line to use the showers we whistled at them, which made them incredibly embarrassed. On the fourth day, we changed our routine. The men bathed first, then went back to their dormitories so the women could bathe privately. We promptly learned that the women liked to take longer showers, who knew why...

We were fourteen men and six women. Although we were adolescents of different genders, we were never distracted. Our relationship was one of camaraderie, and it was very strong, and, frankly, we were so close to making *aliyah*, we never thought of making anything more than a loving gesture, a kiss. Saying *"je suis fous de toi."* I'm crazy for you, was meant platonically, and said in front of everyone. Without realizing it, we were already living in a *kibbutz*, living as a community.

Several incredible weeks passed. For me, this was like being on vacation, something I hadn't enjoyed since 1937 when I went with my mother to Hungary. Although the physical work was intense, the simple fact that I didn't have to wake up every morning and go to work in the laboratory was marvelous.

In the *Ferme* each of us had to do everything. We took turns in the kitchen: we had to peel potatoes, kill, quarter, and cook the chickens. We maintained cleanliness of the dormitories.

The first few days we each made our own beds as best we could. As we were not very good at this, the women took charge of this task. They made fun of us. "You don't even know how to make your bed! You should be ashamed!"

When it wasn't raining, we made a large fire on the patio, and sang songs till all hours of the night. We danced for hours. We also had to study Jewish history, and the history of Zionism.

Uri, who at that point spoke decent French, taught us common Hebrew words and phrases. This is how we spent the first of the three months of *hakhshara*. One Sunday there was a knock at the door. I went to see who it was. I'd been in the kitchen peeling potatoes. It was Buci. He'd driven here. He explained that Yolanka hadn't wanted to come, that seeing me would make her sadder than she already was.

I let him in and offered him a glass of lemonade. He gave me a telegram, written in English, inviting me to Mexico. It was signed by Else and Moritz Lazar Ellenbogen. I vaguely remembered something my mother had told me in Vienna, before I left, that she had a cousin, my aunt Else, in Italy. But this telegram had come from Mexico…

Buci looked at me, and his face was kind, as usual. He asked me: *Nu?* What does it say? He already knew, and his eyes filled with tears: You don't have to go to Mexico, or to Palestine. You can stay with us. *"On t'aime bien et tu le sais."* We love you, you know that. This was the first time Buci had openly expressed sadness over my departure. For Buci and Yolanka, this was like losing a son.

I suppose they imagined that the day would come when we would separate and my parents would reclaim me. They were only my "adoptive parents," after all.

I understood the dilemma, and I didn't want to hurt them more. I told him I wasn't interested in going to Mexico. I was already here in the *hakhshara*, and already had a certificate from the British to legally immigrate to Palestine.

I begged him to understand that to do *aliyah* was the greatest desire for any Jewish youth today. We hugged and he returned to Brussels. I was left with a deep pain in my heart.

I kept the telegram among my papers, beside my bed. We had very little privacy at the *Ferme*. That was the price we paid for choosing this communal lifestyle, which was one we would continue once we'd arrived in Palestine. It was what we longed for, without knowing very well what it was.

We knew from Uri's *sichot* that in the *kibbutz* everyone had to work hard. We slept and ate communally. There was no private property; everything was property of the *kibbutz*. Upon entry, each of us would relinquish our belongings, and later the *kibbutz* bought what was necessary for the community. The children, if there were any, were educated communally. The mothers took turns caring for them. They didn't sleep with their parents.

I decided to say nothing to my peers about the telegram so as not to disappoint them. But I was confronted by a dilemma: Palestine or Mexico. Make *alihh* or travel to a place I knew nothing about and with relatives who'd suddenly appeared out of thin air: *Min ha-shamaim.*

Until then, I'd made my own decisions. I didn't want to hurt anyone. But I felt that no matter what I chose, I'd end up hurting Buci and Yolanka.

The following days passed quickly, events occurring one after the other, making my decision for me.

On Thursday I spoke with Buci on the phone, and he told me a letter had arrived from Mexico. I asked for Berl to bring it on Friday afternoon when he arrived at the *Ferme*.

It was written on the letterhead of Ultramar, the company where my uncle Moritz worked. He wrote in German, my aunt Else in French. The letter, which was quite brief, stated they were happy to know I was alive. They wanted me to come live with them. They'd already processed my visa and bought me a ticket. It was that simple. They had already decided for me.

The following Monday, around noon, there was a knock at the door. Two men were asking for me. I took a break from planting small fruit bushes, which we'd found at a nearby nursery, and went to the gate to see what they wanted.

Much to my surprise, one was Uncle Tibbik, my Aunt Ana's husband, and the other was a uniformed Belgian gendarme who, without even saluting me, asked *"Etes vous monsieur Hans Katz?"* I answered in the affirmative, and he gave me a sheet of paper and asked me to accompany him: *"Vous venez avec moi, lisez d'abord."* You must come with me, but first read this.

My uncle purposefully kept his distance, remaining quiet. Moumous, after seeing the uniformed gendarme, approached the gate. The statement was, in reality, an ordinance by a judge in Brussels according to which my uncle received custody over the "minor Hans Katz" by virtue of the fact that Ana Katz of Thiebert, sister of my father, who was my official legal guardian, was unwell, and would be represented by her husband, my Uncle Tibbik.

I couldn't believe what I was hearing, but that it what was written. The gendarme was waiting. I had no idea what to say; this was unheard of! How was it possible something like this could happen in liberated Belgium? Uncle Tibbik remained silent.

Moumous was the one who spoke, and asked if I was allowed to take more time to let the words sink in. The gendarme agreed. He told me he'd return for me at three in the afternoon, and that he warned me that if I weren't ready or if I fled, I'd become a fugitive from justice. He said goodbye and both men walked away.

Of course, my aunt and uncle learned of my plans through the Lanksners, who complained bitterly of my absence. I'd like to think that my aunt felt a certain responsibility for me. When they found out about my imminent departure they began to think: We should avoid it if possible.

I wanted to cry, I felt so helpless. I had been free until now—perhaps too free—but suddenly, I had to obey the will of others.

Moumous put her arm around my shoulder and told me: Look, we'll go to Brussels and consult a lawyer. *"Ne t'en fait pas."* Not to worry. *"Ca va s'arranger"* This will be fixed.

Inside the *Ferme,* Armand Zaslavsky—a law student—joined us. He spoke with a Jewish lawyer from the Maitre Flame organization over the phone. I read the statement to him. According to the lawyer, the document was valid, as it was an order from a judge. The gendarmerie was only enforcing the warrant. This meant that at three in the afternoon, I'd be driven to the gendarmerie and would be at the disposal of my uncle, who, according to me, was relinquishing my power and autonomy. I began to cry helplessly.

I felt embarrassed in front of my friends, like I had disappointed them. Where was my independence, my free will? Moumous and Armand tried to calm me down; they urged me to comply with the order. But they'd also set up an appointment with a lawyer the following Tuesday to see what could be done legally to object to the custody decreed by the judge.

In the communal eating area, I could barely eat. I'd entirely lost my appetite. Everyone said goodbye to me; Yuri with a *Lehitraot,* "See you later." Deep down I knew I'd never return to the *hakhshara.*

At precisely three, the gendarme appeared again at the front gate, accompanied by my uncle. We walked to the village commissioner. After a brief wait, the commissioner appeared, and after asking for my name and identification, he explained the situation, handing me over to my uncle. We walked to the station where we caught the train to Brussels at five in the afternoon.

During the journey I refused to speak with my uncle; I wished to make apparent my annoyance at the situation. He told me again and again, "Later on, you'll thank me for this. You'll end up in a desert with a bunch of crazy '*Meshugene Idealists'.*" In my head, I went over my life after the liberation of Brussels. The dreams of seeing my parents were just that: illusions. At this point—a year and a half after liberation—I needed to resign myself and accept that I'd never see them again. "My aunt and uncle are taking advantage of me," I thought to myself. Damn it! They had to liberate me from their control, at any cost. I would consult with Monsieur Carton, one of Buci's old friends from the Resistance.

We arrived at the Gare Du Nord. My uncle warned me I was under his tutelage, and that I'd best behave myself and not do anything crazy, like try to escape. If I did try, he would report me to the authorities.

I went to the Rue Des Vierges with my tail between my legs. And such was my glorious return from the *hakhshara.*

Yolanka and Buci were home; they were happy to see me. What I loved about them was that they never questioned me, nor resorted to histrionics. As far as they were concerned, I'd already said goodbye to them, and now I was simply returning. They both kissed me and asked if I wanted any supper.

Their reception of me did me good. It was exactly what I needed: I'd never felt so confused before.

Before, I'd felt so self-sufficient! I thought I knew everything, including the solutions to all my problems!

Now I felt like a sad miscreant, condemned by a judge and hunted by a gendarme, delivered into the hands of my uncle, who didn't care about me, who just wanted to prohibit me from moving to Palestine.

Buci gave me two letters that had arrived for me. So much correspondence! I'd barely received anything since 1942. Now, a telegram had arrived from Mexico, then the letter from the Ellenbogens and, finally, two more: one from Mexico and one from the United States of America.

I opened this last one, signed by Oscar Gruenfeld. I remembered, then, my grandmother Caroline's last name; it was written in English. Through this letter, I became aware of the reason for the telegram and the letters from Mexico. Oscar, my mother's first cousin, lived in New York, where he edited "*Aufbau,*" a weekly German newspaper. He came across my name on a list of survivors in Brussels. He told my aunt Else Ellenbogen who was living in Mexico and who happened to be my closest relative: my mother's sister.

The letter said that, in effect, Oscar was the one who saw my name in "*Aufbau.*" Oscar was able to immigrate to New York in 1938, and began a new Gruenfeld family clan. He was soon joined by Joshy, *Hakoach* player who'd been in Dachau. His wife Emma and daughter Gerty were able to leave Vienna in 1938. Now in New York, they moved heaven, earth, and sea so that Joshy could be freed from the camp. This was only possible with an American visa and an affidavit that guaranteed his economic solvency.

Finally, at the end of 1939, Joshy was liberated from the talons of the Getsapo and could be reunited with his family. His brothers Oscar and Poldi had already immigrated with their respective wives and Oscar and Bertl's daughter Erika.

My mother's cousins had also managed to escape: Gerda and Erich, the children of Leopold Gruenfeld.

Gerty married a Viennese man, Fred Weis. A particularly advantageous football match allowed Emil to be invited to play on the Viennese team in Trenton, where he decided to live. This happened in 1936.

My encounter with this part of my family was like a revelation. Since leaving my parents' house in Vienna, I'd only kept up with my father's family. Now I'd discovered the Gruenfelds, and was thrilled to know how many family members I still had left alive.

Oscar wrote something that drew my attention: the Ellenbogens wanted to bring me to Mexico, and he advised me to accept their offer. In the event that this was not to my liking, I was welcome to live in the United States. He spoke for both himself and his two brothers.

Something else surprised me: I'd read and understood the letter Oscar had sent me, which was in English, a language I'd never studied formally. I'd never spoken it, but it turned out I could understand it.

The letter from Mexico was from Aunt Else, and was written in French. She told me that she and her husband Moritz were waiting for me, and that I would have a very nice life with them. That Mexico was a lovely country, and they were completing the paperwork for my visa, I just had to be patient.

But my dream was still to be a *chalutz* pioneer, and I continued to think *aliyah* was best for me at this time in my life. The success of the *Ferme* drew me towards this lifestyle even more. But perhaps I should go to Mexico with my aunt and uncle…I could always return to Palestine later on.

Moving to Mexico was also a way to shake off the paternal rights that bound me to my other aunt and uncle. They were opposed to me leaving for Palestine, but no one said anything about Mexico.

The lawyer from Matire Flame met with me in his office in the Place Rouppe. He requested the statement and, after perusing it, said that, effectively, the judge's orders were correct. He explained that as an orphan, though this was not stated legally, my first-degree relatives—either on my father's or mother's side—could initiate a process for being granted custody until I was of age. This would impede me from getting married or traveling outside of the Belgian kingdom, but couldn't affect my activities within the country. He told me he could not appeal it because it was a judicial matter.

In the Poale-Zion I was given the task of organizing a group of youths in Antwerp with my friend Phillipe Weinreb. This was a matter of forming a *kvutzah* of youths between twelve and fifteen years old. And so I took the train to Antwerp every Saturday and Sunday: a short, thirty-five minute trip.

We were received by their fathers, also members of Poale-Zion; they were interested in having their children trained as scouts. I went back to work. After an interview with the owner of the laboratory, he agreed to give me my job back after I'd given it up to go to the *hakhshara*. I was embarrassed, but I needed the money.

Amid the confusion, I rushed to answer the letters from my recently-materialized family members, my aunt and uncle in Mexico. I asked them if they agreed to let me study film: I wanted to become a movie director. Nothing more, nothing less. I didn't realize this wasn't a career that could be studied, per se, but rather one requiring many years of experience and practice in the field.

I thanked my cousin Oscar, who "found" me, for his invitation to the United States, informing me I'd also been invited to Mexico.

I returned to my old routine, working during the day, spending evenings at the organization, and commuting to Antwerp on the weekends.

A telegram arrived at the house from Havana. It was from my cousin Sigi! Naturally, I was surprised. Sigi, whom I'd last seen in Brussels in 1941, when he'd married his beautiful fiancé, was now living in Cuba. After his wedding I'd heard no more from him.

It turns out that, shortly after his wedding, he met with a jeweler friend from Vienna, Hans Ventura, whom he'd met in Brussels. They'd planned to escape to Vichy France and cross the Pyrenees into Spain by foot, aided by a Spanish guide.

The Spanish mountaineers were historically smugglers, and they now dedicated their time to helping guide refugees illegally by foot in exchange for a hefty sum of money. But Sigi, his wife, and their friend were spared this way.

And that's how they arrived in Bilbao, where today a transatlantic service still exists to ports in Latin America. Fortunately, they were able to obtain Cuban visas for all three.

Although they'd brought some money from Brussels, it was not enough for their tickets. They'd spent more than they anticipated.

Sigi knew of a jeweler colleague in San Sebastián, with whom he'd had business dealings. The jeweler, a Republican, was forced to close his shop when Franco won the war. They were able to find him, and he lent them the money necessary for their passage in American dollars, as was stipulated by the carrier, *sine qua non*.

The jeweler had buried several kinds of currency throughout his garden. They sealed their transaction with a handshake and no guarantee other than a promise. This is what Sigi told me many years later.

The telegram, written in French, urged me to travel with my aunt Julie, his mother, and to stay in Havana on my way to Mexico.

I'd seen Aunt Julie just once since the liberation, at a very emotional family reunion at Aunt Zilly's house in January, 1945. There, what was left of our family gave thanks to G-d that we had survived. Aunt Zilly was the most religious of any of us, and, hence, the favorite of grandfather Juer. We celebrated with a festive *Shehechyanu* with cakes and wine in abundance. Among the family present were Aunt Julie, Aunt Ana, her husband Tibbik, cousin Hilde, her sons Herbert—my partner at work—and Jack, his brother. Not to mention my cousin Heinrich Wolfthal, his wife Steffi, and their son Louis. They had been saved thanks to Steffi, a gentile, who had a valid German passport. I'd slept many times in their safe house during the occupation.

Louis, one of Aunt Julie's sons, was a violinist, and had been deported, never to return.

I immediately contacted Aunt Julie, who was fifty-eight years old, to tell her about Sigi's telegram and let her know that I would be going with her after all. For me, this was a pleasure rather than a duty. At this moment I had no idea what ship, what port, or even what date I would be leaving, only that we would be traveling together.

In the interim, I hadn't heard more from my aunt and uncle in Mexico. What had happened was that my uncle had found Sigi in Havana, and told him that they were sorting out the paperwork for me to come to Mexico, and that the only boats carrying passengers were from the Spanish Compañía Transatlántica, and they traveled only as far as Cuba. (At this time, Mexico had no dealings with Franco's Spain.) They asked that Sigi buy me a ticket to Havana, and told them they'd reimburse him later. This was the reason for Sigi's telegram to me.

I saw from this frequent correspondence that things were moving quickly, and my departure to the Americas was rapidly approaching.

Two days later another letter arrived from Mexico from Aunt Else, saying that she and my uncle were in agreement that I could study whatever I liked. They were looking into whether a School for Cinematic Arts existed in Mexico. They had agreed to bring me there, they'd paid my way, and agreed to my conditions!

On October 15, 1945, Pierre Laval was executed, along with Marshall Phillippe Petain and others guilty of treason. He was a symbol of Collaborationist France between 1940 and 1944.

I personally blamed Laval's politics, his hatred for and discrimination against the Jews, for the death of my father, and thousands of other Jews and Spanish Republicans—communists and anarchists. Perhaps they'd still be alive if he'd left them in internment camps like Rivesaltes, Gurs, Pitiviers, Vernet instead of delivering them on a silver platter to the Germans. Hopefully this execution would serve as an example for the new French youth, so that no such disgrace would ever be perpetrated again on French soil.

The German war criminals were prosecuted in Nuremburg. This was the first trial of this nature in history, holding accountable those who'd committed warm crimes against humanity.

Photographs of high-ranking military officials on the accuser's bench were published in the papers. They presented a sad spectacle, these Nazi senior leaders and generals in civilian clothing, most of whom were emaciated and older-looking, with cloudy, vacant eyes. So different from their haughty visages years before.

Hermann Goering, Minister of Aviation, directly responsible for the destruction of Guernica, in the Basque country, committed suicide before he was given a sentence. As did Baldour Von Schirach, *gauleiter* or commandant of Vienna.

Of the murderers, of which there were thousands, only two hundred and fifteen were brought to trial, and among those tried, only forty-six were condemned to die at the gallows. The others were subjected to various other penalties, and a prison was prepared in East Berlin specifically for war criminals tried in Nuremburg. It was guarded by soldiers from the four Allied powers.

News arrived from Vienna: the establishment of a "Center for Documentation" on behalf of Simon Wiesenthal, a survivor of the camps. After losing his parents, brothers, and wife, Wiesenthal decided to dedicate his life to locating, pursuing, and collecting the evidence needed to prosecute and punish those guilty of perpetrating the Holocaust. Difficult but necessary work.

In France, Serge Klarsfeld's wife Beate, a German gentile, zealously dedicated her life to the same mission.

The effort made by Simon Wiesenthal, Beate Klarsfeld, and others was truly impressive. Thanks to the collective force of volunteers including the Israeli Mossad, many criminals were apprehended and brought to justice.

The Nazis and the S.S. disappeared off the map surprisingly, and as if by magic. Many were placed in high political office in Germany and Austria, now occupied by the four Allied powers. Hence, the necessary and expedited intervention of the Nazi hunters.

Although the verdicts in Nuremburg set a precedent for jurisprudence, and individuals were prosecuted for the first time for "war crimes" and "crimes against humanity," those indicted were mostly a few senior German government officers, when in reality many more were involved in the planning and ordering of the killings.

Speaking of crimes against humanity, the massacre of innocent civilians, of genocide... according to some frightening statistics compiled in 1945, the Second World War killed 17 million citizens, and that's not even taking into account the military losses on both sides.

This included six million Jews, five million Russians, three million Polish, and three million gypsies, and civilians from nations occupied by the Germans.

Yesterday it was the Jews and the gypsies who were murdered and burned to ashes; tomorrow the Armenians, Kurds, black people, any group of people deemed "inferior."

Unfortunately, many of the criminals were protected by the German people, and so it was virtually impossible to find judges or prosecuting attorneys who weren't directly involved in the NSDAP.

Finally, a very long telegram arrived—three pages—from my aunt and uncle in Mexico, a statement in Spanish, allowing me permission to enter Mexico. I had to get to Paris immediately, which was where the Mexican consulate was located, to pick up my visa. The Cuban consulate was also located in Paris, where I would apply for a transit visa.

I first went with Uncle Tibbik—my guardian—so that he could accompany me to the municipality, where I was given a travel document. I was free of his tutelage. The document was a *Laissez Passer* issued by the Belgian government, an *"Allemand Non Ennemi"*—Austria did not exist when I was born—accompanied by a picture of me and various stamps. Government officials, after all, loved to put stamps on official documents. My uncle did not object to my leaving, *Got tzu danken*. Thank G-d.

Soon after, I went about saying goodbye. At work, this was my second time doing this, but this time it was definite; I also said goodbye to my friends at the organization, and they acknowledged the hard work I'd done in Antwerp. Our goodbye was a very emotional one. Finally, I said goodbye to my family. My Aunt Julie would join me in Paris in a week: her Cuban visa was not yet ready.

I said goodbye to Maurice and the Renous family, my neighbors for nearly eight years.

And, of course, I said goodbye to Yolanka and Buci, who'd finally resigned themselves to my leaving. They wished me well. Buci gave me a blessing, a *Yevarechecha* as he would for a son. This was different form when I departed for the *hakhshara*. I was sad, and felt tremendous love for them. Yolanka and Buci had given me their home, and cared for me for eight years, ever since I'd left my parents in Vienna in 1938. Yolanka was quite shy, and loved me in her own way.

Buci was more openly affectionate, loving, embracing me with arms outspread. He would always serve for me as a paradigm of justice and goodness, a life lived according to the Jewish tradition; completely devoid of egotism, his main goal was always to do good for others. He always found ways to help, a rare virtue in people. Both Buci and Yolanka wept, and I cried in the car as Buci drove me to the train station.

I had to buy a large valise to hold all my belongings. I didn't have much clothing; a new suit I'd bought when they'd raised my salary at the photo laboratory, my day-to-day clothing, and the uniform I wore to the organization.

But I had other things to pack, like my stamp collection, my parents' letters, my camera and tripod. So many pictures and books. I bought a well-known Spanish grammar book known as *"Assimil"* and a French/Spanish dictionary, along with two bulky books to read: *The Forty Days of Musa Dagh* by Franz Werfel, on the Armenian genocide in 1905, and *Jean Cristophe* by Romain Rolland. With this reading material, I'd be ready for my transatlantic voyage, which was going to be a long one.

On the platform, Buci's eyes welled up with tears, but he managed to say: *"A jo isten megyen veledem fiam."* God be with you, my son. The train began moving, and I left Brussels behind after eight bittersweet years. In Brussels, I transitioned from childhood to puberty, I learned to work, to value life, to be responsible, to share, and, above all, to emulate Buci's goodness and humanity. I'd embraced my Jewish identity and became an idealist. Even though my *aliyah* project had been thwarted, my Zionist ideals remained intact—somewhat shaken, but still alive.

When the train made its first stop, I thought about how different this was from our trip to Mons in 1940. This time, the train went straight to Valenciannes, the French border. I couldn't stop thinking of how we'd tried to flee to France, about our pilgrimage over Gallic roads. This time, my journey would be made in less than four hours. Then, we had to disembark and show our documents; now, the border police boarded the train, which barely even stopped, but only reduced its speed. With my *Laisser Passer* and the last telegram confirming I was to obtain a Mexican visa, I had no problems being admitted into France. The French police stamped my transit visa, valid for thirty days. I was incredulous at how easy this was. I felt like I was in another world.

The train rolled smoothly over the French countryside. It was February, midwinter. The trees, bared of their leaves, cast a sad shadow. Everything was new to me, and I was fascinated by everything I saw from the window.

I became absorbed in my own thoughts. Suddenly, without my realizing it, the train was entering the periphery of Paris. After awhile, it made its entrance into the Gare Du Nord station. I was in Paris, where I'd wanted to embrace my father. I felt a knot in my throat. I dragged my heavy valise across the aisle, to the door. I got off the train; someone helped me with my suitcase. I stood on the platform with my luggage, awaiting Hugo Mordkovich.

After most of the passengers had cleared the platform, I observed a man in a hat approaching me; it was Hugo. He immediately gave me a hug, and repeated again and again *"Hansi quel plaisir"*—How wonderful to see you. He helped me with my luggage, and we left the station, which was enormous, much larger than the largest stations in Brussels or Vienna. There were so many people coming and going in one continuous movement.

We walked outside the station. Hugo carried my valise. We crossed a kind of square and arrived at the Hotel Du Nord. He explained, his voice shaking with emotion, that that's where my father stayed when he arrived in Paris in 1938. He'd reserved a room in my name. We were given a key, and we went to our room on the third floor. I was extremely excited; this was the first time I'd stayed in a hotel room. Hugo put my valise on the bed and helped me unpack. Later he told me: "I'd like you to come to my apartment and meet Paulette and her daughter Danielle." I was moved by this hospitality, which I hadn't expected. I put my things in an *armoire*, a type of wardrobe, and we went down to the lobby. Hugo was very thin; he'd not yet recovered from two years in a concentration camp. He was about thirty-five years old.

He spoke perfect French, although with a lingering Viennese accent. He radiated joy, and kept repeating: "Hansi, Hansi, I never thought I'd see you again." *"Je suis si heureux."* "I'm so happy," he'd exclaim, and hug me.

We left the key with the porter and made our way to the street. We walked to the Metro—another new experience for me. As I descended the station stairs I was struck by the strong odor, though not necessarily a noxious one. I later learned that this was the characteristic smell of the Parisian metro.

We took the train, and shortly after switched to another train lines. We arrived at our destination just after noon. After getting off the train, Hugo recommended I memorize the station name—Saint-Germain-Des-Pres—so that I could learn to get around Paris. His house was on the Rue Des Siseaux, 34, in the old part of Paris, across the River Seine, and near the Pont Royal. This area was called the Saint-Germain-Des-Prées.

To get to the apartment, we had to cross a patio, at the back of which was a green door. I met Paulette, his girlfriend, who'd motivated and supported him through captivity, and Danielle, her daughter. Paulette was a thirty-five year old woman with dark hair who dressed simply but elegantly. She gave me a kiss on each cheek. Her fifteen year old daughter was lovely and sweet; she also gave me a hug, which surprised me; I thought that girls this age were timid, but not Danielle. On the contrary, she looked me straight in the eyes when she spoke to me.

We sat on the sofa and while Paulette prepared dinner, Hugo caught me up on his life, and the lives of the Katz family members in Vienna, how he'd met my father in Paris, how they'd fled to Clermont-Ferrand before the Germans occupied the city in 1940. I was fascinated listening to him.

This was the first news I'd heard of my father from a Viennese eyewitness. Hugo spoke well of him, and I could see how much he admired my father. He told me of my father's frustration after dealing with the manufacturers in Lyon, who were reluctant to help him obtain those long-awaited visas to save my mother and I.

My father became very depressed because of this. Hugo also told me how he worked as a translator at an office in Paris. He then told me about the family in Vienna. He knew my grandmother Rifke when her house was a center for family gatherings.

Hugo and the others were my first cousins, but my father had married late, at forty-one years old, and five years later I was born, which explains the age difference among us—almost twenty years. I was still a child by the time they were adults.

The "Katz Clan" at one time consisted of thirty-four people. After the war, the survivors were: Uncle Max (Asher Marcus) in London and Uncle Poldi in La Paz, cousins Fritz and Paul Katz (Curzon) in London. Ernest and Else in Melbourne, Heinrich Wolfthal, Aunt Julie, Aunt Ana, Aunt Zilly and Hilde in Brussels, and Sigi Stark in Havana. And me, of course.

Hugo continued recounting his adventures in the Foreign Legion: how he was apprehended, and later deported by the Vichy Surete—almost all of his regiment consisted of German, Austrian, and Hungarian Jews who were deported to a work camp in the Sahara, many dying from the climate, the scarcity of food, and strenuous construction of the Trans Saharan Railroad. Very few survived from the Ain el Ourak.

Paulette called us to dinner. Danielle went for the baguettes—how delicious is the bread in France? Not to mention the food. Paulette prepared some steaks on the grill, called *"pavé"* and some *pommes frites*—french-fried potatoes— and a delicious salad. And, of course, red wine, which immediately went to my head. In Belgium, I'd tried only kosher wine on Shabbat and dessert wine on Jewish holidays. The French wine was much drier. Very delicious, but so strong it practically blurred my vision.

After dinner, we chatted awhile, and made plans for the following day. Danielle offered to take me wherever I needed to go. She was on vacation and had plenty of time to spare. I loved that idea.

The following morning, we went first to the Mexican consulate, launched just after the war. There was no furniture, only desks and two government employees.

I showed them the telegram I'd received from Mexico; they had actually already had the order that would grant me an immigrant visa. They asked for my *Laissez Passer* and passport. I explained myself to them, but they remained unconvinced. They asked me for two photographs. All they needed were photographs! I'd taken a dozen before I left. They asked me to return the next day.

Afterwards, Daniele and I went in search of the Cuban consul, who dispatched from the room where he lived in the Hotel Claridge in the Champs Elysees. He received us personally and let me know that it would be no problem whatsoever for me to obtain a transit visa. I only had to return with my documents from the Mexican consulate.

I would return once Aunt Julie had arrived, and he would provide us with our visas.

A person without a passport in Europe was a nobody. I swore that one day I'd have a passport just like everyone else.

Aunt Julie arrived four days later. Meanwhile, I asked Danielle to show me around the city, and to show me the Jewish neighborhood. Apparently, there were many Jews living in Paris, both because of the war and because of the deportations. Danielle seemed to read my mind: I wanted to get to know Paris.

Paris, *La Ville Lumiere*. The city of light was a capital city if ever there was one. So much more so than Brussels, provincial by comparison. So much larger than Vienna, which had impressed me so much as a child. Paris was vibrant: people everywhere, cars driving up and down the boulevards, struggling to move because of the congestion. I enjoyed the way French was spoken here, with better, clearer pronunciation than in Brussels. Until then, I had not known the difference.

Danielle was an enthusiastic tour guide. In four days, I saw places I'd only known before from books and photographs...I'd read *"Arc de Triomphe"* by Erich Maria Remarque; but to walk beneath this iconic Arc impressed me greatly. I enjoyed Paris for its many monuments that formed a part of the foundation of Europe and of Western humanity.

We visited the *Jardin de Tuilleries* where Louis XVI would stroll, and the *Place de la Concorde* where he was decapitated, and the *Ancien Regime*, the old order, alongside him. *Les Invalides*, Napoleon's mausoleum. Nearby was Rodin's house, where Danielle showed me a garden full of life-size bronze statues. Also the *Tour Eiffel*, a proud vestige of the *Exposition Universelle* in 1889. The *Pont Alexandre* constructed on behalf of Tsar Alexander's visit to Paris. Danielle was an avid reader of history books and she knew a great deal about her native city. She explained everything to me.

What would have happened to Paris if General Dietrich von Choltitz had carried out the orders of the Fuhrer? *"Alle bracken sind zu sprengen, alle monumente warden zerstoert."* You must blow up all the bridges over the River Seine and destroy every monument. This is an order."

Later on we went to the Jewish neighborhood, to the Pletzl in the Marais; we visited the Rue de Rivoli, packed with fabric stores and stores full of Allied military surplus items. G-d only knows how the Jews managed to obtain and sell them. And the people were buying; merchandise was moving. She showed me the *Rue Des Rosiers*, full of little kosher restaurants and Jewish bookstores. A little over a year and a half after liberation, after the most ruthless persecution of Jews in Paris, the Jewish people had demonstrated their perseverance and great capacity for regeneration.

Walking in the Jewish neighborhood, situated in the *Troisiemme Arrondissment*, where there had been a Jewish presence since the 15th century, when the city was still known as Lutecia, I felt, for the first time, a sense of communion with my people. I felt at home, *Heimish*. My eyes filled with tears thinking about my coreligionists, many of whom, on returning from the camps, were now busy, eager to earn a living. I said as much to Danielle, and squeezed her arm to communicate my emotion. She said to me: *"Je comprends"* and squeezed my arm in return. It felt good to be at her side.

Instead of returning home, we ate at an inexpensive bistro Danielle knew about. It's worth noting that the word "Bistro" is of Russian origins and means "quick" and dates back to Tsar Alexander's visit to Paris. It is said that the Russian secret service in charge of watching over the monarch asked the busy servers to hurry, exclaiming "Bystro, bystro." Which is to say, faster, faster! And this is how the "French" word originated.

The next day, I received my visa. It said "immigration form" and included my photograph. Hugo had already received receipts from Sigi for my trip to Havana. He brought to my attention that in the "immigration form" the religion of the passenger was designated. In my case the machine had put down "Israelite," which was correct. This practice was discarded in postwar Europe.

I felt happy; everything was ready for my trip overseas. The only things missing were Aunt Julie and my visa for Cuba. We went to the Spanish Embassy, where I was startled by an immense photograph of Franco, beneath which was the slogan: *"Una y Grande."* I'd been told I needed a transit visa, which turned out not to be true. The receipts from the Compañía Transatlántica Española were sufficient.

I spent five marvelous days in the city. One night we went to an enormous theater called the Olympia. We heard Edith Piaf sing: What an incredible sight to behold firsthand! I'd only heard her on the radio before.

The money I'd brought from Brussels was running through my hands like water. I spent like I'd never spent in Brussels. Go to a restaurant? Why not...it was only a Bistro. A concert? Pay for two tickets? I was a bit worried.

The following day, Hugo informed me that Sigi was sending money for Aunt Julie so that we could travel to Bilbao. I felt uncomfortable about it, but I had no other choice.

In the meantime, I was enjoying Paris and Danielle. I was reminded of a saying I'd heard in Vienna, and that until now I didn't understand, which referred to one who'd spent his time "like G-d the father in France." *Wie der liebegott in frankreich.*

My Aunt Julie arrived. Hugo and I went to pick her up at the station. She stayed in the same hotel.

The following morning, we went for our Cuban visas. Later, we bought train tickets for Bilbao. Poor Aunt Julie did not want to go anywhere. She was exhausted from her trip and preferred to remain at the hotel.

Hugo and Danielle accompanied us to the Gare de Lyon. My cousin helped me load my luggage. I noticed that Aunt Julie was carrying a chamberpot. That's how she travelled!

The train set out westward, and I sat in my seat ruminating over my glorious memories of Paris.

Aunt Julie was content to reunite with her only son left alive. She married Daniel Stark at a young age in 1907. They had three children: Karl, Sigi, and Louis. Daniel owned a *Greislerei*, or grocery store, which I visited with my father on two occasions. It was located in the Gruenetor Gasse near the Bergasse and the Donaukanal.

By June of 1944 there were very few Jews in Brussels, but the Germans did not slack in their effort to eliminate those who were left. My aunt and Louis were arrested and sent to the dungeons of the Gestapo, to testify.

By June of 1944 there were very few Jews in Brussels, but the Germans did not slack in their effort to eliminate those who remained. My aunt and Louis were arrested and sent to the Gestapo dungeons. To witness the transfer of a group of detainees found that night. They appeared before Mr. Schneider, the owner of a jewelry shop, who was a Judenrat official appointed by the Germans.

Immediately, Julie and another older woman—Lilly Stark's mother— were separated from the group. Schneider obtained permission for them to be sent to a hospital maintained by Queen Elizabeth in Laaken, near Brussels. The pretext being that these women, due to their deteriorating health and their age, were unable to travel. This turned out to be a miracle. Thanks to the intervention of Mr. Schneider—who owed Sigi many favors—they were saved. They survived in the hospital in Laaken until the liberation in September 1944.

Julie's son Louis was arrested and deported in convoy number 26, the last convoy leaving from the Centre de Rassemblement de Malines. 26,000 Belgian Jews were deported from this location. In 1945, only 562 returned.

Aunt Julie told me on the train that she was glad I'd waited for her so that we couldtravel together. She'd suffered so much, and had become nervous and apprehensive from the traumas she'd faced. She'd lost her entire family, after all. All that remained was one son in Havana. She was glad the war had ended, and happy to leave Europe. She was grateful to be alive.

The train traveled quickly, stopping briefly at the station in Tours, and later inPoitiers. Night fell, and the train continued its journey. I slept. The following morning we awoke in Bordeaux. From there, the train traveled to Biarritz, near the sea. I'd never seen anything so vast and splendid. I'd only been to the port in Antwerp, and it was entirely different. This was my first time seeing the open ocean.

The train stopped in Saint Jean de Luz. The next station would be Hendaye, on the Spanish border. Suddenly, the train came to a halt. Everyone was impatient and wanted to know what was happening. Aunt Julie was getting nervous.

We were on some kind of clay promontory, from which we could see the ocean.

People were getting off the train. I tried to find out what was going on, but nobody knew anything. Some said the borders were closed and that was why the train couldn't pass through, that we'd probably end up staying in Hendaye. We had to get through at any cost because our boat left from Bilbao on March 3. This was our problem; all the other passengers had their own problems in turn. After an hour, uniformed French customs officers arrived on motorcycles. Several other passengers and I approached them.

They informed us of what had occurred: just yesterday, leftist demonstrators placed a bomb in the Spanish Embassy in Paris. In retaliation, the Spanish closed the border between France and Spain. The French authorities were currently negotiating with their Spanish counterparts to see if we might be allowed to cross on foot. The train would remain, for the moment, in Hendaye.

How could this be happening to us? Granted, worse things had happened to me before, but what mattered right now was getting to Spain any way we could.

After approximately an hour of waiting, we were informed that the passengers who wished to do so could cross the border on foot. With two valises and my Aunt Julie in tow, walking was incredibly taxing. We arrived at the border crossing. The Frenchallowed us to pass without looking through our luggage, only our documents.

"Baruch Ha-shem," we were now at the mercy of the Spanish authorities. They wore olive green uniforms and strange black lacquered tri-cornered hats. This was the Spanish Civil Guard.

At the Spanish border crossing station in Irun, Aunt Julie, extremely anxious and exhausted by the walk, was able to sit and rest. I calmed her down as best I could, and hoped we would eventually be granted our visas. All the while, we were watched with utmost severity by the Civil Guard.

An immigration officer checked the picture on my Vish. He motioned for my aunt to remain seated. He studied our tickets and, finally, our papers.

Now, if I'm to recount these events from A to Z, they proceeded to confiscate some French magazines I had, which, according to them, constituted "subversive material," I imagine. They let me keep my books, my photographs, etc. *"Zol zain,"* I thought. So be it. What mattered most was that we were granted entry into Spain,and could proceed with our journey to America.

From there, with the help of a porter, of which there were many, we set out on foot to the train leaving for Bilbao in half an hour.

Even by 1946—eight years after the Spanish Civil War had ended—its effects could still be felt. Not to mention we were in Euzkadi, one of the most pro-republican areas at the center of the conflict.

At six in the evening, we finally arrived at the Hotel Toledo, where Sigi had reserved us a room.

At the station in Bilbao, we were assisted by another porter, who helped us figure out how to find our hotel. I hailed a taxi. With the money from Aunt Julie, I felt like being generous, *Groszuegig*. My poor aunt was exhausted by the day's hardships.

The offices of the *Compañía Transatlántica Española* were located on the main street in Bilbao. There, I swapped our receipts for two second-class tickets, and I was informed about the arrival of $200, which my aunt had to collect in person. We truly didn't need any more money, as we'd spent very little, but it was very kind of Sigi to take care of his mother.

We would sail for Cuba on the *Marqués de Comillas*, which would set sail at noon on the sixth.

We spent three days in Bilbao, situated in Spain, a country we'd both heard, and read, so much about. Spain torn apart by the Civil War; Spain, subject of the dramatic photographs in- *"Mourir a Madrid-"*, a banned book, of course. Censorship prevailed for eight years during the war. However, there were no restrictions on tourism. There were civil guard officers everywhere. Indigent, shabbily-dressed people, as well as "good" people selling lottery tickets—now, under the new regime, they were displaced, with very few employment opportunities. We also saw many children without shoes.

Here and in Catalonia were large textile factories, comprising much of the vast industrial parks in Spain. This part of Spain had always been the heart of Spanish manufacturing, and these were some of the most prosperous provinces in the nation.

In the Hotel Toledo, we ate well. Every day, the guests congregated in the entryway to the dining room, which opened around one in the afternoon. The two occasions I went with my aunt, we met a tall, husky man, probably around forty years old, who always looked hungry. I made friends with him: as it turned out, he was going to be traveling with us on the same boat. He was Russian, and his name was Misha. He'd come from Paris, where he'd worked as a *portier* in the Russian cabaret "Rasputin."

He was setting out to try his luck in Havana. Misha always eagerly awaited the moment when it was time to eat. He'd exclaim *"Poidiom!"*- "Let's go!" and rushthrough the doors to secure his table.

Misha spoke some Spanish, and with a strong Slavic accent. On the third day, *"Poidiom"* became *"Podyemos"* which sounded just like Russian. He was a friendly and helpful man, and we were fast friends.

One day he invited me to accompany him to Portugalete, the port in Bilbao. At the pier, "our" majestic ship was anchored and in the process of being loaded. I'd never seen a boat like it: it was incredible. And immense! I kept thinking: "In that boat I'm going to America!"

The following day, he invited me to San Sebastián, a spa near Bilbao, with hotels so elegant they were practically palaces, although they were empty of people. It was the beginning of March, after all, the off-season.

Misha explained everything in detail. I was impressed by this beautiful, luxurious place. I found out much later that, along with Biarritz and Paris, it was one of the places most preferred by rich landowners in Mexico. A place where they'd spend swaths of time during the era of Don Porfirio Díaz. Including when they accompanied him in his exile during the Mexican Revolution. I thanked Misha for taking me on this excursion, as there wasn't much to do in Bilbao..

In the hotel we were told a Pullman would come by for us at ten in the morning and bring us to Portugalete.

The Pullman was an old truck, probably a "vintage" 1935, with no discernable color. We gave them our suitcases and climbed inside. For the most part, the few automobiles driving through Bilbao were old, from before the Civil War.

I didn't see Misha. He would likely be on the next bus. The bus arrived at the dock, where there was a gangplank. Two officials wearing stately dark blue uniforms sat at a large table, consulting lists with the passengers' names. My turn came; the official asked me for our tickets. He consulted his list and stamped our tickets. He then gave us tags to attach to our valises, which had our cabin number written on them.

Meanwhile, Aunt Julie remained seated on her valise. All of the excitement was too much for her. I went to get her and we boarded the ship. I'd never been aboard a ship before, and I found myself extremely excited. A sailor took us to our cabins. Everything looked clean, like it had recently been painted.

Later, during the voyage, I realized that there were sailors constantly painting some part of the ship. I suppose it was to keep it clean and avoid oxidization.

I left Aunt Julie in her cabin, as she wanted to rest. I went up on deck to observe the spectacle of our departure.

More and more passengers were arriving at the dock. Some by car, others by taxi. The bus returned carrying other passengers, probably from other hotels.

At twelve o'clock on the dot, a kind of whistle was blown—I think it was powered by steam—and the gangplank was finally raised.

The *Marqués de Comillas* began to slowly move in the water. And so I embarked for America, the new continent.

The ship moved through a canal before coming into open water. I watched with the other passengers as the coastline grew farther and farther away. I stayed on deck at least a few hours, fascinated by this spectacle, a new experience for me.

At dusk the ship entered the port at Vigo. I learned that it would also stop in Gijón and Cádiz before traveling to the Canary Islands. This was the ship's itinerary, and at every port goods were loaded on board. The *Marqués de Comillas* carried a mixture of cargo and passengers. Now I understood why crossing the Atlantic took so many days—eighteen, to be exact—almost as long as it took Christopher Columbus!

My bunk was comfortable, and the food served in the dining hall was abundant but extremely greasy. Luckily, at meals and at all hours they served cheese and fresh-baked bread. I'd never eaten so much cheese before. The soups were delicious.

I saw Misha on deck. We talked at lenth, and he told me of his life: how, after the revolution and a terrible famine, he fled with a group of white Russians to Poland,
and later to France. In Paris, they joined a colony of Bieli Russkii also able to escape from the Soviet Union and, like the Jews, began new lives in the Gallic capital city.

First, he was a taxi driver, and then a butler for a wealthy family of Russian immigrants. Finally, a porter at a cabaret. Russians were known in Paris as *"les émigrés."*

On deck I met and became friends with a young Jewish man, a bit older than I—around twenty-five. He spoke Yiddish and I answered him in German. We understood each other quite well. My German at that time was a bit rusty; during the war I was careful not to speak it. It was peppered with Yiddish words I'd learnedat the organization in Brussels.

We got on very well, and from that moment on he sought my company. He came to my cabin every morning and we'd go to breakfast together. He helped me with my aunt Julie. He was a very kind person.

My new friend was named Mordechai Morgenstern but liked to be called Mordi, as he was known at home. He was from Praga, a suburb of Warsaw. He came from a good family.

His father had been a gynecologist, and his mother a teacher at a Gymnasium. He had two older sisters. His father served as a doctor in the ghetto and, thanks to his skills, the family enjoyed certain privileges for a very short time. Mordi was separated from his family and sent to an *Arbeitslager*: Monowitz, near the hell that was Auschwitz. I.G. Farben had large facilities to hold forty thousand forced laborers, practically slaves. This is how his life was spared, although his entire family was deported to Treblinka and exterminated.

After the liberation in Gross Rosen Germany, he returned home. He found it as they'd left it in 1940, with furniture, books, silver, porcelain tea services, etc. Two Polish families were living there: one came and went through the front door, and the other through the servant's entry. When he knocked, no one opened the door, and no one allowed him inside. Most likely they were frightened.

They yelled: *"Szyd Nie Do Viarei."* They wanted him to leave them alone. He went to Warsaw, to the other side of Vistula. Everything was in ruins. Where the Ghetto had once been were mountains of blackened bricks. No one was walking in the streets.

He spent around a year in various Displaced Persons camps in Germany. He had a UNRRA Vish like I did. He was traveling to Venezuela, where he had family. They'd sent him money for his journey. We talked about Jewish matters, about geography. He had an atlas, and pointed out to me where we were, and the trajectory of our journey across the Atlantic. He knew a great deal, not just about geography.

I introduced him to Misha, and we became a trio. When the ship stopped in Africa after a leg at the last European port in Cádiz, he slid his finger across the map, to the Mediterranean Sea, and showed us how Palestine could be reached.

The next stop of the *Marqués de Comillas* was Tenerife, capital of the Canary Islands. We went on land. It was hot, but the heat was a pleasant one.

Mordi told me it was because we were nearing the Equator. There were palm trees, which before I'd only seen in photographs. The vegetation was green and luxurious. Trees and plantsgrew everywhere. During this stopover, we were served tropical fruit for breakfast every day.

We were, in fact, following the itinerary of Christopher Columbuus and his three caravels, La Niña, La Pinta, and La Santa María. And so we replenished our supply of fresh water and produce in the Canaries before embarking onto the open seas.

I enjoyed the smell of the sea. For me, it was something new. I'd finished *The Forty Days of Musa Dagh*, which I enjoyed, being a Viennese Jew. In it, Franz Werfel dealt with the historical details surrounding the Armenians and their traditions. Perhaps my being Jewish allowed me to access their mentality. The Armenians had also been persecuted throughout history, up to the present day. Although they had one advantage over the Jewish people; they have their own territory. The Republic of Armenia covers at least part of their ancestral lands. The remainder lies in the hands of the Turks, who massacred them in 1905.

A short time after the war in Europe had ended, the persecution of the Jews, the destruction of their cultural values, began again in the Soviet Union, and resulted in a bloody culmination in 1952. The Jews had been gunned down or exiled to the Gulag between 1936 and 1939, during Stalin's great purges. But long before, Yosef Stalin was a hero to the Jews who'd fought in the International Brigades in Spain. They fought for their "cause" regardless of the sacrifice. How ironic! Now, Stalin's anti-Semitic campaign was directed at the "cosmpolitans" and "Zionists," the Yevrei Burshuii. The campaign reached its peak in August of 1952 when twenty-six members of the "Anti-Fascist Committee," created during the Patriotic War, were arrested and sent before the firing squad. Without a trial or any semblance of justice. Among them were intellectuals and Jewish writers like Perez Markish, ItzjakFefer, David Bergelson, David Hofshtain, Leib Kvitko, Samuel Persov, and Benjamin Zuskin, who was director of the Moscow State Jewish Theater. The distinguished Jewish actor Salomon Michoels, who had received the esteemed Order of Lenin and who visited Mexico in 1944, was assassinated by the NKVD in 1948.

The writer Isaac Babel, author of *Konarmina* or *Red Cavalry*, and *Tales of Odessa*, was among these prisoners, and died in prison in 1940. He was arrested for his "overtly Jewish" tendencies and for being too "cosmopolitan."

And finally, the so-called "Doctors' Plot." A group of eight Jewish doctors selected by the Kremlin to serve the Soviet senior officers were accused of having murdered Shdanov and Scherbakov, two Soviet leaders, and of attempting to murder Stalin.

The accusations were made by Lavrenti Beria, the *Bete Noire* of the Kremlin. Stalin eventually died despite of the Jewish doctors' best efforts.

The Jewish situation improved momentarily when Khrushchev came to power. A Ukrainian peasant famous for pounding the table with his shoe during the United Nations Assembly in 1954.

After 200,000 Jewish soldiers in the *Krasnaya Armiya* fell on the battlefield duringthe Patriotic War, anti-Semitism worsened in the Soviet Union, precisely because of the creation of the State of Israel, which they saw as a danger, a "fatal attraction" for Russian Jews.

Like most of the Jewish minorities living in the Soviet Republics, Armenians were not very Orthodox. Nor were those in Birobidzhan, a Jewish state conceived as an experiment by the Soviets during the 1930's. In the Soviet Union one had to be a communist and an atheist above all else. Nationalities were merely "window dressing."

Years later, another state-sanctioned anti-Semitic incident perpetrated by the Soviet Union. Natan "Anatoly" Sharansky was a mathematician highly regarded among the "Refusniks" and the seasoned partner of Nobel Prize-winning Sajarov, who couldn't receive his Nobel Prize personally because he was imprisoned in Gorky—his wife, Yelena Bonner, a Russian Jew, went to Stockholm to receive the award in his place. Sajarov was a "prisoner of conscience" and exponent of the "Refusniks" in the Soviet Union during that time.

Sharansky was arrested for "conspiring against the state" and was locked away in Lefortovo Prison in Moscow. He was later sent to the Gulag in Siberia, where he spent two long years.

His wife Avital—also Jewish—immigrated to Israel and, from there, organized an international protest to help free her husband. Finally, Sharansky was exchanged for an East German spy and set free. Now both of them live in Israel. Sharansky serves as Minister of Commerce in the government of Benjamin Netanyahu.

Now we were navigating through open waters, not stopping until we hit North American shores. Europe lay behind us. Luckily for me, I'd remained in good health up to this point. Many of the passengers on board became seasick, vomiting constantly. There were few people in the dining room when it came time to eat.

That day, for the first time, I ate fish directly from the sea. I'm not sure what kind, exactly, but it was delicious. The meat was a bit firmer than the river or lake fish in Europe. I suppose this fish wasn't kosher, for it had no scales or gills.

Perhaps after our stopover in the Canary Islands the flavor and quality of the food had improved. Or perhaps I was just becoming accustomed to it?

I could see nothing but the immensity of the sea, and the occasional faraway boat, never close enough for me to really see and identify.

How large and vast our planet is! How immense are its oceans! And, by comparison, how small our boat, how miniscule each of us human beings on board! Everything governed by a Supreme Being!

Every time I mispronounced a Yiddish word, Mordi would laugh. He'd say: *"Du Apikoires, Du yeke."* German offender! And he'd correct me, which I thanked him for doing. I learned correct Yiddish pronunciation, thanks to his help, as well as many new words. When I was happy, I'd always say *"A Mechaye."* Delightful! If something displeased me, I'd exclaim: *"Oof Kapores"* or *"A broch."* I vaguely remembered hearing the latter phrase in Vienna. *"A Shlemazl"* for good luck. My father's family spoke what was known as *"Gyuedlt"* among themselves. Essentially German with Yiddish words mixed in. We spoke only German at home. *"Hochdeutsch Gottbehuete."* My mother would never have permitted anything else in her house.

"Hochdeutsch," or the German spoken in Vienna and throughout Austria is, in general, smoother, sweeter, and less *harsch* than the German spoken in Germany, with the exception of Bavaria, where it's also sweeter-sounding.

The difference lies also in pronunciation. There are certain words used only in Vienna, such as *"Schmaeh." Es Geht dich einen Schmaeh an"*, or "Quit being so dramatic!" "What's it to you?" or "It's none of your business!" *"Blamash"* is an insult. *"Ein Busserl"* is a kiss. *"Schlamperei"* is a mess. But what most stands out is the Viennese greeting *"Servus"* from the Latin which means "I'm your slave" or "at your service." Friends and lovers greeted each other in this way. It's considered an intimate salutation.

"Servus" is sweet: *"Sag-ruhig Servus"* is what lovers say as an intimate form of address, an invitation. This expression dates back to Roman times. It's also very common in Hungary, where the plural form is employed: *"Szervusztok"* like "Ciao" in Italian, which is a bastardization of the Venetian word *"Schiavo."* A more formal salutation is *"Ich Habe Die Ehre"* which means "It's a pleasure" or the ever present *"Kuess die hand,"* the equivalent, of course, of kissing one's hand. To say goodbye, we said *Adieu*.

So many words and expressions were used only in Vienna, like *"Umberuien Toi, Toi,*

Toi," spat three times by old Jewish women to ward off the evil eye, or *Yeitser Hara.*

A *"Majloike"* is a conflict. *"Barcjes"* is a *"Challah,"* bread eaten during Shabat. *"Napetzn"* is to take a nap. *"Kititzn"* is someone who cheats during a game of cards.

In the Wienerisch, words came into existence and were employed only by Viennese Jews, like *"Grobian"* used to refer to a rude individual. *"Schmutzian"* was for some worse than rude, similar to *"saligot"* in French. *"Plaite"* referred to bankruptcy. *"Schlamastik"* was an affair (or entanglement).

"Eine 'Petite'" meant fraud. *"Ein Gschpuserl"* was to have an extramarital affair. *"Ein Verwaelkter Krehn"* was someone very old and wizened. *"Ich wer ihm die levit'n vorlesen"* means "I'll set the record straight," perhaps relating to the many precise duties expected of the Levites in the Temple in Jerusalem. *"Ein Matzehfresser"* was a pejorative term for Jews, essentially meaning "one who eats matzo."

"Hier gibt's kein koshere wurschtl'n" was said when a restaurant server refused to serve a Jewish diner. This phrase alludes to sausages, preferred by the Viennese, but in this case kosher for Jewish clientele.

Mordi attempted to teach me new Yiddish words so that I wouldn't speak like a *Yeke*. He said *"Svet Dir Helfn vi a toiten, bankes,"* which is to say "Not gonna help anything." The exact meaning was explained to me later, in Mexico, by Dr. ShaikeStrigler. *"Bankes"* are leeches used to cure disease before antibiotics were invented, which, most of the time, weren't very helpful... *"Lo, mit an Alef"* in the negative. *"Bobbe maises"* meant stories. *"Ich bin kimat gefaln in Jaloshes."* I almost fainted from shock! *"S'is mir geworn nimess."* "I got tired of waiting." *"A nejtiger tog"* to indicate something is worthless. *"Ich hob gerissn shtiker"* "I tried my best." *"Ich hog im in d'rerd."* "I don't give a damn!" And many more...

Later on, in Mexico, while studying Yiddish seriously, I learned that my travel companion spoke what was known as *"A saftikn Yidish"* an eloquent, lively form of the language.

It was interesting to observe the Jewish passengers, who somehow recognized and approached one another. It must have been something intuitive, as there were so many people of varying nationalities on board. But the Jews managed to tell each other apart from the rest.

My friend Mordi counted them up on the third day of our journey. He said *"Sis do oif zwei Minyonim"*: "There's enough for two *minyanim* as for a double *minyan*, or double prayer shift. Effectively, including women, there were thirty Jewish passengers aboard the *Marqués de Comillas*.

When the boat stopped in Spain, we read the daily paper. Or, rather, Misha read it to us and translated it. It was the ABC but since we'd left the Canaries we hadn't heard any news. What was happening in the world?

There was a radio in the great hall, but it was only tuned into Spanish stations and a United States Navy broadcast, which was in English.

We found out that the British had intensified the naval blockade in the Mediterranean and had captured more and more Mosad refugee boats. They even set up an internment camp in Cyprus for Jews apprehended on the high seas.

After the fall of the German regime, which lasted from 1933 to 1945, care must be taken to qualify the nature of a "camp." In comparison with those in Germany, those in Cyprus were like summer camps. Yet it remains an embarrassment to the civilized world that young Holocaust survivors, crowded into dilapidated boats bound for their ancestral lands in an attempt to live normal lives among their fellow men, were thus detained by the British.

How ironic, to have the Promised Land in plain view, but be unable to set foot on its shores. But economic interests like oil were at the root of British policies. By 1946, the United Nations was in existence, but nothing was done in the face of this abuse.

Misha, curious and adventurous by nature, occupied himself by looking forexcitement on the ship. He invited us to come along and explore with him, *"Moiem Drugozi,"* he'd say, "my friends." He organized a visit to the engine room. I was struck by the noise of the motors, the strong odor of oil, the infernal heat. The machine operators had to remain here day and night. *"Yenes gesheft,"* said Mordi wryly. "What a way to spend your life!" We went up to the cockpit, where we saw the captain and his officers dressed in dark blue uniforms. They showed us the rudder and stabilizers, allowing the vessel to resist the movement of the waves.

When I wasn't reading, I walked on deck or took photographs. Aunt Julie was muchmore relaxed than she'd been before we left. She would lounge on a reclining deck chair and nap. The ocean air agreed with her. For my part, I took care of her; after all, I wanted to deliver her safe and sound to her son in Havana.

Elbows resting on the railing, I searched for any indication of a coastline in the distance, but there was nothing but ocean. It must have been like this for Christopher Columbus and his caravels.

One morning, I woke up, washed my face, and went on deck to discover there was land in sight! We were approaching Venezuela, our first stop on American soil. We were arriving in La Guaira, where Mordi would live with his family in Maracaibo.

We said goodbye over breakfast. The truth is that Mordi was a dear and indispensable friend, and the perfect travel companion. He also got on well with Misha, the other friend I'd made during the trip.

We couldn't disembark in La Guaira due to immigration laws. The ship was not docked at the pier, but rather remained at sea, the passengers conducted to land by motorboats. Hours later, the *Marqués de Comillas* resumed its journey. Our next stop was Aruba. We resumed cabotage at the American ports, as we had in Spain. It was always fascinating to see and experience these new places, especially when we were allowed to disembark and explore them.

Aruba was a Dutch colony, and the location of two large Shell refineries. Crude oil came from Venezuela, was converted into fuel for ships, and was then exported to Central America. We were able to get off and walk around. It was a lovely place, and everything was incredibly clean. The homes were one or two stories, with the façades painted yellow or blue. Aside from a few Europeans the inhabitants were black. As Mordi was no longer there to explain everything to us, an official from the ship served as our guide. Mischa was our interpreter.

He told us that the Caribbean Islands were centers for slave trafficking in the eighteenth century. The slaves arrived in ships from the West African coast, wearing chains to prevent them from jumping into the water to escape. The conditions aboard the ships were subhuman. On land, they were distributed to the Spanish colonies or to the thirteen American colonies. Many remained on the Caribbean Islands and constitute their populations to this day.

I ask myself: how could a human being debase oneself by selling other humans as though they were animals?

A large number of passengers disembarked in Aruba to visit the city, as the climate was very agreeable, and the sun illuminated still more the already bright facades of the small painted houses in this Dutch city. We moved through the narrow streets and were struck by how clean they were, as were the sidewalks.

Mischa had already determined the address of the "red light district", which is where we were headed. Interestingly enough, the houses here were much the same, but with shop windows featuring some women as G-d made them, others semi-clothed. "Like in Amsterdam," said Mischa. Most of them were mixed race, some were white, and few were black. Of course, in Brussels, I'd never seen anything like this.

The *Marqués de Comillas* set sail again. We were bound for our destination: Havana. I observed the color of the water. Here in America it was more beautiful than in Europe, bluer and sometimes emerald green. The following morning, the Cuban coast was in sight, and I could make out "El Moro," an imposing lighthouse. The ship advanced towards land, maneuvering itself so that it could align with one of two piers.

Aunt Julie had already packed her things. Simultaneously joyful and nervous, she was to see her son again after five long years. A barge full of Cuban immigration officers approached the ship. Almost all the passengers were on deck. The officers came on board and set up a large table. They began to review everyone's documents. The ship continued moving, now very slowly, before docking.

Little by little, the passengers were getting off. I was at the tail end of the line, in front of the government officials seated at the table with my and my aunt's papers in my hands.

Suddenly, Sigi appeared on deck. He'd received permission to board in order to receive his mother. I pointed to where she was seated.

They went over my paperwork and asked me if I was to continue on to Mexico. I answered in the affirmative. The functionary stamped the usual seal onto my documents. Sigi was already talking to them in Spanish. Fortunately, there were no problems, and we were able to disembark.

Lilly was on the pier waiting for us with a man who turned out to be their chauffer. She received us with kisses. Sigi was busy catching up with his mother. We approached the customs desk, but since Sigi spoke Spanish, they barely opened our valises before letting us pass through.

We all got into a large car and drove to the Stark house. After around twenty minutes, we arrived at a beautiful, great house, a kind of "villa" like I'd seen on the outskirts of Brussels. Sigi's youngest son Georgie, less than two years old, was in the arms of a black nanny.

During our car ride, Lilly explained the areas we were driving through. There were many black people, but not as many as in Aruba. There were palm trees everywhere. Lilly spoke to me in French.

Sigi told me he'd communicated with my Uncle Ellenbogen in Mexico because he wanted me to stay with him in Havana for a week. Would I accept his offer? Of course I would! I was fascinated by what little I'd seen since arriving in Havana. I was sure there was much more to experience.

I spent many wonderful days in Cuba as my cousins' guests. I was happy, first because I hadn't been expecting this at all. I thought I'd immediately continue on my journey. In addition to my vacation on the ship, I'd have more on this Caribbean island. My cousin Lilly bought me a bathing suit, my first since I'd gone to Baltonlelle in Hungary. They brought me to the pool at the Hotel Nacional. I'd never seen such a grand, elegant hotel before. They took me to the beaches at Varadero and to the Yacht Club. For me, this was an altogether new world full of countless luxuries I'd never known before. Since when does a black valet clean my shoes without me even asking?

Havana during the 40's was a world I'd never dreamed of, a world of Club Tropicana, a cabaret with incredible shows. A world of the *"Bodega de en medio,"* a cantina frequented by Ernest Hemingway, author of *For Whom the Bell Tolls*, which I'd read in Paris. My cousins took me to Carmelo, a very popular, stylish restaurant. Sigi also took me to a Jewish restaurant near the pier called *"Moishe Pupik"*, curiously named, but the food was delicious. He introduced me to his friends, among them Mr. Cates, formerly Katz, but no relation. Here, I met Sigi's partner Hans Ventura, with whom he'd escaped Europe in 1941.

I enjoyed playing with Georgie, a precocious child for his age, who spoke to me in Spanish. Of course, I didn't understand any of it. But aside from "formal" communication, we understood each other well enough.

After eight days of going to the beach, it came time to continue on my journey to Mexico. I was once again surprised when Sigi told me I'd travel there by plane. I had, of course, never been on an airpane. I'd only seen them in movies and in France during the war. Surprises followed one after the next.

On April 2 at 10:30 A.M. my Mexicana de Aviación propeller plane, a DC-3, left for Mexico City. Back then, the flight was six hours long, with a stop in Mérida, Yucatán.

Sigi and Lilly brought me to the airport. My cousin thanked me again for accompanying his mother, whom I'd surely made more comfortable and happy on her trip.

Sigi had given me two suits, so my suitcase was completely full. Ours was an emotional goodbye, and he wished me the best of luck.

Everything was new and strange to me—first of all, the cabin, which was very small, and the narrow seats, having to use a seatbelt. The stewardess "making rounds" to see that everything was in order. The narrowness of the cabin, the noise of the motors. It was an entirely new experience.

The plane began revving up its engine. We took off after a few minutes of infernal noise, and before I knew it, we were already in the air! Awesome! From my window, everything on land was dwarfed as the plane ascended. My stop in Mérida had been a short one.

I continued to marvel at what I could see from the windows. Mexico was an incredibly green, mountainous land. I was very impressed. A man around thirty years old was seated next to me, and we began chatting—or, at least, we tried. He was a North American schoolteacher. He'd been teaching at a bilingual school in Chile and was returning to his home in Mexico. He spoke English and some Spanish.
I realized how different spoken English was—or at least, the kind he spoke—from the English in Oscar's letters, which I could read. I ended up speaking to him in German, and he answered me in English, syllable by syllable.

He told me he'd been discharged from the American army in 1945. He was now teaching English and literature classes at the Colegio Americano de la Ciudad de México.

I told him I was invited to Mexico by my aunt and uncle, who'd spent the war in Europe, and that I'd lost my parents. I spoke of the Jews who wanted to leave war-torn Europe at any cost.

We didn't stop talking until the plane landed in Mexico. I was nervous and anxious about what would happen. How would my aunt and uncle be? How would I manage living with them? How would my life be in Mexico?

They had known me when I was a child, as they'd lived in Vienna, and surely they were going to recognize me, but I didn't remember them at all. The Ellenbogens had left Vienna in 1937, first for Switzerland, where my Aunt Bachruch lived, wife of my deceased uncle Julius, and their daughter Ruth. From there they went to Torino, Italy, where my uncle ran a light bulb manufacturing business until 1940. With visas they obtained through the Guatemalan Consulate in Rome, they immigrated to Central America, where they stayed one year. In 1941 they were able to move to Mexico.

I followed the other passengers to a room to wait for our luggage; there were at least thirty of us. Soon I was approached by two men around fifty years old. One of them addressed me: "Hans?" I knew how to say "sí" in Spanish. It was my uncle. He continued in German: *"Ich bin dein onkel Fritz Ellenbogen."* He gave me a wet kiss on the cheek. The two men took me to the immigration office. I learned that one of them was my father's lawyer, a Mexican by the name of Garza Lozano.

We stayed in the immigration office for some time, almost an hour, while my documents were reviewed, alongside the documents the lawyer had brought. The immigration chief began speaking with the lawyer.

Finally *"el jefe"* returned with my papers, which had been authorized. They kept my Vish but gave me an FM-2, with my photograph. It was a residence permit, renewable every year. I left with the lawyer to meet my aunt Else Ellenbogen, who was very well dressed and wearing a hat. She kissed me profusely, her eyes filled with tears. Everyone else—everyone in the waiting room, that is—were dressed very differently: the men wore straw hats, and the women wore shawls. As it turned out, all the men wore hats, in some form or another. My aunt was dressed in a very European style.

My Uncle Ellenbogen drove a large, black car, which I later learned was from the brand Packard. In Europe, there were no cars this large aside from the Mercedes driven by German officers during the war.

My aunt sat alongside my uncle, who drove. I sat in the back. She spoke in French. After a half-hour trip, we passed through a beautiful tree-lined avenue, El Paseo de la Reforma, heading toward Las Lomas. We stopped at Sierra Paracaima 860, which was where they lived. Everything was intensely green, a new kind of landscape, the greenery coexisting with drier spots, where grass and wildflowers grew.

We went inside the house, where two *"muchachas"* wearing uniforms were waiting for us. One of them took my suitcase, and we went upstairs to a lovely room facing the street. The afternoon sun shone through the windows. This would be *"mi cuarto."* My aunt bid me a brief goodbye from the doorway: "At seven, we eat supper."

The room was wonderful, and everything was clean. My bed had already been made. I sat down to think. I thought of everything that had happened in just one day: in the morning I found myself in another country, on an island: now I was in a different country, among majestic mountain ranges and volcanoes I saw from the window of the airplane.

I reflected back on the reception my aunt and uncle had given me, which, although adorned with kisses, was quite formal after all, and a bit cold. They were so different from Yolanka and Buci, who were, in turn, different from Sigi and Lilly.

Fortunately, I'd arrived at my destination after nearly a month of traveling. How would I fare here? I unpacked my things, hung what needed hanging, and I thought of the hotel in Paris. My aunt and uncle would appear when it was time to eat.

I went downstairs at the appointed hour—I knew it was seven thanks to an alarm clock on the bureau, as I didn't have a watch. I attempted a Russian accent with my meager Spanish-speaking abilities to parody Misha, my friend from the ship. *"Podyiemos comer?"* Apparently, they were not amused by my attempt at communicating with them.

We sat at the table, luminous and perfect with a freshly-starched tablecloth and perfectly-aligned cutlery. My aunt served me tea; on the table there was bread, cheeses, and ham, as well as Liptauer cheese, which I hadn't tasted since I'd been to Mrs. Schneider's house—the jewelry shop owner's house in Brussels. There was also Leberwurst, a type of liver pate.

They asked me about my stay in Havana, but not about my life in the past ten years, although I wished they would. Declaring I must be exhausted from my trip, they announced it was time for bed. They conducted themselves strangely, and far too rigidly. I realized they did not sleep together—each of them had their own bedroom.

After several days much like the last, my uncle informed me I was to meet Dr. Mauricio Luft, who would help me enroll at *Colegio Israelita*, a school where I might learn Spanish.

Dr. Luft was a plump, friendly, and affectionate older man around seventy, a Jew from Leipzig. We got along well. He told me I'd begin my studies the next Monday. It was a bilingual day school, the most appropriate for my needs.

Because I lacked documents verifying my level of schooling—in reality, I'd hardly completed fourth grade—I was told that if I passed the corresponding examinations, I would be awarded a certificate for having completed the requirements for primary school, and that I'd then be allowed entry into a secondary technical school. *"Ojalá,* I hope I pass!" I thought to myself.

Early Monday morning, Dr. Lutz came for me and brought me to the school in *la Colonia del Valle*, which was large and beautiful. We went straight to the office of the principal of the primary school, Professor Vélez. He took down my name and admitted me immediately, thanks to the help of Dr. Lutz and Wutzia and José Rubinstein. And, of course, my uncle had paid for my enrollment.

The principal brought me to a classroom, where the students were in the middle of a Bible class. The teacher's name was Professor Kowalsky. I sat down. He asked me: *"Redst du yiddish?"* and I responded *"A bissl."* A little. He welcomed me, *"Baruch ha-ba."*

This was the extent of our conversation. The other students were staring at me: I was sixteen, they were twelve. This was the sixth grade. The teacher began to read aloud. I didn't know how to read Hebrew letters, as I'd never formally learned Hebrew. There were times in Brussels when Yolanka wanted to teach me so that I could learn to read the Seder prayers.

At recess, the Yiddish teachers came over to say hello, or, rather, to "examine" me, the school's first *Pelet*, or survivor from Europe.

And that's how I met professors Bayón, Rotenberg, Fein, and Rifke Golomb. Those first few days I was the attraction of the moment. But then everything went back to normal. My fellow students were very kind to me. They helped me learn my new language. In fact, I soon began speaking the language. "Speaking" is saying a lot, but I could already form sentences, although with many grammatical errors. It helped that I already knew French. At the same time, I learned to speak, read, and write in Yiddish.

I remember some of my classmates: Marcos Strygler, Isaac Backal, Issac Wolin, Yuri Tartakovsky, Bromberg, andFried, to name a few. Years later, they came to be very well-regarded working professionals.

Life at my aunt and uncle's house continued as always. One of the problems I confronted was obtaining permission to come home late at night. The Ellenbogens treated me like a little boy. I had to be at home by seven o'clock. What would I do if I had to go to a lecture that began at nine? They couldn't understand this…They also couldn't understand that I would always be a free person, that I had never had to ask permission from anyone.

I discovered many things to do and see in Mexico. I was hungry to learn, and I wanted to live in ways I wasn't able to during the war. Of course, I wanted to do it all in one day.

After the attack on Pearl Harbor in 1941, and the United States' entry into the war, Mexico considered itself an allied country. Especially after German submarines sank the oil tanker "Potrero del Llano" in March of 1942. Although Mexico still had relations with Germany, they declared war on the Axis nations—Germany, Italy, and Japan—in May of 1942.

The Aztec nation represented a very special case in German diplomacy. First because of its proximity to the United States. And secondly, because Mexico contained a relatively large German colony. Thirdly, because Germany was interested in Mexican oil. Germany maintained an embassy with a large staff, as Mexico was thought to be an ideal point for an eventual invasion onto American soil.

Today, this notion seems utterly far-fetched, but back then was thoroughly analyzed by the German Ministry of Foreign Affairs in the Wilhemstrasse in Berlin, according to top-secret documents found in Berlin after the war by Dr. Friedrich Katz.

According to the German secret service in 1941, 80% of Mexicans were Germanophiles, not only because they loved the Germans, but also because of strong anti-American sentiments.

Once war was declared, Mexico's particular involvement in the conflict had to be determined. In May of that same year, the president of Mexico, General Manuel Ávila Camacho, met with Franklin Delano Roosevelt. Camacho proposed that Mexico would provide fifty thousand soldiers to fight in Europe. This proposal was rejected due to language and various idiosyncrasies. Instead, it was decided that a select group of three-hundred men from the Mexican Air Force—including thirty pilots—would be sent to fight. And so the famous "Escuadrón 201" was born, commanded by aviation captain Antonio Cárdenas Rodríguez, who fought in the Pacific—in the Phillipines and in Okinawa until the end of November, 1945.

After declaring war on the Axis powers, and following the example of the United States, who imprisoned Japanese "enemies" in detention camps in California, Mexico detained the Germans who lived in Mexico, especially the coffee growers in Chiapas.

I'd read about this in "*La rebelión de los colgados* by Bruno Traven, anti-fascist German writer exiled in the United States. These people were arrested and sent to a farm in Perote, Veracruz, where they were detained until the end of the war.

The first Jewish family I met was the Rubinstein family, Don José and Doña Clara. My aunt and uncle had met them through Dr. Luft, whose son Max was married to Raquel, or "Raya" Rubinstein. Generally, my aunt and uncle's friends were German-speaking Jews, but the Rubinsteins were Russian. They had four children, the aforementioned Raya, along with Jacobo, Boris, and Anita. Boris, or Bubi, as everyone called him, was my age, and we've been lifelong friends. Theirs was a musical family: Don José and Jacobo played violin, and Raquel and Anita played piano.

I began going to classical music concerts at el Palacio de las Bellas Artes with Bubi. I also learned a few "tricks." Since we didn't have much money, we bought gallerytickets, and during the intermission, we'd go down to the first floor and sit in unoccupied seats. On the first floor were the most distinguished people in the Jewish community. In contrast, we were *"los paisanos,"* the Mexican word for "peasants," but we thoroughly enjoyed the music.

Carlos Chávez was the conductor of *la orquestra sinfónica de Bellas Artes.* Scarcely a year after the war ended, a constant stream of prestigious European and North American soloists and conductors were coming to perform in Mexico.

I saw Aaron Copeland conduct his *"Salón México,"* and also Leonard Bernstein, Eugene Ormandy, and Leopold Stokovsky. David Oistrach, Russian violinist, Szygeti, Hugarian violinist, Yasha Heifetz, Arthur Rubinstein, and Yehudi Menuhim, the most famous peformers of that time. Mexico was certainly in the international circuit of quality performers, and there was always an audience for them.

Two concert seasons served as an experience of higher learning for me, an introduction to a marvelous world I'd never known before.

I met other immigrants at my aunt and uncle's house, some of whom had arrived in 1937, others more recently, in 1942. Their social life revolved around playing cards. They generally invited couples over, and after a bit of conversation, on to the game! Bridge, Gin Rummy, or Canasta.

I met Arpad and Mitzi Berci from Vienna, whose son Kurt, was a few years older than I and eventually became my associate in the manufacture of lighting. I met the Escandón's—the Stiglitz's in Vienna—who Mexicanized their last name. I met the Warschavsky's, former movie producers from Berlin, the Samuels, the doctors Hermann Glaser, Leo Deutsch, and Oscar Stern, the last of whom was Miroslava's father, and many others.

I would briefly participate in the conversation, and would then retire to my room. My aunt Else took pains to prepare sandwiches, Brotchen, tea and coffee. The maids in their brand-new, starched uniforms, would serve the guests. My aunt's lengthy *Kartenpartien* were truly impressive. Probably similar to those she'd organized in Vienna before Hitler.

Mexico is a fascinating country, a country of great contrasts, where misery and opulence coexist. This is true to this day. Back then, the capital city's population was around two and a half million. It was an impressive city. Commercial life was generally limited to the downtown area—traffic came and went from *El Centro*.

There you'd find all of the government offices. The more remote, provincial government, in the old *Palacio Covian*, on the streets in Bucareli; Foreign Affairs, on the Avenida Juárez and Ministry of Health on Calle de Lieja, very close to the Chapultepec Forest. The other secretaries were a few blocks from the *Palacio de Gobierno*, in the Zócalo. The banks were at Isabel la Católica, and the luxury stores and jewelry shops were in Madero.

I went to the movies with my aunt and uncle, usually once a week. Afterwards, we'd go eat a light dinner at the *Restaurante Chapultepec*, the Weinstein brother's place. We also frequented *la Flor de Lis* or the *Café Viena* owned by Mrs. Bruder, in the Plaza Iztaccihuatl. In el Centro you could find the *Restaurante Borda* owned by Mrs. Kis; Sanborn's in the Palacio de los Azulejos, and the elegant Prendes on Avenida 16 de Septiembre.

One Saturday afternoon, they brought me to a function organized by the group *"Austria Libre"* on the Avenida Albaro Obregón. There, I met the Bruder, Kafka, Shwartz, and Horecky families, along with Mrs. Bonyhady, Mrs. Wolinsky, and Robert Kolb. After the regular Monday meeting, there was a performance of Shakespeare's *A Midsummer Night's Dream*, acted out by the members. Robert Kolb, who was head of the Librería Internacional, on la Calle Sonora, was an Austrian gentile, and he founded the group in 1938. In total, thirty families were members, all of them Austrian. Before the meeting, they played a Felix Mendelsohn overture, which was funny and well-done, although the actors were amateurs.

My aunt and uncle brought me to Cuernavaca one Sunday, a small city south of the Distrito Federal, the political entity where the capital is situated. On the way, I glimpsed the imposing mountain range encircling the city, and the view was incredible. After stopping in a small village called Tres Marías, and after a ninety-minute journey, we arrived in Cuernavaca, which was incredibly green, with a lush tropical climate. It was further south, and 1480 meters above sea level. Mexico City, in contrast, is on a plateau 2440 meters above sea level.

We ate in the *"Pensión Muller"* run by German-Jewish immigrants, so the food they served was European. Most of the patrons were immigrants, save for a few local Jewish families.

The Jewish community was a large one, with around forty thousand souls, and organized into communities according to place of origin. The

Sephardim, who'd come from Turkey, Greece, and Bulgaria, had immigrated around the end of the last century.

The *"árabes"*, so-called because they came from Syria, Lebanon, and other Arabic-speaking countries, were the first Jewish immigrants from the modern era. They arrived in Mexico in the middle of the last century. The Ashkenazy, mostly from Russia, Poland, and Lithuania, arrived at the beginning of this century. The 1930's brought a new wave of Jews from Germany, Austria, Czechoslovakia, and Hungary.

This was a much smaller immigration wave than those that preceded it.

We spent all day in Cuernavaca, and we returned to Mexico City around six in the evening. Our trip was very nice: I was able to swim in the pool, although the water was cold. What struck me the most was the vegetation, the trees with bright red and yellow flowers. Everything was an intense shade of green.

In school, I progressed quite well. At home, I read as many newspapers and magazines as I could, and watched Mexican movies to familiarize myself with the sound of the language. I still could not read books—I was still not proficient enough in Spanish for this. I spoke, although I made many mistakes, which were mostly grammatical and syntactical.

Every morning my uncle drove me in his car to the corner of Calle de Sonora and la Avenida de los Insurgentes, in front of the American School. From there, I took the tram, which brought me to the Avenida Coyoacán, one block from the school in San Lorenzo. Returning home, I got on the same tram, which dropped me off at Avenida of la Reforma, where I took a bus toward "Palmas", which dropped me off near my aunt and uncle's house in Sierra Paracaima.

Transit in Mexico was very cheap. The tram cost *"un diez,"* or ten cents. The bus bound for Las Lomas was first and cost *"una peseta,"* or twenty-five cents. The fifty cent coin was called a *"tostón"* and it was enough to buy two sodas. My uncle gave me ten pesos each week. This was every Sunday, or *"domingo,"* in Spanish.

The Colegio Israelita ran a Seminary for teachers, or, rather, for female teachers—almost all of the students were young women, and I was the only boy. They treated me very well. There, I met Jaya Rodov, Feige Kuba, Toibe Segal, Gitel Konigsberg, and Java Berkman. I learned a great deal about Judaism. I attended as often as I could, and when my classes let out at two in the afternoon. The Seminary classes lasted until four, sometimes five. I felt grateful for this deference.

Profesor Abraham Golomb and his wife Rifke taught classes at the Seminary. I made friends with both of them. They had a son, Berl, more or less my age. We became very good friends. Although the Golombs were Yiddishists, Berl studied at the Colegio Americano.

They invited them to their home on Calle de Cuautla; they were incredibly friendly and hospitable. Mr. Golomb was from Vilna, and had immigrated to Palestine in the 1930's, and later lived and worked in Winnipeg, Canada. He was a brilliant, but very conflicted person, and sometimes an extremist with respect to Jewish education.

Rifke, his wife, was also from Vilna, and was an excellent pedagogue. Only Yiddish was spoken in their home. For me, spending time there was a natural way of learning the language correctly.

My first friendships were not always pleasing to my aunt and uncle. In the first place, because I spent a great deal of time away from home; and furthermore, the friendships themselves weren't deemed "adequate" for me. My uncle, originally from Romania, arrived in Vienna as a boy and was a typical assimilated Viennese Jew. It was clear that he and my aunt shared the same values. Their ideas regarding Zionism were similar to those of my Uncle Tibick in Brussels. For them, Zionists were "a bunch of crazy idealists going to an inhospitable desert." Their views on Judaism were that "Jews should assimilate themselves in the countries they live in." As for Yiddish, they claimed that "it should remain a jargon—a dialect—to be forgotten and cultivated no further." In Vienna, as here in Mexico, my aunt called my uncle Fritz, because it was more "Viennese." His real name was Moritz Lazar, Moishe Leizer, but that sounded far too Jewish.

I believe my friendship with the Rubinstein and Golomb families made them jealous; those families provided me with support and security. I was grateful for their affection and care, the respect with which they treated me, which was precisely what I was lacking at home.

With weekly readings of the German newspaper "Aufbau" published in New York, which my Aunt Else subscribed to, I once again became reacquainted with Viennese Judaism, popular in the "City of Iron", the legacy of my cultural hometown. I was also able to polish my German, which was very rusty at that point. One thing brought to my attention by this newspaper was the suicide of the writer Stefan Zweig in Brazil in 1942.

Stefan Zweig, whom the Anschluss surprised in London, never returned to Vienna. He was able to immigrate first to England, and later to New York, in

1939. He was a writer of international fame; his writings were translated into more than twenty languages. He felt European more than Austrian —in his own words, "a Citizen of the World." Once in exile, he wrote *Die Welt Von Gestern*, *The World of Yesterday*. His world had fallen apart, and he plummeted into a terrible depression, from which he never recuperated. Exile wasn't easy for any of the Viennese Jewish intellectuals for various reasons, from the cultural to the economic. The composer Arnold Schoenberg, who lived comfortably on the salary of a Viennese music teacher at the *Musik Akademie*, suffered from the severe and unrelenting economic conditions. Upon arriving in the United States, he was paid just 100 dollars per composition class at Princeton University: he only taught twice a week. Later he earned a teaching post at UCLA, with a salary of 400 dollars a month. This was in 1944.

    I don't know why Stefan Zweig didn't go to New York, where a great deal of Viennese, German, and Czech immigrants lived. Perhaps due to some kind of personal problem. Although married, he was romantically involved with a woman much younger than his wife. At first, the three lived together in a *ménage a trois*, which after a while no longer worked out. Erwin Himmelfarb, a Judeo-Viennese immigrant who'd made a fortune in Brazil, invited Zweig to stay with him there, along with his new wife Lotte, who was the daughter of a German rabbi. They stayed in Petrópolis, a wooded area located on the Rio Grande do Sul plateau, which had a very pleasant climate. It was there that Zweig was reminded of *"Isch en el Tirol."* There was also a large colony of German Jews.

    In Petrópolis he made friends with the Chilean poetess Gabriela Mistral. Apparently, her humanism comforted him in this faraway land. But it wasn't like this; in my opinion, what went wrong with Stefan Zweig was his own relationship to Judaism. Thanks to his secular education—his parents lived as assimilated Jews—he grew up lacking Jewish values, which I imagine would have given him a *"raison d'etre"* as a man, as a Jew. He who lacks roots can't properly transplant himself in new soil, as many others can. Nor could he hold on to his beliefs. When a young Brazilian rabbi invited him to give a *Drosche,* a speech in the Temple on Yom Kippur, he declined, saying that "like other Viennese Jews, my education was far-removed from Judaism, and so I'm not the person to speak before an audience of true believers."

    In February of 1942, dejected and increasingly depressed by the news— the triumph of the Germans and the initial defeat of the Allies—he and his wife committed suicide together by injecting themselves with a lethal dose of Veronal. On his desk, he'd left a letter to the Brazilian authorities thanking them for providing him with asylum and hospitality, explaining he was tired of running, exhausted by traveling from one country to another in search of refuge. He also left a letter for his first wife, Frederika.

He lived out his personal tragedy without thinking of the real tragedy: death at the hands of the Nazis, or to be trapped on European soil with no way out.

In New York there was, as I mentioned, a large concentration of Jewish immigrants from Austria, Germany, Czechoslovakia, and Hungary—who'd arrived between 1933 and 1940. Among them were left-wing political refugees. The majority of them returned to Europe after the war. Those that remained had problems during the era of McCarthy and his cohort Jewish lawyer Roy Cohen. A boycott was instituted against them. Many lost their jobs, which necessitated that they migrate once again (1951).

The great "City of Iron" was teeming with German culture. Hermann Leopoldi, Viennese political cabaret actor, performed every night to a full house at the Hotel Almanac at 71st and Broadway. He sang "Over there I was a Bernhardiner and here I am a kleiner dakl." He brought into vogue the phrase "Join the Jews and see the world," a parody of forced immigration.

Many Viennese and German restaurants were opened by recent immigrants. My cousin Joshy Gruenfeld opened one at the Hotel Beacon on 73rd and Broadway in 1942. Most German speaking Jews lived on the Upper West side, from 70th Street all the way to Washington Heights, an area bounded by the Hudson and Harlem rivers.

One night I came home late. It all started after school, when the Katz family invited me over for dinner. Dr. Leo Katz was from Vienna, and his wife was a German Jew. They had a son, Friedrich, whom I'd met at an assembly of *"Alemania Libre,"* a group similar to *"Austria Libre,"* but with more people my age. He and his parents—who were social researchers—arrived in Mexico in 1938 from Germany, where they lived as political refugees. In addition to being Jewish, they were Communists.

Through them, I entered into the nucleus of leftist intellectuals living in Mexico between 1938 and 1946: Ana Seghers, German writer and social activist; Egon Erwin Kisch, writer from Prague; Brigitte Alexander, actress; Lenka Reinerova, Czech writer; Hans Eissler, musician; Walter Reuter, photographer of the Spanish Civil War; Bodo Uhse, German writer; André Simone, Czech activist; Hannes Meyer and Max Cetto, architects, and many others. When I arrived in Mexico in April, 1946, most of them had already returned to Europe. But the Katz family remained in Mexico until 1947. I would go to their house on Calle de Toledo to talk to Friedrich. They were very hospitable and friendly.

I called my uncle from the Katz's house to tell them I'd be late. His only response was to hang up the phone on me. I was used to this sort of thing; it was irrelevant to ask permission for something that was already "against the rules."

I went with Friedrich to the assembly at *"Alemania Libre"* on Calle de Río Elba. There, I met Doris Katz, a young German Jewish girl, as well as Rodolfo Stavenhagen and Susana Alexander, who years later became a sublime Mexican actress.

The assembly let out at eleven at night, and I arrived home to Sierra Paracaima around midnight. The "Reforma" left from the Fountain of Diana in Chapultepec and traveled through the Paseo de la Reforma to a place called La Suastica—who knows why.

From there, I had to walk some twenty minutes before arriving at home. I had keys, although I could see that my uncle, whose bedroom overlooked the street, had turned on the light. As soon as I turned the key in the lock, the light went off, and I entered without a sound and went straight for my bedroom.

For my uncle, leaving the light on was tantamount to a silent but effective reprimand, a reproach to make me feel guilty. In other words, as if to say to me: "because of you, I couldn't sleep, and tomorrow I have to get up early to go to work."

Neither my uncle nor my aunt said a word to me at breakfast the following morning. This "punishment" lasted two more days, "for good measure." So be it, for I preferred to attend meetings anyway. I couldn't fully understand the mentality espoused by my aunt and uncle.

Dr. Mauricio Luft, who visited my aunt and uncle, observed what was happening with their "European nephew," as I was called. One day he came to get me and we went out for coffee at el Restaurante Chapultepec. He told me of the tragedy the Ellenbogens had suffered with the death of their only daughter, Daisy, in Mexico in 1944. Although I did not remember Daisy, we were together in several old photographs. We were two and four years old. She died from an untreated appendicitis that became peritonitis. This obviously caused the family profound sadness.

Although it seemed, according to Dr. Luft, "they were already strange before this happened." Daisy was a very intelligent young woman; she went to the university in Mexico. To make matters worse, she professed liberal and leftist ideas. She developed friendships with leftist intellectuals. My aunt wanted a daughter who was "impeccably ladylike, well-educated, and well-dressed," and Daisy was nothing like this. She studied and read voraciously, and went to political assemblies. Such a shame I never knew her, as I'm certain we would have been great friends.

"You must understand, they are incredibly bitter people," my friend Dr. Luft told me. "I will always help you if you have problems with them. Talk to me, and I'll intercede on your behalf."

I was moved, but also confused. I wasn't aware that so much tragedy had befallen them. But why did they have to take it out on me?

In the six months since I'd lived with them, they'd never once mentioned this fact. That's what I came to resent, the fact that they never spoke of the dead. They never spoke of my parents, of whom I was dying to hear anecdotes. Any mention of the dead was prohibited, completely taboo.

One day I made my first excursion without my aunt and uncle. Kurt Berci invited me. I arrived early at their house on Colonia Hipódromo Condesa, where cars left for el Paso de Cortes in Amecameca a beautiful, forested area. It was there that Cortes and his comrades glimpsed from afar the valley and lakes of Tenochtitlán. The Spanish surely must have been filled with wonder and incredulity, according to Bernal Díaz del Castillo in his *Historia verdadera de la conquista de la Nueva España*. Today, the landscape resembles the work of José María Velasco, which I've seen at the Museo de San Carlos: they are diaphanous and luminous. Of course, I brought my camera and took my first photographs of the Valle de México.

Our group consisted of Kurt and his wife Liesl, the Brimers, the Kafkas, the Wolinskys, and me. Liesl Berci brought delicious sandwiches, hard-boiled eggs, and on the way we bought fruit. It was the first time I rode on a horse; you could rent one for two pesos an hour. It was interesting to see that these recent newcomers from German-speaking countries, unlike the majority of Mexican inhabitants, knew a great deal and were interested in learning more about the country's pre-Hispanic culture. I learned so much from their commentary.

I'd been completely fascinated by everything I'd seen in Mexico thus far. It's a beautiful country with breathtaking panoramic views. Everything was grand. That day I saw the Iztaccihuatl volcano for the first time, the sleeping lady. Its neighbor, the Popocatepetl is commonly called *Popo*. For me, this word was funny, because in Vienna it meant buttocks.

Kurt brought me home. I, of course, made sure to arrive on time, before my designated curfew. I never knew how my aunt and uncle would react. They said nothing; I told them what I'd seen that day. Although they often went to Cuernavaca and Cuautla, they didn't know certain places, nor did it interest them to know, usually due to *"umstaendlich,"* inconvenience. They preferred more convenient, comfortable destinations, which abounded near La Ciudad de los Palacios.

I continued to make progress at school, although in some subjects I had to study very hard, for they were new for me. I enjoyed going to classes at the Seminary. There, Feige Kuba introduced me to her boyfriend Isaac Pikovsky, with whom I made friends. He owned an electronics store on Calle de Corregidora downtown.

Pikovsky was a Russian Jew, widely known to have inherited their political affiliation from their parents.

One day he invited me to a reception at the Embassy of the Soviet Union. I went with him to the mansion on Avenida Tacubaya. It was packed with people, all of whom were standing, as there was nowhere to sit. They served drinks and some hors d'oeuvres—*zakuski*—which were very good. Obviously I didn't know anyone who'd been invited. We stood among them, glasses in hand. Pikovsky knew a great deal of them, and he introduced me to a few. They were mainly Mexican intellectuals: Vicente Lombardo Toledano, Margarita Nelken, Fany Rabel, David Alfaro Siqueiros, Narciso Bassols—Minister of Education during the regime of Lázaro Cárdenas. The ambassador at that time was Konstantin Umansky, a Jew. The reception was being held in order to present to the delegation of Soviet filmmakers and, in particular, the director of the movie "Stone Flowers" which I'd seen at the theater on la Avenida Juárez.

It was a very interesting experience; I thanked Pikovsky for inviting me. I'd never been to a diplomatic reception before.

Kurt Berci, a Jew originally from Vienna, was a multifaceted man. A bit like the men of the Revival, who were autodidacts in various disciplines. He studied medicine and architecture in Vienna, graphic design and interior design in Zurich, without receiving formal training.

In México, to which he came via Uruguay, he worked first at a leather goods shop with Hans Bruder and Julius Horecky, both of whom were Austrian Jews. He later served as theatrical director at the "Heinrich Heine Klub" in the city. Then he became a furniture designer and interior decorator. He decorated many buildings and homes in el Distrito Federal, Puebla, Cuernavaca, and Acapulco.

He also designed the lighting facilities at el Archivo General de la Nación, at the old Palacio de Lecumberri, at el Centro Cultural de Acapulco, and at the Nezahualcoyotl Concert Hall of UNAM, in various banks and department stores throughout the capital, and some cities in the countryside.

My aunt and uncle—who almost never spoke of family—informed me that I had a cousin in Switzerland, the daughter of my uncle Julius, my mother's brother. My cousin Ruth Bachruch had not been brought up Jewish, as her mother was Swiss.

She never knew her father, my Uncle Julius Bachruch, because he died when she was only two years old. Now she was actively searching for her Jewish roots, and, what's more, considered herself Jewish.

She'd always lived in Switzerland, and was therefore spared during the war. She worked for most of her life at Ciba-Geigy laboratories in Basel, which is how she met her husband, Wilfried Eicheberger—also Swiss, and a gentile. They traveled periodically to Vienna in search of news from the Bachruch family. On their first trip in 1960, they found there was no family left. Everyone had been deported or had immigrated elsewhere.

She fixed up the grave of our grandfather Berthold Bachruch in the *Zentral Friedhof* Jewish cemetery in Vienna. It was she who discovered Isabella Bachruch, who died at twelve years old, who no one knew about. As I've already said: "In the Bachruch family, no one discusses the dead." She was able to collect information on the deportations from Vienna to Teresienstadt, and found out about my grandmother Caroline, as well as information on my mother, who was deported to Opole. For this information came to *Wiederstand und Dokumentation Arkiv der Opfer des Faschismus* in Vienna.

I received a letter from Palestine from my two friends in Brussels, who after finishing their *Hakshara* immigrated to Eretz Israel. They were living near Beer-shevba, in the Negev. They built a kibbutz manned by French-speaking youths from Belgium, France, and some from Piedsnoir in Algeria, where things were "looking ugly" for Jews because of the resurgence of Arab Nationalism. In Algeria, Jews were equated with the French, who were in power for two centuries. And so it was that many *djimmies*, as Jews from Maghreb were called, emigrated to France and Palestine.

The kibbutz was called "Mishmar Ha-Neguev." They included photographs with their letter. I was so excited they'd remembered me. They recounted their adventures, the problems they confronted as they acclimatized themselves to the difficulty of living in the desert. But everyone was glad to have made aliyah. I began to feel a bit nostalgic. If it hadn't been for my Uncle Tibick, I would have been there with them. But such was not my destiny. We maintain a correspondence to this day. I was able to visit them personally on my first trip to Israel in 1962.

Fortunately for me, I sustained a healthy correspondence with my friends in Europe. Moreover, I wrote one letter each week to Yolanka and Buci. It was really Yolanka I was writing to; Buci never sent me anything, for he hated to write. My correspondence with the Lanksner family helped preserve my Hungarian, and even helped me learn to write it better. *Per Forza.* Yolanka corrected my grammar like a teacher would her student's. For her birthday, the 14th of May, I sent her a money order of ten dollars, money I'd saved from my "*domingos.*" This was very rewarding for me, and from then on I sent what I could every month.

Time passed quickly. I paid attention in school and kept to my studies, as I didn't want to fail, and furthermore I was eager to receive my coveted sixth grade diploma. I read often: my aunt and uncle had a substantial library. I went to the movies more often than I did in Brussels. I enrolled in the IFAL, French Institute in Latin America, in Río Nazas.

This institute was founded during the war by Jaques Soustelle, a French intellectual and official representative of General de Gaulle, who lived as a refugee in Mexico.

IFAL was more progressive than the Alliance Française, founded in Mexico in 1882. I enrolled in a literature class in which we read Victor Hugo's poetry. I learned to recite. I made two good friends, Alain Resnais, a French teacher, and Julien Pomard, a doctor of medicine. Basically, IFAL was a destination for young Mexicans wanting to learn the French language. There were many other activities. Recent movies were shown there, theater productions performed, there were conferences, an excellent library, periodicals, and diction classes. These were the ones that I frequented.

Among French immigrants, who were called *"La Colonia Francesa"* there occurred a phenomenon similar to that of the Spaniards. Those who settled here before the Second World War clustered around *"l'Alliance"*, and those who'd come more recently around the IFAL, sequestering themselves in the excellent *Liceo Francés*, an incorporated day school with a solid academic reputation.

The Spaniards of the old guard, or *"Peninsulares"*, were contemptuously called *"Gachupines"* or *"Panaderos"*—many of them dedicated themselves to the art of breadmaking. The Spanish settlers who'd lived in Mexico for many years had their own groups: *El Centro Asturiano*, *El Centro Vasco,* and *El Casino Español*. And those who'd immigrated during the Spanish Civil War had theirs: *El Centro Español, El Orfeo Catalá, la Escuela Luis Vives, El Colegio Madrid*, among others. These latter people were known simply as *"refugiados."*

I attended *La Casa de España*, later the *Colegio México*, for an interesting conference on the Golden Age of the Jews in Spain. There, they offered an assortment of classes taught by the most distinguished Spanish intellectuals who'd come to Mexico during the Civil War, who dedicated themselves to cultural investigation. This wave of immigrants was very profitable for Mexico.

It's interesting to note that many Spaniards who'd come during the war formed solid friendships with Jews from Germany, Austria, Hungary, and Czechoslovakia, and who'd also sought refuge in Mexico. They had affinities and interests that united them, and many of the same economic problems—not to mention both groups were European, and products of the same cultural values.

Among the German Jews who lived in Mexico was Dr. Erich Fromm, originally from Frankfurt, who lived in Cuernavaca. He taught classes in psychoanalysis and therapy to Mexican youth and to the doctors who flocked to Mexico from all over America to specialize in psychoanalysis.

Dr. Leo Deutsch taught classes in la Universidad Nacional, and Dr. Max Luft worked as a volunteer at el Hospital de los Shriners. At that time, a medical society *"Ars Medici"* was formed, to which nearly every Jewish doctor in Mexico belonged. This society provided free medical services to any Jew in need. The medical center OSE, directed by Dr. Yavnozoh, from Lithuania, was also already in existence in Mexico, as well as the Ashkenazi organization Hilfsfarein, headed by Boris Volkovich.

In 1946, there were already a great many Jewish doctors in Mexico, some of them born and raised there. They were rapidly gaining favor among Mexican patients, not just Jewish ones. There were very well-known immigrant doctors, such as Dr. Samuel Fastlicht, dental surgeon, author of *La odontología en el México Prehispánico.*

Among these doctors were also Walentin, opthamologist from Hungary; Lisker, a Russian Jewish dentist; Dr. Roberto Ruff, a pediatrician from Alsace; Jaime Constantiner, surgeon; Boleslav Ratniewsky, who was Polish and immigrated to Russia, where he served as a doctor in the Soviet army; Fishleder, a Russian Jew who arrived in Mexico via Cuba; Rudolf and Leo Zuckerman, cardiologists; Oscar Stern and Sidney Ulfelder, general practitioners; Prof. Alexander Von Lichtenberg, urologist; and Stefan Bieringer, opthamologist.

Doctors Hermann Glaser from Vienna, a general practitioner, and Luis Feder, founder of the Society for Psychoanalysis in Mexico; Samuel Zacarias; Yuri Kutler, endocrinologist; Dumont, pediatrician; Karczmar, gynecologist; Siegfried

Becker, cardiologist. Kunewalder, dermatologist. Egon Loewe and Gad Shih, radiologists. And others.

From the generation born in Mexico emerged Doctor Teodoro Cesarman, cardiologist and student of the famous Dr. Ignacio Chávez of el Institute de Cardiología. Shaike Strygler, Horacio Jinich, Rubio, Baraptalo, Lichtinger, and Dr. David Brucilovsky.

The Jewish community in Mexico, which at that time was made up of approximately 32,000, was extremely well-organized. The Central Committee, its governing body, was formed during World War II and was presided over by Dr. Sigmund Bibring, Romanian Jew from Czernovitz. There was also the anti-defamation committee *"Tribuna Israelita"* headed by Salomón Kahan, a musicologist from Poland, and by Dr. Eugenia Hoffs.

Even from the beginning, and with few supporters, the community made many contributions to the sciences and arts, with the presence of those like Dr. Marcos Moshinsky, physicist from Kiev, and Dr. Mauricio Roussek, biologist, who both worked at the Universidad Nacional.

In architecture, along with those I've already mentioned—Max Cetto and Hannes Meyer, successors of the social urbanistic Bauhaus School—was the architect Vladimir Kaspe, from Jarbin, in China, whose parents had emigrated from Russia in 1920.

Also from the new generation was Boris Albin—although born in Odessa, he grew up in Mexico and was a Civil Engineer at UNAM—who began constructing local factories and designing housing projects, along with apartment buildings, in a starkly modern style. These constructions were inspired by the Bauhaus school, and by the works of architects Richard Neutra and Mies van der Rohe.

Albin worked hand in hand with Kurt Berci, who was in charge of interior design. A modern home aesthetic was becoming very popular in Mexico.

Mathias Goeritz, born in Danzing, was taught in the Bauhaus school. He was much more comfortable as an artist than as an architect. He produced various decorative works throughout Mexico. In his mind, his magnum opus was already germinating, the famous *"pirámides"* that he'd build much later. These were constructed at the entrance of the Ciudad Satélite development.

In poetry, we have the aforementioned Salomon Kahan, author of *Bosquejos Musicales*. We also have various orchestral directors, such as Ernest Roemer from Vienna, who directed in *Bellas Artes*, a cycle of Viennese music highlighting several Strauss waltzes. Abel Eisenberg, Polish musician and conductor who completed his studies in composition and conducting at Oberlin University.

Within the booming film industry were Jaques Gelman, Jew from Warsaw, producer of Mario Moreno's popular "Cantinflas" films; Gregorio Wallerstein, from Galicia, producer of the Mexican Cinema classic "La Perla" with Pedro Armendariz, a film featuring Hans Rohner, Viennese Jew; and the daughter of the aforementioned Oscar Stern, Miroslava, an actress who was already famous. She was discovered because she'd won the title of princess in the *"Blanco y Negro"* dance. Martha Roth, in *"Vitola"* and other works. The French Jew Julian de Meriche, husband of India María, and Nono Arzu who later became a star in the fledgling medium of television. Alfredo Ripstein, born in Mexico, a producer of many wildly successful movies in Mexico, a producer of many wildly successful movies.

Gutierre Tibon had already published his book *Gog y Magog*. Arnoldo Belkin, who'd emigrated from Canada, had painted his first mural in Mexico; Fanny Rabel began making murals on government-owned buildings.

Eduardo Weinfeld, a Jew originally from Slovakia, and Isaac Babani, from Bulgaria, published the *"Enciclopedia Judaica Castellana"* in ten volumes, a monumental work in Spanish on the history of the Jewish people, which circulated rapidly in Mexico and throughout Latin America.

Entrepreneurs also emerged, creating their own businesses. It was impressive what these people were able to accomplish in just a few years, and not just in terms of their personal successes: they indubitably helped the country that gave them asylum.

Dr. Emerich Somlo from Hungary founded the Hormona and Sintex laboratories, where, with the help of doctors Rosenkranz and Marker (also Hungarian Jews who'd arrived in Mexico via Cuba), he was able to synthesize cortisone from barbasco, a plant common in Veracruz and Tabasco.

Marcel Revesz, Hungarian Jew and former director of Gideon Richter in Budapest, founded a pharmaceutical laboratory in our country.

Hans Koenig from Vienna founded the ingenious *"El Potrero"* in Veracruz. Igor Ohrenstein, Viennese, began the first Rubber Factory in Mexico; Georg Warschavsky, German Jew, film director in the UFA in Berlin, founded the Lakeside laboratories.

In 1936, Mateo Beja and Andrés Sevi, Jews from Salonika, founded the industrial company Orizaba, in Veracruz, which produced cotton poplin reknowned around the world for its quality.

Ernesto Meyer, from Mannheim, Germany, who came to Mexico via Spain, founded a plastic factory, Plásticos Internacionales. Among other products, they made panels for Volkswagen in Puebla.

Imre Magyoros, Hungarian Jew, began manufacturing electric irons in Mexico. His brand was called Mogum, and his irons were exported to Central America and the Caribbean.

Emil Polak, Dutch Jew, founded the Polaquim company, responsible for producing raw materials for the chemical industry.

Luis Neumann, originally from Offenbach, Germany, founded the Mercurio tannery, a pioneer in the leather-tanning industry.

In 1940, Mauricio Lask and Mauricio Pier founded the Mexico tannery, with the same end.

Gaston Muller, from Alsace, began the Moderna tannery, specializing in fine leathers for women's purses and jackets.

In 1931, the Hermanos Gurvitz tannery was founded by Samuel, Moisés, and Elias Gurvitz, originally from Lithuania. In 1941, Moisés became partners with Mr. Bogomolny, and they created the Rex Tannery. Meanwhile, Samuel founded the Vestón Tannery with Carlos Krazer and Jaime Peretzman.

Abraham Kreimerman opened a foundry and steel manufacturing plant for the production of silverware, the first in Mexico, called Cufisina.

Max Shein, Jew from Galicia, in the Austro-Hungarian Empire, arrived in Mexico via the United States and founded Cipsa, an industrial emporium for articles made of plastic and acrylic, with plants in various states throughout Mexico. Today, he is a true philanthropist: he donated facilities to the Albert Einstein Primary School, to a vocational secondary school, and also to a rural center in Panzacola, in Tlaxcala, among many other beneficent works.

Najman Zeidenweber, León Bialik, Abraham Leiter, Max Goldsmith, and Roberto Schoenfeld, all of whom were Polish Jews—except for Shoenfeld, who was Sephardic—founded *Encajes Mexicanos* with machinery from Switzerland, England, and France. Their lace became internationally known for its quality.

Francisco Ferry, a Slovenian chemist who fought in the International Brigades in Spain, founded Fester together with Alfredo Stern, from Germany. They began producing waterproofing agents and additives for paint. Their company was subsequently directed by Murray and Irene Dorit, who immigrated to Mexico from Poland via Palestine. Irene was the daughter of Dr. Karcmar, famous gynecologist, who rebuilt his career in Mexico.

Harry Steele, from Galicia, came to Mexico via the United States, and started the first wristwatch factory. The brand was Haste, and today operates under the direction of Norman Gottlieb.

The brothers Pablo and Israel Brenner, born in Mexico, began Fud, a meat processing plant in Pénjamo. Ham and sausages were packaged in Guadalajara and exported to the United States.

Max Grinstein, from Lodz, Poland, imported machinery to the United States during the war. He began the brand Non Pareil, manufacturing nylon pantyhose for women.Simón "Shimshon" and Mike Feldmann, his brother, began a metal smelting plant, La Consolidada, during the war.

Elias Sourasky, a Jew from Bialystok, came to Mexico via the United States and founded el Banco de Cédulas Hipotecarias (BCH), which granted mortgages to thousands of Mexican families. A great philanthropoist, he created *el Premio de Ciencias*, an award for science which bore his name, and was given annually by the President of the Republic.

Before the creation of the Comite Central in 1938—a centralized governing body—the immigrants were organized in *Kehilot* according to their countries of origin. The Jews of Eastern Europe are still grouped according to *Kehilá Nidjei Israel* to this day. Sedaka and Marpé, for the Jews from Aleppo. Those from Damascus, the Mount Sinai congregation. The Sephardic from Turkey, Greece, and the Balkans joined Yehuda Ha-Levy.

The German Jews had Hatikva-Menora, and the Hungarians, Emuna. A small group of ex-American G.I.s who settled in Mexico after the Second World War founded *La Congregación Beth-Israel*. The congregation was incredibly diverse, but everyone participated in a rich Jewish community life. It had, of course, a committee for charity and a *Chevra Kadisha*, a committee responsible for burials, according to thousand year old Jewish tradition.

There were also Jewish day schools incorporated into the SEP : the aforementioned Colegio Israelita "La Yidishe"; La Yavne for Orthodox Jewish students; El Monte-Sinaí for Jewish students from Arabic nations, el Tarbut and el Hebreo Sefardi for Sephardic students, with a special emphasis on Hebrew.

Finally, the Magen David school for students from Aleppo. The lodge *La Espinoza de la Bene* was founded in 1934, and was comprised mostly of German, Austrian, Hungarian, and Czech Jews, although they included some of their "brothers" from other communities.

Long before the existence of el Centro Deportivo Israelita, which was founded in 1950, there was el Club de Jóvenes Judíos on Calle Tacuba 15, in the city center. There was also the Macabi Sporting Club, which had an excellent soccer team, incorporated into the second-division Mexican league.

The Zionist Federation brought together people of all political stripes: from the left, the Mapam and the Klalim, and from the right, the Irgun.

Newspapers were published in Yiddish and in Spanish, as were literary magazines. There was also a publishing house. In Latin America, Mexico was second only to Argentina in the editorial field, Argentina being one of the oldest literary—as well as one of the oldest and largest Jewish—communities in North America.

Of course, the Jews from the Diaspora spoke many different languages, depending upon their countries of origin. The Sephardic Jews, expelled from Spain in 1492, spoke Ladino; the European Ashkenazis, Yiddish, and the Middle Eastern Jews, Arabic. The use of Hebrew, *Lashon Kodesh*, the holy language, was restricted to prayer until the nineteenth century.

At first, both Ladino and Yiddish were written in Hebrew characters. From an early age, the Jews—in a world in which the majority of people were illiterate—went to Seder after age five, and then to Yeshivá, so that they were literate and well-versed in Jewish culture by the time they turned thirteen.

"Ladino" comes from *"mal latino"* or the vulgar Latin spoken in medieval Spain and Portugal during the fourteenth century, long before the emergence of Castilian

Spanish we know today. Its syntax is Hebrew, and the language itself contains up to twenty-five percent of the Hebrew language, and also borrows from Turkish and French. Ladino was formed and used, for the most part, in the Ottoman Empire.

When Ludwig Zamenhof, Polish Jew, devised and propagated Esperanto as an "International Language" from 1887 to 1892, the Sephardic community adopted Latin letters for Ladino. The adoption of Latin letters was also influenced by *La Alliance Israelite Universelle*, by the distinguished philanthropist Sir Moses Montefiore and Adolphe Cremieux, a French Jew, who founded westernized schools in Bosnia, Bulgaria, Greece, Turkey, Syria, Palestine, Iraq, Egypt, and the North African countries of Maghreb. This is why today Ladino is written in Latin characters.

Yiddish was born in the first Jewish communities living in German and Alsatian villages. It subsequently became diffused in Silesia, Bukovina, Bessarabia, Poland, Hungary, Romania, and Russia. Nearly twenty-seven percent of Yiddish is comprised of Hebrew rounded out by Russian and Polish vocabulary. It essentially comes from Altdeutsch, the German spoken in Alsace and the Rhineland during the sixteenth century. Its syntax is Hebrew, and much of its idiomatic influence is Slavic.

The oldest Yiddish writings include prayer books, or *Sidurim*, the *Tanakh*, or Pentateuch, which were *Farteischt*, translated from Hebrew in the seventeenth century for the use of Jewish women. To this day, it's written in Hebrew characters.

The nineteenth century brought forth a rich Yiddish literature written in Galicia, Poland, and Russian. Outstanding writers like Mendele Moijer Sforim, Yud Leib Peretz, Sholem Aleichem, Sholem Ash, Chaim Nachman Bialik, Isaac Bashevis Singer, winner of the Nobel Prize in Literature in 1978. More recent authors include Peretz Markish, Itzik Feffer, Unger, Abraham Sutzkever, Niger, and others.

The Yivo founded in Vilna, now based in New York, is an institute dedicated to the investigation and archiving of the Yiddish language. It also serves as a Yiddish language academy.

Until 1958, there were two daily publications in Yiddish in the United States: *Forverts* and *Der Tog*. In the Soviet Union, until 1953, there were *Einikait*, published in Moscow, and *Emes*, in Birobidshan. In Mexico, there was *Der Veg*, founded by Moisés Rosenberg in 1930. After his death in 1942, it was edited by Jaim Lazdeiski until the 1980's. It was discontinued in 1990. *Di Shtime* was initially founded and headed by the writer and journalist Moises Rubinstein, and, when he died it was passed on to Abraham Rubinstein, a typesetter, founder, and co-collaborator with Moises for more than fifty years. *Di Shtime* also ran until 1990.

In 1938, Moises Rosenberg translated and edited *The History of the Jewish People* by Heinrich Graetz, together with Prof. Salomón Kahan. A monumental work in nine volumes.

Unfortunately, the Yiddish language received a mortal blow with the annihilation of the Jewish population in Poland, Russia, Romania, and Hungary during the Holocaust.

I visited Cuernavaca with Berl Golomb, invited by the Goldenberg family, who had a large home with a garden in this subtropical paradise. They had a daughter, Assia, who was of marrying age, and they'd often invite young Jewish boys to visit so that she could keep company with men her own age.

Samuel Goldenberg was a Russian Jew, and a man of great fortune. In his home, he spoke Russian and Yiddish, and he was greatly interested in Jewish culture. In the afternoon he always read aloud: that day, we were instructed to listen to a few paragraphs from a novel by Sholem Aleichem, a survivor of Bergen-Belsen who'd recently arrived in Mexico. His novel described the life and customs of the *Aler Heim* in the *Shtetlach* in Russia.

I greatly enjoyed this Yiddish author, who wrote and described everything with a wonderful sense of humor: ball players, the Lufmenschen of Odessa, the dairy farmers and tailors of Yehupetz, the waterboys from Kazrilevke. After the literary portion of our day was done, we went swimming in the pool. The water in Cuernavaca is extremely cold, but also refreshing, likely because of the altitude, 1,300 meters above sea level.

Mrs. Goldenberg, accompanied by a maid, brought us tea and *Lekach*, a kind of honey-based dessert. Tea was served Russian style, in a glass, not in a teacup. Mine was so hot I could barely stand it. Instead of sugar, it was sweetened with *varenie*, a kind of strawberry jam, which was very delicious. Goldenberg drank his tea by placing a lump of sugar on his tongue, then sipping, something I'd seen my father do. I told him that, and spoke a bit of my grandmother, from Odessa. *"Er is nit kain hundertprozentig yeke,"* said Goldenberg to his wife, *"Sis do a russische bobe."*

After swimming, the musical portion of our evening began. Mrs. Goldenberg played the piano, and her daughter Assia sang *"Katyusha"* in Russian, and we sang along with her.

Mania, the woman from Bergen-Belsen, and I sang *"Zog nit keinmol as du geist dem letzn veg"* and *"Tumbalalaika,"* songs I knew from Brussels. And then *"Oif dem pripetchok,"* which is a Ukrainian Jewish song. We also sang *"Main shtetele Belz,"* a song about Belzec, in Poland. And then I performed a duet with Mania of *"Partisaner lid,"* anthem of the partisans.

We had a wonderful time, and we were invited to come back the following Sunday.

"*Nu reb Yoel vet ir kumen?*" "Of course," I said in Spanish, "*con mucho gusto.*" "*A molodietz,*" Goldenberg said to his wife. Berl and I went to the literary gatherings in Cuernavaca several more times. There was good food to eat, a first-rate swimmingpool, and excellent company. What more could I ask for?

Of course, in the interim, I learned to swim at the YMCA, known as "Guay," at the corner of Balderas and Independencia. First, I went on Saturdays and met with a swimming instructor for two hours. On days when I didn't have school, I went early in the morning. The pool was covered so that it wasn't affected by the weather. Sometimes I ate breakfast at a Chinese café on Revillagigedo. These "cafés" were very popular and could be found everywhere around the city. For a peso sesenta centavos, you could get a large cup of café con leche, two biscuits or pan dulce, Chinese style, of your choice. In addition to being cheap, it was very tasty.

After four months of swimming lessons, I was finally able to swim the front crawl and breast stroke. "La Guay" was a popular institution, with a membership fee of three pesos per month, which allowed you access to all the facilities anytime you wished to use them. It was open until nine p.m. except for Sundays, as it was a Christian organization. I was happy I knew how to swim, for in Mexico this was a very important skill, much more so than in Belgium.

Berl took me to the Coyoacán neighborhood south of the city. I was impressed by the cobblestone streets, the beautiful carved wooden doors, and the colonial style homes. Everything looked as if no time had passed since the arrival of the Spaniards. Coyoacán, so called because of its location at the shore of the great Lago Mayor.

We visited el Palacio de Cortés. We saw the house where Leon Trotsky—Lev Davidovich Bronstein—lived and was assassinated in 1940.

There had been a previous attempt to assassinate him in 1939, a complot headed by the painter David Alfaro Siqueiros, which was squelched by Trotsky's bodyguards. Those involved with this plot were forced to flee, so as not to be apprehended by the Mexican authorities.

The second attempt on his life was better-organized, and was perpetrated from within by Ramón Mercader, a Spanish communist. Mercader, who worked with Trotsky, little by little was able to gain his trust. The rest is history: Trotsky was killed with a "piolet" or a pick used for climbing. The Russian communist leader was slow to die in the wake of a blow to his skull. The arm of Stalin extended easily all the way to the distant lands of the Anáhuac. I say "easily" because Stalin was served by Communist cronies throughout the world who carried out his personal vengeances. Trotsky, having sought asylum in Mexico, represented no threat to the security of the Soviet Union in 1940, but Stalin longed to put an end to him for his gesture of militant desertion. The Fourth International attracted them to fight Trotsky in the international revolution.

The fear and hatred Trotsky inspired in Stalinist communists bordered on paranoid. The rift began during the Spanish Civil War. Stalin, through his resident commissioner V. Raskolnikov, claimed that the Trotskyites were supporting the Anarchists. An aside: in Russia, The Fourth International was called "Bronstein's International" which pejoratively emphasized the Jewish origin of his last name.

In the Soviet Union, the Jews served as a scapegoat for the masses until Stalin's death. To this day, the *Pamyat*, or "the right," still believes that during the communist era between 1917 and 1979, the Jews were responsible for Russia's prevailing misery. The Russian people diverted their discontent and foisted it onto their scapegoat—in this case former Jewish leaders: after Glastnost, Gorbachev indicted them as capitalists. Who can understand why! After the German invasion in 1941, less than a third of Russia's Jewish population remained. Approximately 1,000,200 died at the hands of the Germans, including the 200,000 who died in battle camps as Soviet soldiers. Around a million emigrated after the war, and even more left after Glastnost, mostly to Israel, the United States, Canada, and Australia, and also to Eastern European countries.

Today approximately one million Jews live in Russia, the majority of them over sixty years old, which indicates they're likely retirees. The rest are intellectuals, architects, engineers, doctors, and well-regarded medical and scientific researchers. Capitalists? Hardly.

Come on now, Mr. Szirinovsky, men of the Pamyat! Vestiges of the same anti-Semitic tradition of the czars and communists. Isn't it comfortable, easy, politically, to blame the Jews for the country's problems? Admit it!

After the Second World War, the communists, emboldened by their victories at the polls in the democratic Eastern European countries—especially in parliament, where a great many communist representatives were elected, as well as in cabinet and administrative positions—were unable to see that their Eastern European counterparts in the so-called socialist nations were falling under a dictatorship, that people were being robbed of their most elemental freedoms.

The idealists among the communists couldn't see that they were being manipulated by Stalin for his own aims. The dogmatism of communist ideology is the only way to explain how he was able to so effectively deceive them until the Prague Spring of 1968, when the Soviet armed forces, hailed as liberators and the

Czechs in 1945, invaded the Czech Republic, arresting Prime Minister Dubcek, along with his staff. Thus began the party's mass defections.

I spent the high holidays—Rosh Hashanah and Yom Kippur—in Mexico for the first time. In reality, I didn't consider myself very religious at sixteen years old, or currently, for that matter, having never completed my Mitzvot. I always worked on Saturdays. I rarely went to Temple, nor did I wear a yarmulke. I did not keep kosher, etc. Certainly, there are 613 Mitzvot a Jew must observe. As far as I can remember, I went with my father to temple in Vienna during the major holidays : Rosh Hashanah, Yom Kippur, Sukkot, and Simchat Torah. I remember going with him once to a *Yartzeit*, or prayer vigil for the dead—that time, it was for his father, my grandfather Juer. But I never accompanied him to Kaddish, to pray for the departed, because children who still had their parents were not allowed to participate. During the celebration of *Yizkor*—a commemoration of the dead—the children are forced to leave the premises of the Temple. I always felt that during these celebrations my place was among my Mexican brethren.

In Brussels I went to temple with Buci. During the German occupation all places of Jewish worship were shut down, resuming operation after the liberation. I remember how Buci always kept a bar of chocolate in his jacket pocket. After fasting for Kippur, once the *"Adonay Hu-Elohim"* was repeated seven times, an indication that the fast was over, we would split it. Our own tradition!

I was told of a temple on la Colonia Polanco, at Calle Eugenio Sue, and I went there to pray. In 1946, it was a provisional temple. Today, in its place, stands the temple Bet Itzjak, built by the architect Boris Albin. It housed a small Orthodox congregation that joyously—and noisily—celebrated holidays. Very similar to the temple I knew in Brussels, but the polar opposite of the solemnity and silence of the Stadttempel in the Seintenstaettengasse in Vienna. "Wild West," my father would have said." Very disorganized."

My aunt and uncle didn't go to temple, but my aunt prepared food for me before and after my fast. *"Sehr aufmerkasam,"* respectful of my customs.

There was a Mr. Timberg, a Dutch Jew, in the temple, who occasionally pounded the pulpit. He stood next to the rabbi, to maintain order. *"Sha zol zain shtil."* SILENCE, he would scream to make himself heard over the clambering masses. Another thing that drew my attention was the sale of *aliyot* to the "highest bidder," the opportunity to mount the *Orn Kodesh* to read a *parasha,* or chapter from the Torah. This was an honor generally granted to pious Jews, and those who practiced *tzedaka*, or charity.

Here in the Templo de Polanco, the beadle or *Shame*, offered this honor to parishioners who offered the highest bid. *"Sis do maftir far drai toisnt."* The possibility of an *aliyah* for three thousand pesos! The result was a veritable marketplace, and everything came to a head at the hour of *neila*. Mr. Timberg rasied his watch, so that everyone could see the time. He shouted: "He who strictly opposes this can start praying before six in the evening." Which is to say, worship could not begin before the setting of the sun, as indicated by Talmudic law, or *Halakhah. Jalile vejas!* G-d save anyone who'd contradict religious precepts. As he understood it, the elderly man had been awarded role of inspector. He thought of himself as "God's representative in el Templo de Polanco."

The Jewish religion is entirely individualistic. Each Jew speaks directly with G-d in whatever way he wishes to, and interpreting G-d as he pleases.

I passed all my subjects at the Colegio Israelita and was granted my Primary School Certificate, complete with a photograph and everything! *Got tzu danken a Dios gracias*, I now had my certificate. With it, I could apply to enter Poli, the National Polytechnic Institute in January, I was informed, open enrollment commenced. I'd already researched various schools, and in Mexico there wasn't anything comparable to a "career in cinematography." And so I decided to study electro-mechanical engineering, which required eight years of training. I hoped to finish and become an engineer one day.

During vacations I offered to work for my uncle at his business. This made him very happy. In subtle and sometimes not so subtle ways, I was made aware of how much it cost him to bring me to Mexico. The price of my transatlantic ticket, the plane ticket, the lawyer's fees, *"viel geld,"* a great deal of money. He told me bringing me to Mexico was an investment for him. And now I wanted to repay him, even if just in part, for what he'd spent on me. I felt it was the right thing to do.

The two of us drove to the office in his car before eight in the morning. He taught me the ins and outs of the importing business. At that time Ultramar, S.A. was based on Calle Durango, in a neighborhood called Roma. Ultramar imported all sorts of essentials in great demand in post-war years during which merchandise was arriving in Mexico from Europe. They imported hardware, mostly from Italy, such as padlocks, battery-operated flashlights, poultry shears, gardening shears, clamps, screwdrivers, and machetes. From England, they imported cashmere; from Switzerland, cotton poplin for shirting, picture frames from Denmark, and many other essential articles.

All of these items had to be sold, and this is what my job consisted of doing. Thus, after a short learning period, I went out to sell.

At that time, all commercial activities took place downtown. So I filled a regular-sized suitcase with poultry shears and went out to sell them. Most of the hardware stores were on Calles de Corregidora and San Juan de Letrán, today Eje

Central. Most were owned by "paisanos." I was very successful, and on the first day I sold three dozen of the ninety scissors I'd brought with me. Some stores bought by the dozen, others six pieces at a time. My uncle instructed me to leave the scissors with an order form for the client to sign. The following day, I'd bring the client an invoice and then they'd pay us. This was an effective system that the clients enjoyed because it showed we trusted them. And so I learned marketing skills from Uncle Ellenbogen.

After two months of work, he told me to take a vacation. This was very generous of him. He gave me two hundred pesos, "so that I could go wherever I wanted for a week."

And that's how I went with my friend Alain Resnais from IFAL, my French teacher, who had vacation from Christmas to New Years. We went to Acapulco.

In 1946, the trip could be made in ten hours on the Estrella Roja bus, which made stops in Cuernavaca, Taxco, and Chilpancingo.

Acapulco was very different than what it is now. A Pacific port, the second port established by the Spanish after Veracruz on the Atlantic. It was a very important port in the Colonial era—where the Nao from China were able to dock with their silks, ivory, and porcelain from the East. It was also the port that enabled communication between Mexico and the Philippines, the first Spanish colony in the South Pacific.

In 1947, it was still an important maritime shipping location, but, more importantly, its beaches were becoming a tourist destination for Americans and Latin Americans.

After going through an area that looked as though it were burnt by the sun, we arrived at "tierra caliente," where the climate and vegetation were entirely tropical. We had descended about 400 meters. From there, we could see the majestic and impressive Pacific Ocean. This was my first time seeing it.

It was extremely hot on the bus and we began removing some of our clothing. The bus brought us into the terminal in the center of town. There was a plaza with a church, which was quite ugly. We headed straight for the boardwalk. Alain spoke of a place where you could rent cots for six pesos a night, where we could store our things. These were called "cachivaches." A room wasn't really necessary in Acapulco, and because we'd be spending all day at the beach, there wasn't really any need to bathe—according to Alain—so this was the ideal place for us. It was also extremely cheap. Of course, we could barely afford a hotel with the one hundred and seventy pesos that remained after I'd bought my round trip bus ticket; Alain had brought more or less the same amount of money.

All said and done, we arrived at the place, paid for the first night, changed our clothes, and I went to the market to buy *huaraches*, a kind of woven sandal, and we went to the beach. At that time there were two beaches that were popular: Caleta at one end of the bay and Hornos, near the hotel Papagayo. We spent the morning at one and went to the other in the afternoon. This was customary.

In addition to going into the water and then drying ourselves on the sand, I discovered that near the hotels there were fresh water showers for guests, where we could wash off the salt and sand.

We went to eat in the marketplace. Very delicious, but everything was incredibly spicy. I had had my "encounters" with Mexican food, but I was not yet accustomed to the spicy food.

What I loved most in Mexico were the fruits: papayas, mangos, prickly pears, zapotes, chirimoyas, chico zapotes—fruits I'd never tried nor heard in Europe. In Acapulco, I learned to love ceviche and grilled red snapper. Everything was delicious.

The following day, we ate breakfast at a Chinese-owned café on the boardwalk. Alain, who'd already been to Acapulco, had already devised an itinerary for the day: finding women. *"Tachles,"* he said in Yiddish, with a purpose: to make their acquaintance and enjoy their company. We walked along the beach with our eyes and ears perked for vacationers of the opposite sex, primed ourselves for making friends, swimming, chatting, and Lord knows what else.

The first day we had no luck. We swam and spent time on the beach. The following day, *"God Hot Geholfn,"* G-d intervened: we met three American tourists. There were a great many tourists from the US in Acapulco because it was their vacation season.

Later we made conversation. They were three young teachers from Baltimore, and, as Alain was also a teacher, there was much to talk about. They were typical tourists, likely in search of their first "adventure" with a Latin Lover in a foreign land—or at least a country totally different from the Eastern United States.

We spent the rest of the day together and became friends. They invited us to dinner at their hotel and then to a dance accompanied by the Hotel Caleta orchestra. I had no idea how to dance—I'd never really danced before—but the circumstances forced me to rise to the occasion. So I did the best that I could.

My friend Alain impressed them most, as he was French and handsome. He had just the right "savoir faire," a way with women (I learned a few lessons from him on this vacation) that left them quite smitten. I also spoke French, and so I served as intermediary. They asked us what hotel we were staying at, and when we told them we'd rented a cot for the night, they burst out laughing, and, after consulting amongst each other, they invited us to stay with them. *Wunderbar!*

I was dancing with one of them, a redhead named Evelyn. According to her, she was staying in a "single room" but really it had a double bed. Alain stayed with the other two. We spent three nights in an "elegant hotel," the Hotel Caleta, and we were still saving on the cost of the cot.

We spent a marvelous few days in Acapulco in the company of our friends, until it came time to leave. The women were Jewish and very friendly; elementary school teachers in a public school. They were fascinated by all things not American. "Foreign and different," they kept saying. I'm not sure what they thought of us—two European men, not exactly the "dark and handsome Latin Lovers" they were looking for. They only thing "Latin" we had going for us was the Spanish language: one of us was a Celt, the other a Jew.

My first vacation away from the city was wonderful. I had an excellent time in Acapulco, and I greatly admired its natural beauty.

I enrolled in the Polytechnic Institute the second week of January. School began on February 2nd. The campus to which I was assigned was on Calle Carlos B. Zetina, in Tacubaya, directly across from the Alexander Von Humboldt German School. Classes began at eight in the morning and were completely free.

I was very happy about this, and eager to begin classes in two weeks. Meanwhile I was still working for my uncle in sales, visiting new clients.

The situation in Palestine was growing tense. Several projected plans for the country's future were presented to the United Nations. One of them was to form two states: one Palestinian, the other Jewish. This was immediately rejected by the Arabs.

Meanwhile, the British blockade was impenetrable. Almost all ships carrying European refugees were intercepted. The "camps" in Cyprus continued growing, there were now 75,000 detained Jews there. Was there an end in sight?

The Yishuv in Palestine had no expectations. Sooner or later, with or without the British, they would have to confront the Arabs, who'd sworn to "throw the Jews into the sea."

The Muslims had declared a Jihad, or Holy War, against the Jews. Volunteers arrived from Iraq, Libya, Syria, and Jordan, armed fanatics who'd come to help their Muslim compatriots. The only peaceful front was that of Lebanon, a country more interested in prosperity and hard work than entangling its people in useless squabbles.

Christians—who were a majority in Lebanon—maintained good relations with the Kibbutzim in Galilee. Many Lebanese went to Jewish clinics and hospitals in Palestine. Many Lebanese youths completed their degrees at the Hebrew University in Jerusalem.

The British, who'd received reinforcements from troops stationed in Germany, reinforced the blockade on the streets, always on the lookout for hidden Jewish arms supplies. This was not effective, nor were many soldiers inclined to fight. Really, they wanted to return to their homes. The war had ended almost two years before, and still they were forced to take up arms.

The British officials sent by the Foreign Office in London were most certainly pro-Arab. These were the politics of the Ministry in London, and their hero was still Lawrence of Arabia, Arab leader from 1918 to1920. It was the Arabs who'd negotiated the details of the Sykes-Picot agreement, which divided Syria and Lebanon, converting them into a French protectorate, and Palestine into a British one. In 1924, the British delivered the Transjordan on a silver platter to the royal house of Hashim, without any regard for its people. The Balfour Declaration was signed in 1917...

In Palestine, the Haganah was in place, a defense force constituted by the members of the Kibbutzim, or agricultural communities, to defend against the Arab bandits. Secretly, they'd been organizing small factories for the manufacture of small caliber weapons and ammunitions under the command of Iztak Sade, veteran of the Haganah. Later on, they organized the Palmach, an organized and disciplined task force. During the XXII Zionist Congress, the Executive of the Jewish Agency took hold of the provisional government of the future Jewish State.

David Ben Gurion was to head the National Defense, and Moshe Shertok was the future Foreign Relations Minister. Chaim Weitzman announced his resignation from his presidency.

Of course, there were other armed groups in Palestine; the strongest was Irgun Zvai Leumi of Menachem Begin, Betar and Lochamei Herut Israel, headed by Dov Gruner, were regarded as "terrorists" by the British.

From Geneva, the Jewish Agency sent buying agents to every European country in search of arms of all sorts, in preparation for the looming battle. Czechoslovakia and Poland were the only countries that allowed them access and sold them arms, which had to be transported secretly and with false documents in order to be brought into Palestine.

The Yishuv armed itself, prepared to be on the offensive once the British were gone. The imminent proximity of battle could be felt in the air.

My father visited Palestine in 1923, which I learned only after the war. This would explain the presence of an engraved seashell he'd given me when I turned eight, and which I always kept with me, through all my adventures. It's one of those white-speckled shells that abound in the Mediterranean. The letters etched on it are embossed in the style of Daum and Galle vases from the turn of the century. They read: *"Zikarun Olam, Dr. Benyamin Yacov Herzl, v' Rishon Letzion."* The shell, which I still keep at my side during Seder prayers, is one of the only things I have from my father.

My father, who was neither a Zionist or an activist, was invited by my cousin Joshy Gruenfeld to join the Hakoach team, which visited and played matches in Palestine, against the Rishon Letzion team. He stayed in Palestine for three weeks. At that time Palestine was not an attractive prospect for immigrants, especially for someone living in Vienna. One needed much more than a migratory curiosity to settle there. One had to be an idealist, a pioneer, a Chalutz, like those who settled in Texas or California when those territories belonged to Mexico.

In Palestine, no one gave the pioneers their land: one had to buy the property of so-called "missing" Arab landowners, which remained idle and, for all intents and purposes, abandoned. These landowners generally lived in Jerusalem, Jaffa, Haifa, and Damascus. Others were in Beirut. All of these lands were bought legally.

The ship "Exodus" set sail in May of 1947, from Sete Port, with four hundred eighty-three European refugees on board. Even before leaving, it was known that the ship was bound to confront the blockade. This was intended to alert the general public and call attention to the mistreatment of Holocaust survivors in search of their own nation. The British received direct instructions from Bevin, Minister of Foreign Relations in England, to not allow a single ship to pass through.

Mission accomplished! England found itself in an impossible predicament when faced with strong opposition from the public. Furthermore, the Jewish Agency, which had observer status in the United Nations, finalized important diplomatic maneuvers to support the proposal for partitioning.

Finally, on November 29th, 1947, the General Assembly approved—with the required majority of two-thirds—the creation of two states. One Arab, the other Jewish. Mexico abstained from voting.

Various Latin American republics voted in favor, such as Guatemala, El Salvador, Costa Rica, Nicaragua, and Panama. However, several countries with powerful Arabic populations refrained from voting.

Among the fighters in this diplomatic arena, summoned by the Jewish Agency, was Jorge Neumann, from Guatemala, who became, years later, my father-in-law. He was in charge of bringing Jorge García Granados, the Guatemalan Minister of Foreign Relations, to Lake Success, in New York, the seat of the United Nations. Granados had to serve as a "filibuster" in charge of distracting the other delegates to give the Jewish delegation more time to convince those who were still undecided. Jorge Neumann, following instructions from Shertok, and with the approval of the President of Guatemala, flew to Bogota in an American military plane.

Jorge García Granados was at a conference in Bogota, where he'd installed an armed movement. This plane, with its motor left on, waited until the travelers returned alive and well, to embark on their voyage to Lake Success.

Problems began to arise in Mexico. Until 1948, Jews and Arabs residing on Mexican soil—and in America in general—had "gotten along well." They were business associates, best friends. They were noted and identified by their common origin. According to the Bible, they both come from Shem, son of Noe. An aside: the term "anti-Semitism" was used for the first time in 1879 by Wilhelm Marr. In Mexico, no one noticed the difference between Arabs and Jews. For Mexican people, they were one in the same, seen as *"barchantes"* not far removed from the *"Baisanoo Jalil"* by the Judeo-Mexican producer Gregorio Wallerstein. Suddenly, the friendly relationships and businesses that had existed for fifty years dashed to pieces by the situation in the Middle East. Not to mention, they were viewed as dangerous.

On February 2nd at 7 in the morning, I woke up very early, because classes began at 8. It was winter, so everything was still bathed in darkness. I took my bus from Palmas and got off in Chapultepec, and from there I took another, to Revolución and Avenida Jalisco. From there, I walked the remaining two blocks to school. In the courtyard of the prevocational, the lists of students were tacked to the walls. I found my name, and walked to the corresponding classroom on the second floor.

I found myself in an entirely new world. It was very different from Colegio Israelita. The school was located in what was once an old shoe factory, Carlos B. Zetina, in Tacubaya, which had been very important during the Porfiriato. The buildings date from that era and looked as though they hadn't seen a single repair since its expropriation in 1923.

I found myself in another Mexico, or rather, I found myself in the real Mexico. The Mexico of Colegio Israelita was practically an illusion.

Mexico is a country of mestizos, resulting from the mix of indigenous peoples with white Spanish conquistadors.

The country claims to boast a society in which no racial discrimination exists. Perhaps, with regard to official matters, this is true; but in day to day life, in practice, it's an altogether different story. Nevertheless, there was a truly indigenous president, Zapotec Benito Juárez (1858-1872), Porfirio Díaz, a dark-complected mestizo, although he powdered himself every day after shaving. In government offices, most of the officials were mestizos, but not their bosses.

It surprised me that many, on speaking, classified their partners according to their skin tone. One dark-skinned person was "prieto"; the next "más prieto". And the third, less dark, was called "güero." I was referred to by this last moniker. To be a "güero" was ideal for my classmates, for whom the word "indio" was most disparaging. And, ironically, it was used frequently among these same mestizos. When I'd go to the market to buy something for my aunt, the "marchantas," the salespeople, would always say to me "mire guerito, which fresh fruit would you like today?" To a woman at my side, probably of Spanish origin, they would say: "mire güerita, which wonderful mangos can I get for you?" I noticed how the customary adulation in each transaction was based on the color of the buyer's skin. In the prevocational, everyone was mestizo. In my class of thirty-two students, there were two güeros: Teodoro Hoppenstedt, with whom I established a lifelong friendship, and me.

The first day, we sat on whichever benches were free; everyone had a look of fear on their faces. Later I learned that there was a tradition of shaving the "rookies." We were waiting on the arrival of our first professor. A tall, slim boy was seated to my right. He smiled at me, and later we began to talk. His name was Javier Arriaga Muñiz, and he told me not to worry about the "shaving" rite of passage; neither he nor I was going to get shaved. He had a strong, tall "bodyguard" to protect him. And from that moment on, we were friends, and our friendship evolved into a brotherhood which lasts till this day.

The first class that Monday was Spanish, taught by Profesora Catalina Herrera. After greeting us and introducing herself, she wasted (or, at least, it seemed to me as though she wasted) at least fifteen minutes of class calling roll.

She came to my name, and paused. She attempted to pronounce "Katz," and it sounded strange, but when she tried "Bachruch," she couldn't pronounce it at all.She raised her head and said "Hans, (which she pronounced "Jans") how do you say your full name?" I pronounced it for her, but she couldn't repeat it, and she continued on down the roll. The same happened with Hoppenstedt, whose second last name was Zimbrón-Levy. She called him by his first name, Teodoro.

Second period was math with Professor Enrique Zepeda, an excellent pedagogue who viewed teaching as ministry. Zepeda had been in the revolution; he'd taken orders from General Felipe Ángeles. After the revolution, he was exiled to the United States in1923, along with Prieto Laurens and others, "honored" for choosing not to follow the National Revolutionary Party. He remained in exile until 1930. Seven long years away from home. Instead of teaching math, he dedicated our first day of class to discussing the "sublime Mexico," which is to say, the ideal Mexico of the future: the working man, responsible and full of virtues, just and self-assured. The men would be *caballeros* and the women, *doncellas*, or maidens. He was a man with a gift for words, and spoke like a Roman captain.

Third period was physics. I don't remember the professor's name, but he was very stylish, well-dressed, and the class was quite engaging.

Afterwards we had a fifteen-minute break. Almost no one left the classroom, as everyone was terrified of being shaved.

My first day at my new school ended without much ado—I hadn't been "shaved" yet, thanks to my new friend Javier Arriaga. Of the five professors on my schedule, I'd only met three. The other two hadn't showed up. I'd thought that only students could mess up; but, as it turned out, so could teachers.

Another difference between the Polytechnic Institute and the Colegio Israelita, not to mention my Belgian primary school on the Rue des Six Jetons in Brussels, was that here, the doors were always open. One could enter and leave freely.

Once, when our Ethics teacher failed to show up, we all went to Chapultepec, about four blocks away. *"Ecole Boussoniere"* was known here as "ditching."

Classes were very interesting, especially the workshops. We had four hours of workshop per week: one was smithing with forge and hammer. Another was mechanics shop, where I learned to weld with a gas torch. There was also a carpentry workshop, where I learned to sand and cut wood to make tables. And, lastly, I leanred about electricity, how to make connection nodes like the Boy Scouts, and to wind up motors. In spite of everything, I was a *"lemech"* with two left hands.

Javier introduced me to the school principal, Mr. Verdugo, and to the Assistant Principal Mr. Arredondo. They also taught classes. Although the "most important" person was Sr. Larrañaga, dean of discipline, who manned the entrance to the school but occasionally would allow us to play hooky.

I had a great relationship with my classmates. Everyone was curious about me and my story. They corrected my Spanish when I misspoke, but they always played fair and never made fun of my mistakes.

April 2, 1947 was my one year anniversary of moving to Mexico. While living in Brussels, I'd never thought I'd someday find myself in a country so vibrant, culturally, politically, and artistically.

I experienced so much more than I could have hoped for. A recently-politicized country, eager to make manifest what was fought for during the social revolution initiated in 1910. It's interesting that in Mexico there were no communist or socialist parties organized or comprised by the masses. Yes, there were numerous labor movements, like la Casa del Obrero Mundial, founded in 1923, from which emerged leaders like Luis Morones and, later, Vicente Lombardo Toledano, creator and leader of the Confederación de Trabajadores Mexicanos, known as CTM.

There was a group of left-wing intellectuals known as "Salon Komunisten" who had a great deal of influence on the government, who often received appointments, including ministerial positions. One might say that, apart from Elías Calles, President of Mexico between 1924 and 1928, the government was largely left-wing, in some cases leaning toward socialism, advocating the expropriation of churches and convents. Unfortunately, these weren't always converted into libraries or schools: sometimes they were turned into parking lots.

In Europe of 1946, very little was known of Mexico. Europeans roughly knew about Mexican history, and, more recently, the Mexican Revolution, but only anecdotally. They were familiar with various personalities like Emiliano Zapata, Francisco Villa, "the bandit," but nothing more. It was known that Mexico was a wealthy country with an impoverished population and that they were in possession of an abundance of petroleum, a resource expropriated by English and North American bigwigs who were pioneers of the oil industry.

The expropriation of oil companies El Águila and Standard in 1938 gave way to the creation of a state monopoly, Petróleos Mexicanos, PEMEX. To compensate the original owners, a national appeal was organized. The Mexican people, along with a number of socialites and village women, contributed money and jewelry to help in any way they could, a gesture of solidarity with the Mexican government.

PEMEX is a matter of national pride for the Mexican people, or at least it was for my classmates. It's also a matter of faith and hope for all, to have recovered national sovereignty and control of this resource, which had formerly been in the hands of private foreign investors.

In the countryside, there was a cooperative—a communal agricultural production center—a type of "Koljosz" in the Russian style. There were cooperatives for the fishing industry as well, and also for the processing of sugarcane, as well as for minerals. These co-ops had broad financial support from the state. Often, money was lost, usually due to corruption or disorganized administration.

There were also well-organized unions for electricians, oil workers, and sugar mill workers. University and Polytechnic students were very political and, obviously, leftists.

Back then, I noticed that although the population was almost entirely Catholic—and very devout—the government was non-religious. In contrast to other Latin American countries, no president or secretary of state was publically seen attending church, although at times their wives could be seen privately attending mass.

The Revolution broke out in 1910 without any concrete political ideology—as a bourgeois political movement beneath the banner of no re-election—headed by Francisco I. Madero, from a family of landowners, one of the richest families in the country, who owned vineyards and vast tracts of land in the north of Mexico. Madero, like his followers, was against the policy of reelection. They initially wanted to overthrow the Porfiriato and its exponent General Díaz, who'd been in power for almost forty years.

After having read several books on this topic, I came to a conclusion that the system of government was more like a monarchy than a republic.

"In Mexico, nothing happens until it happens," said Porfirio Diaz when the Revolution broke out. Among other things, the Revolution fought against the Church, which owned large tracts of land, convents, and churches throughout the country, evangelizing and accumulating vast riches since the time of the conquistadors. It was the most powerful force of capitalism in Mexico, truly second in command, and the goal of the Revolution was to relegate it to its more applicable spiritual function.

In 1917, the constitution was promulgated in Querétaro, Mexico, reaffirming the separation between Church and State. This constitution is, to this day, one of the most progressive and enlightened in the New World.

But Mexico, as a people, would never abandon Catholicism. The veneration of the national patron saint, the Virgin of Guadalupe, is and has always been the essence of the country's religious life. Every December 12th, pilgrimages are organized from every corner of the country to the sanctuary of La Villa. The accompanying festivities are most impressive. Thousands of villagers and farmers would walk, sometimes for days, until they arrived and prostrated themselves before the image of the Virgin in the Basílica de Guadalupe, located in el Cerro del Tepeyac, near the capital. All of this is well-documented in the film "Que Viva México" by the Soviet filmmaker Sergei Eisenstein (1934).

One little-known fact about Mexico is the contribution to its cultural life by Irish immigrants like the O'Farrils, the O'Gormans, O'Learys, O'Heas, O'Reillys, O'Sullivans, etc, all of whom were descendants of Irish Catholics. Many of them were involved in the Battle of San Patricio, and fought alongside Mexicans in the battles waged in favor of the independence of Texas in 1847. These brave youths preferred to fight on the Catholic Mexican side, the Guadalupanos, than live under the government of Anglo-Protestants. After the defeat suffered by Antonio López de Santana, they retreated with the Mexicans and remained living in Mexico.

Among those descended from these people were two brothers: the painter and architect Juan O'Gorman, and the historian Edmundo O'Gorman—among his works was "La Invasión de América."

There were also the O'Farril brothers, important industrialists from Puebla. Romulo O'Farril, part of the same family, was founder of the Novedades newspaper, and later became the vice president of Televisa.

Another group of immigrants that stands out is the Lebanese, who arrived en Masse from 1880 to 1890, long before the Jews. The "Bled" migration reached its peak in the 20's, as the Ottoman Empire was crumbling. In Mexico, they became known simply as "Árabes." They are descendants of the Phoenicians, and are mostly Maronite Christians. Some became Catholic after arriving in

Mexico. Physically, many of them resembled Mexicans, and so they didn't appear foreign.

Most of them began working in business and moneylending, like many Jews. Some rapidly achieved unparalleled economic success. Many of them settled permanently in various provinces, where they live to this day. Puebla, Merida, Coatzacoalcos, Torreon, Chetumal, Monterrey, and others.

Many Lebanese began to achieve notoriety in cinema, such as important director Miguel Zacarias and his producer brother Mario. Jose Yazbek, Antonio Matuk, Antonio Helu, Said Slim, and Jorge Trad also worked in this budding industry. Gaspar Henaine "Capulina", Antonio Badu, and Mauricio Garces were all popular actors. Tufic Yazbek, renowned photographer, worked in Mexico City.

Others achieved great success in the industrial and commercial fields: the Ganems began the Rayovac battery factory; the Simons, the silk factory La Joya. The Rihans the pen company Esterbrook; the Marocs, the Mariscal and Manhattan shirts; the Yazbeks found success in intimate apparel; Miguel Abed in textiles. The Aboumrads managed a bank. Fajer was the primary manufacturer of knitwear in the country. The Slims owned many stores through the downtown area, and were also active in the real estate business.

Neguib Simon was the owner of many movie theaters throughout the Republic. He also participated in the construction of la Plaza de Toros Mexico, located on la Avenida de los Insurgentes, in the capital.

Many Lebanese living in Mexico associated themselves with the Jews, like the Beja with the Aboumrad; the Zaga with the Fajer, etc. The relationship between these two groups was a strong one, a solid bond of friendship, and, above all, mutual respect.

There was an Orthodox Church, where Maronite Lebanese worshipped alongside the Greeks. As far as I remember there was never a Muslim Mosque.

After the last day of class, Javier invited me to his house, which was within walking distance from school on Calle Sinaloa. The Arriaga Muñiz family consisted of Javier's father (also named Javier), a railroad worker at FF.NM.MM. Mexicans inherited this form of abbreviation from the Spanish, repeating the first letter of a capitalized word to indicate it was plural. For instance, la Secretaria de Relaciones Exteriores was SS.RR.EE. Javier Arriaga worked for the weigh station in Buenavista. His wife Doña Consuelo, was a homemaker. There were four sisters: Guadalupe "the baby", Consuelo, Lila, and Angelita. They took me in as a son, offering me food and asking me about my life. Mexican hospitality customs were very sincere. "Esta es tu casa," they said to me, as soon as I walked in the door.

"Now, don't forget, this is your home, too," they told me when they said goodbye. I was struck by the kindness and courtesy of the Mexican people.

I also took note of the large clay Michoacán pot in the entryway of their home, through which standing water was filtered. At that time, people in Mexico City were accustomed to drinking rainwater. It was potable and could be drunk without concern.

We spent many pleasant hours chatting, and then my friend brought me to the bus stop in Reforma. I had to return to my aunt and uncle's house before seven in the evening.

This was the first Mexican family I'd met, and their hospitality surprised me, though it was a normal occurrence here, as I learned as the years passed. I've lived many years alongside them, and they've always made me feel at home. As though I'm part of their family.

One autumn afternoon in September, I went to Calle Amsterdam in la Colonia Hipódromo-Condesa. Better known as the Parque Mexico where a British style hippodrome had existed since 1913. During the Revolution, this spectacle was brought to an end. A North American in the real estate business received a grant to urbanize the extensive grounds between Avenida de los Insurgentes and the Plaza de Toros, where today stands the Palacio de Hierro Durango where the Hacienda de Miravilla stood until the end of last century.

The hippodrome was called "De la Condesa" in honor of the Condesa de Miravalle, who owned the land, also known as la Hacienda de la Condesa. In Calle Amsterdam was the local B'nei-Akivo. All the "grine" or newcomers, were invited.

There, I met Isaac Kelerstein, with whom I instantly became friends, and we remain friends to this day. Isaac is also a concentration camp survivor. His left arm bears the infamous tattooed number. He had a brother, Israel, who was also in the camps. I also met the Flegman brothers, from Hungary, and Moishe Shuster, a Krasnaya Armiya captain; Leon Bukrinsky, soldier from the red army; Luzer Stein from Bichava. I met Shoshana from Kovno, who later married Mr. Cimet. I also met Dunia, Sr. Wasserstrom's wife, both of whom were survivors of Auschwitz-Birkenau. I ran into Manya, whom I'd met in the Goldenberg's house. There were many other people, all of whom had recently arrived in Mexico, whose names I no longer remember. The idea behind this social activity was to have us meet one another. We would periodically reunite as a group. We formed a *chevre*.

At the Polytechnic there was a society of students, and Javier Arriaga was elected president. Aside from political meetings there weren't many social activities for students. Professor Enrique Zepeda, The Apostle, as I referred to him previously, took the initiative to form a club for excursions called el Ilhuicamina, or Aztec Archer of the Sun. It was to my great surprise that I was voted "Tlatoani," the club's president. Me, a foreigner, a güero who hardly knew how to speak proper Spanish? Apparently, they had faith in me. They knew about my scouting background, which is why I'd won the election.

Enrique Zepeda poured his soul into this endeavor. Many times he invited those of us on the executive committee to his house. Like at the Arriagas, he told us the first time we came: "Muchachos, take note: this is your home." There, we drew up the statutes and regulations of the club, during "tamaladas" in which his wife and daughter served us tamales, Aztec-style frothing hot chocolate without milk, and different kinds of atole. The result was a political exercise that was also a wonderful time for all.

One Sunday we organized an excursion to Monte de las Cruces. We boarded a train in Buenavista bound for "Salazar" where we set out on a hike along the same route traversed by Padre Miguel Hidalgo, head of the Independence armies fighting against the Royalists, in turn commanded by General Calleja. Hidalgo, flashing his banner of Guadalupe, slowed down his people to avoid possible riots in the city. This was in 1810.

Finally—after three years of bloodshed—an alliance was agreed upon, whereby Mexico obtained its independence from Spain on September 27th, 1821. The Trigarante Army—at the command of Agustin de Iturbide and Viceroy O'Donoju—marched triumphantly into Mexico City. Mexico was independent!

Our excursions with Professor Zepeda were more than just trips; they were challenging and stimulating classes on Mexican history. Zepeda recounted historical facts as though they'd happened yesterday. He had a brilliant and vast body of historical knowledge and was conscious of the force of history in our generation.

After eating—we always brought sandwiches—some of us went horseback riding and others started a bonfire. Salazar is a forest east of the city, with a cold climate. These excursions were extremely popular among the Poli students. At times we numbered forty, sometimes even seventy, students.

During our December vacation, we organized a camping trip for four days in Tecolutla, Veracruz. Our civics teacher Raúl Fernandez, who was also chief of transportation for the Secretary of National Defense—most teachers had two jobs, as a teaching salary was not enough to live on—procured for us a bus with a driver and everything. We stopped in Huasteca first, at the hydroelectric station in Necaxa; later, passing through Villa Juarez, where coffee was grown, we reached the coast of the Gulf of Mexico. What landscapes, what a variety of climates! We set up our tents, also courtesy of the army, and went to sleep.

When I caught my first crab in a trap, I proudly presented it to our "cook," the young Luis Valdes, excellent speaker who went on to become the Mexican Ambassador in Germany in 1982. We threw the crab into a pot of boiling water and covered it, anticipating the delicious meat we were about to eat. After some fifteen minutes, I went to check on our succulent meal—but, to my surprise, I found that it had escaped from the pot!

We had a wonderful time. We ate seafood and rabbits. Of course, none of this was kosher.

I was truly quite happy in Mexico. Much more so than I could have imagined. Of course, I had issues living with my aunt and uncle, but everything else was great.

I had begun my career path at the Poli. I had great relationships with my classmates and my teachers. Above all, I was surprised by how they'd received me, a foreigner who didn't speak the language very well. I was received with such warmth, and people went above and beyond to help me: they explained something when I didn't understand. They accompanied me everywhere. Incredibly, I had friends already! The Jewish families I met here were very hospitable. They wanted me to tell them about myself and my experiences. They listened to me. After two years, I had a variety of friends and I felt welcome in their homes.

Isaac Kelerstein had arrived in Mexico in February 1947. He first worked with his uncle Najman Zaidenweber, as his father did. After a short while, he began working independently, and started a dressmaking shop on Calle del Carmen. That's where I met him. In his shop there was a long table—about four meters—where he cut pieces of cloth which he'd later give to seamstresses to sew. He worked sunrise to sundown in his shop, where he also lived with his brother and his father. At night, I'd stop in and we'd go eat at la Copa de Leche on San Juan de Letrán, today Eje Central Lazaro Cárdenas, a Chinese owned café, near the Zócalo. Another time we went "to the movies"—or, rather, to find girls. We also loved to go to the Teatro Blanquita, at that time very famous for its comedies and musicals. Joaquin Pardave, Jasso, Resortes, Viruta, and Capulina all performed there.

During our visits to the theater we visited Isaac Ivker who played in the orchestra. We also frequented more "serious" theaters, like Manolo Fabregas. There, we saw "A Streetcar Named Desire" and "Of Mice and Men," directed by the Japanese Seki Sano. Among the actors were Virginia Fabregas, Manolo's grandmother, and Fanny Schiller, her mother, an Argentine Jew. I also remember the newly released "La Gran Dama" by Salvador Novo.

When we were out late, we went to the "Caldos de Indianilla" on the Colonia de los Doctores. Near the old electric tram yards of the now-defunct American Electrical Tramway Company, inaugurated by General Porfirio Diaz in 1900, and which was now Transportes Eléctricos del D.F., we found a small makeshift hole in the wall restaurant that served delicious chicken soup. Chickens hung from the ceiling, already de-feathered and gutted. The soup was served in a glazed earthenware bowl, with fragrant accompaniments, herbs like oregano, cilantro, onion, chili, and lemon. The soup itself contained garbanzo beans, rice, and shredded chicken, and it cost two pesos. People also came here for soup to nurse their hangovers.

La Plaza Garibaldi was near Avenida San Juan de Letrán, a place known for the best Mexican mariachi music. The plaza was named after Guiseppe Garibaldi, the Italian revolutionary, head of the Redshirts in Genoa. There as a monument dedicated to him on Avenida Chapultepec. Garibaldi was in Mexico a short while between 1840 and 1842, and afterwards went to Brazil, and died in Isola Di Caprera.

Near Garibaldi Plaza was the capital city's red light district, which could be found on Calle Organo and Dos de Abril. There were "women of ill repute" on other streets throughout the city. There were also brothels, discretely known as *casas de citas*, one of the most famous of which was *"La Casa de la Bandida,"* or Bandit House, frequented by politicians and the well-to-do. This was situated at Durango and Salamanca, a block from the Plaza de Toros.

We generally went out with four or five friends, all of them "grine," or newcomers. A very special friendship was born between Isaac and I; we discovered we had much more in common than we'd previously imagined. We were both European, we'd both endured the war in some way or another. We both knew what happened. We were both profoundly interested in the history of our people. We spoke Yiddish to each other, as I had now mastered the language, and was comfortable reading and writing in it. Isaac was a big-hearted young man, and incredibly sensitive. He was hard-working and a good businessman, and through his hard work, he quickly made a name for himself. *"Mazl is a gute zach, ich will nur a bisele."* To be lucky is a wonderful thing, and I just want a little." We became best friends.

This was not the type of friend my aunt and uncle thought suited me. They probably wished I'd become friends with the Rockefellers, Vanderbilts, or Rothschilds, whom I obviously didn't know, nor was I interested in knowing people like this. But deep down they reproached me for this friendship that was too "Jewish."

The high holidays came around once again. Since I went downtown almost every day, I decided to go to the Nidje-Israel Temple on la Calle de Justo Sierra. Back then, this was the center of the Ashkenazi Jewish community . There was also a kosher restaurant there.

The night before Yom Kippur, during the Kol Nidre prayer, the temple was completely packed, to the point where not a single person more could fit inside, although somehow I was able to get around the Shamash, who reluctantly let me enter without a ticket.

The Kol Nidre prayer, which originated during the time of persecutions and forced expulsions in Spain, is more than just a prayer; it's a confession of the Jewish soul forced to recant their fate. And, from there, an oration of repentance and sorrow. Another transcendental night prayer is what is called "Al Chet," in which one enumerates his sins, either intentional or unintentional, in the hopes he'll be pardoned by G-d, our only true judge, the only one who can decide who will live or who will die, who will be successful, and who will fail.

It's interesting to note that in the Jewish religion, the pardon which G-d eventually grants is in no way an automatic pardon. On the contrary, a Jew must confess, present his sins to G-d, and he must recognize them first—this part is very important—and later leave them in a kind of administrative office, for G-d to review. The pardon—if it comes to pass—comes much later.

Isaac didn't attend Synagogue. Like other Jews burdened by how tremendously they'd suffered in the camps, he was convinced that G-d had abandoned him. Where was he when the Jews were mistreated and massacred? A difficult question to answer, no doubt. Isaac waited for me outside of Temple. The day after after the Closing Prayer marking the end of a twenty-four hour fast, we went to eat dinner.

I attended a wedding at that very same temple, Justo Sierra. Isaac knew the groom and had invited me. The Nidjei Israel community was traditional Orthodox, as was the bride's family. Before the ceremony, the men from the couples' families gathered in a room within the temple, a kind of chapel, in order to celebrate the Tnoyim, the marriage commitment. In this ceremony were specified the conditions of the matrimony: what each of the two young people would bring to their marriage.

The Tnoyim, the couple once married, were inseparable. The celebration was concluded with the breaking of a plate, usually a porcelain plate, which sealed the pact, in remembrance of the destruction of the Temple of Jerusalem.
After this, the religious ceremony began, under the chuppah. Inside the sanctuary there were a lot of people, all elegantly dressed for the occasion. At the Justo Sierra

synagogue there was no gallery. The area reserved for the women, the Ezrat Ha-Nashim, was to the left. The men sat to the right. On the Bima was the chuppah. The hazzan holding a glass of wine, sang the blessings. Then the family, the parents, siblings and grandparents walked around the bride and groom seven times. Then the rabbi said the seven blessings, the bride and groom drank the wine and finally the groom used his right foot to step on a wine glass wrapped in a napkin. That is in remembrance of the destruction of the Temple.

I heard that a Jewish-Mexican friend had passed away. I had never been to a Levaya, a Jewish funeral. Simply, my mind blocked out that idea. Not because I am a Cohen- it had been explained to me that Cohanim were not allowed to enter a Bet Olam, or cemetery. No, it wasn't that. It must have been something inside me that told me not to go. Maybe it was because there was no cemetery where I could pray at my parents' graves. I don't know.

After the vote in favor of the creation of Palestine, the Security Council met several times and the vote was unanimous. England accepted a timetable, through which they agreed to end their mandate and abandon Palestine on May 14, 1948.

The joy in Tel-Aviv, the largest Jewish city at the time, at the Kibbutzim and the Moshavim was short lived. Now, they had to plan and organize their defense. What would the Arabs do? Would they stay with their arms crossed? That was the Jews' biggest concern.

The British continued their blockade of the coasts. The Arabs, for their part, had many advantages. They could receive, and were receiving, aid and arms through Jordan, Syria, and Egypt. The proclamation of a jihad in the Holy Land was a calling to all neighboring states.

There were many intense months of emotion for the Yishuv. Then, as in the time of the Maccabees, the Jews took up arms in defense of their own land; all less than fifty years after the publication of the book by Theodor Herzl, *Der Judenstaat*. He was a type of modern prophet, who foresaw fifty years prior the resurgence of the Jewish State, sovereign and free. It was he who said "Im tirtzy ein dzu agada," or "If you will it will not be a dream."

In Basil, where the first Zionist Congress took place in December of 1897, after leaving the venue, Herzl declared "Today I created the Jewish State. Many will laugh at me, but probably within five years and surely within fifty years it will be a reality."

The Jewish Agency who had become the provisional government, secretly invited—since it did not want to gain the attention of the worldwide public opinion—Jewish volunteers from the entire world. There arrived pilots from the USA, marines from France, artillery experts from Canada, radio and telephone technicians from Holland, and ballistic specialists from the UK. Almost all had served in their countries' armies during the Second World War.

Secretly, too, so as not to arouse suspicion from the British, the Jews of the Yishuv trained for combat. And 1947 came to a close.

I finished my first year at the Poli with good grades. To finish the school year, the Club de Excursionistas took a last trip, of three days, to Cuernavaca. Really to Palmira where there was a teachers' institute. Profesor Zepeda put us in contact with them and we were invited to visit them. We brought our volleyball team for an exhibition game and also planned a round table to discuss problems with education. Zepeda had the good idea to include the Dean, Ing. Verdugo, with which this became more of a sanctioned trip.

We traveled by train. We arrived in Palmira just before sunset. At 6 o'clock in the morning, the next day, we went to the salute of the flag. I had to give a speech on behalf of the Poli. In my bad Spanish I did as best I could. To this day, whenever I see any of my former classmates, they will remind me of my speech. The audience started to laugh when I said: "It is a privilege for us to be here for the raising and lowering of the Mexican flag."

We spend wonderful days with the girls, who were between thirteen and eighteen years of age. I had invited Isaac Kelerstein and Berl Golomb so that they could see the "real" Mexico.

During the vacations I continued to work for my uncle, with whom I continued to learn more about the business. With what I was paid I was able to more than cover my expenses.

Even though I did not study at Colegio Israelita any longer, I continued to meet with some of the people I had befriended there. Mostly with the Golomb family, at whose house I spent some time, especially with Berl. They motivated me to stay involved with the community, especially with Yiddishkeit. They were obsessed with the topic, and they spoke about the Yivo, the Academy of the Jewish language. They insisted that any Jew who did not speak that language was not really a Jew.

Abraham Golomb was a well prepared and cultured man. He was fluent in Russian, Hebrew, English, and Yiddish. Along with his wife Rifke they injected dynamism at the school and the parents' association. All this to preserve Yiddishkeit.

At the beginning of 1947 they founded in Mexico the youth organization Hemshech, which means community. Basically it was comprised of students of Colegio Israelita. They asked me to head the group, along with Jave Berman and Taibele Weisman. And with this I found myself quite busy creating scout type programs for the teenagers. We met at the Kadima on Avenida Mexico, across from the park. We had meetings every Saturday morning. Sometimes we would celebrate Shabbat together and on Sundays we would go on trips to Xochimilco, Cerro de la Estrella, Xitle, and Desierto de los Leones.

At the end of 1947, we decided to create a literary group, "Yugnt Shriftn", whose first edition was published that Rosh Hashana. I contributed two articles. One about the liberation and the other about the situation of Jews in postwar Europe.

Those were my first published articles. I was, by the way, very proud of that.I opted for a pseudonym. I had to somehow define my name. I had left the name Hans behind, except at my uncle's home and with their friends. I did not like the name as it sounded too German. Peter was the name that I was known by at the Poli, but that too sounded too German.

Jean, my name during the war, sounded too foreign and above all it did not match the name on my immigration papers. So, I chose the name Joel, which at the time I believed it to be my paternal grandfather's name.

I did not know that in reality his name was Juer. I had nobody to ask. My aunt did not know or professed not to know. Sometimes she would reprimand me, "Du und deine Juden" —"You and your Jews" —as if I was speaking about a group of lepers. It seems that her disdain for all that was Jewish was constant.

I signed my first article as Joel Katz. And thus was born what frequently and during many years became a confusing issue with my friends and later with my children. What was my real name?

For my second article, I adopted the pseudonym Yud Kojav. Yud for Jewish and Kojav for star—the Jewish star, which during the war the Nazis had used as an infamous symbol. The star by the Stern group, a word which means star in Yiddish and in German, which I admired in their fight for the Jewish liberation in Eretz Israel.

The Hemshech, "A glid un der goldener keit"—a link in the Jewish gold chain—worked well, at least in the beginning. What is more, we even organized concerts in the Palacio Chino on Calle Humboldt. I liked above all the Oneg Shabbat at Kadima. We would sing Jewish songs like *Hevenu Shalom Aleichem*, *Oyfn Pripetchik*, *Shein vi di Levone*, *Main Shtetele Belz*, *Der Rebe Elimelech* and many more. But it did not last too long. In 1949 the group ceased to exist due to lack of interest. Or maybe it was because of a lack of inspiration from the leaders, myself included.

It was a season of much creativity. I again felt in my element organizing activities for the youth, which reminded me of the work I had done with Rosh Kvutzah in Brussels.

During that time, organizing the Hemshech and the publishing of the first and last edition of "Yugnt Shriftn", I had a short relationship with Taibele Weissman. A red haired young woman, she was quite attractive. We spent a lot of time together planning and editing the literary magazine.

Of course, she was the expert in Yiddish and I was the apprentice. We would often go out for coffee or, more often, ice cream. When we went to the movies for the first time, cloaked in darkness, we declared our love.

The interesting part of the relationship is that between us we only spoke Yiddish, as she was one of Abraham Golomb's protégés and as extremist as he was in linguistic terms. "A Yid wos redt nit kain Yiddish, is nit kain Yid". Our conversation was mostly structured on the sentences used in novels from the twenties, obviously old fashioned like those if Yud Leibush Peretz and Sholem Aleichem. We would say "Ich bren mit libe far dir," I burn with love for you, or "Lomir zij tzekushn," we should kiss.

The recreation of the Yiddish tongue reminded me of the Holocaust and all that the world had lost forever. These were the words that would have been used by a million and a half children massacred as they reached puberty!

The Jewish work "Di Yidishe Velt" covered the Baltic Sea, the North Sea, the Adriatic, the forests of Alsace, the steppes of Ukraine. The Jew who decided to travel throughout this land would always find someone he could communicate with in this language and spend the Sabbath with a Jewish family who would have considered this an honor.

This "world" was destroyed, as we know, by fire and machine guns. The trees that had flowered over centuries were yanked from their roots, the synagogues burned to the ground. A peoplewas massacred and, with it, the Ashkenazi culture that had flowered for more than a millennium.

Kurt Berci invited me one Saturday to Kurt Stavenhagen's house in San Angel, who agreed to show us his Pre-Hispanic art collection. There we met up with Paul Westheim, an art critic of Judeo German art, who had arrived in Mexico in 1941. There he specialized in Pre-Hispanic art. He was a well-prepared man.

During the Weimar Republic he published his critique of Oskar Kokoschka, the popular Austrian painter, and also wrote about Egon Schiele and Gustav Klimt, both controversial artists as well. He escaped to Berlin, then to Paris. There he wrote his novel *Rassenschandle,* or racial embarrassment, published by a group of German refugees.

In 1935 he was stripped of his German citizenship, along with Berthold Brecht and Lion Feuchtwanger. He arrived in Mexico in 1941 thanks to a visa obtained for him by the Mexican Consul in Marseille, Gilberto Bosques. This was a liberal and humane man, practically the "Savior Angel" for many Jewish and Spanish refugees.

In Mexico, Westheim was already considered an expert in the field. He traveled and spoke at many North American universities. That was his modus vivendi.

For me this visit was a sort of revelation. Kurt Stavenhagen was showing us his collection while Westheim spoke about the pieces and their history. There were figurines from Colima, Costa Chica, La Venta, some Mayan and some from Teotihuacan. The most impressive was the collection of clay toys. There was also a collection of clay figurines showing all kinds of illnesses, from dental illnesses to orthopedic deficiencies. And, of course, many fertility deities.

It was an honor to meet these two German Jews, both scholars and lovers of the art in their new adopted country.

Sometimes I would go shopping with my Aunt Else. At the time there were few delicatessens in Mexico. There were some downtown like La Puerta del Sol on Avenida 16 de Septiembre and La Negrita in Calle Lopez. These stores were owned by Spaniards who carried many items for their Mexican, French, and Spanish clientele.

There were at least two delicatessens owned by German families who had immigrated to Mexico before Hitler. One owned by Señora Lukens, where they carried Dutch ham, Lebkuchen, sauerkraut and delicious sausages, hams, olives, Tilsiter cheese, and French pates.

For the Jewish clientele there were the Tafelov and Burakoff stores in Colonia Hipodromo. They carried "Jewish" or dark bread, rye bread, Lekach, kosher wine, sour pickles, halvah, chrain (horseradish), gefilte fish, and all the delicacies that these immigrant families desired. For the German, Austrian, Hungarian, and Czech Jews there was a store owned by Señora Bruder on Oaxaca Street and Parque España, were I went with my aunt. This, of course, was not a kosher store.

One time, we were at Señora Bruder's store, waiting our turn. Ahead of us was a short and stout Jewish man who spent time looking through the refrigerator's glass door. He then asked her, without raising his head, "Frau Bruder, hat ir a sheine brust?" The woman—knowing my aunt was there—replied while looking down at her chest, which by the way was ample, "Ja ich glaube schon." One was referring to the meat and the other, having some fun, referred to her own.

Señor and Señora Bruder—Karl and Edith Bruder—had a daughter who was about 10 years old. A beautiful blond girl whom I played with when I accompanied my aunt and uncle to visit their house on Calle Amsterdam. I remember that she was a very sensitive young girl and with whom I felt at ease. Today, that girl, Hanni Bruder, is the owner of the prestigious and popular Restaurante Bondy on Calle Galileo in Polanco. To this day we are friends.

By the way, Bondy was the last name of a Jewish Austrian chef who had arrived in Mexico in 1939 and had been hired by General Enriques to be the chef at this luxurious hotel in San Jose Purua in Michoacan.

Since I had become friends with Isaac Kelerstein and with the Grines, we would often go swimming to the Baños del Peñon on the old road to Puebla. With three pesos for admission and two extra for a private changing room, which we shared, we could spend all day there swimming and sunbathing. Ever since I had learned how to swim at the "Guay," I loved that sport.

That is also were I became friends with Moise Shuster, Henryk Ciuk, and Leon Bukrinsky.

The climate in Mexico City was marvelous. It was almost always between 18 and 20 degrees Celsius. It was never too hot, the temperature would reach 28 degrees Celsius for three or four weeks during the year. During the winter months, January and February, the temperature would go down to 10 degrees Celsius and that did not last more than three weeks. The sky, at that time, was clear. The name of *Region mas transparente del aire*, or the most transparent region in the air, was coined by Alexander Von Humboldt upon visiting the city. Also called "*Ciudad de los Palacios*," or the city of palaces, which was still a reality.

From el Peñon you could see the volcanoes. The other side of the city was visible. Mexico still afforded its beautiful panoramic views, man had still not destroyed its beauty.

From 1918 to 1920, when the large Jewish migrations to Mexico started, the commercial life was centered downtown around the Zócalo. From there the picturesque donkey-pulled trams would depart.

By that time the city had a million and a half inhabitants. There had been Jews in Mexico since the time of the Conquest. It is said that there were two "conversos" who arrived with Hernan Cortes and who were convicted of being Judaizers. Since 1580 there had been Jewish converts living in this country.

Now in this century, Wilhelm Kahlo, a Jew from Arad in the Austro-Hungarian Empire, and Frida Kahlo's father, tells that upon his arrival to Mexico, he had worked for a German Jew, Gottfried Loeb, owner of La Perla jewelry store. Many years later, Franz Mayer arrived, a scholar and collector of many works of arts.

At the end of the century, too, there were Sephardic Jews from Istanbul, like the Montequio, Pappo, and Benveniste families. Many jewelry stores in Calle Plateros, then San Francisco and Francisco I Madero, were owned by Jewish families. Many of them attended the festivities surrounding Mexico's Independence Centennial in 1910.

I remember Señor Arturo Stein, a jeweler originally from Hamburg, who had immigrated to Guatemala where he later died. Señor Stein told me that in one of his visits to Mexico during the Centennial celebration, he had visited many jewelry stores, among them one owned by an Alsatian Jew. He spoke in detail about the festivities and parties hosted by the great families of the city, the parades with the army in French style uniforms. All the important people of the world had come together in the city. Many of these families spent long seasons in Europe. He told me that before coming to Mexico, he had been in San Francisco where he had had suits made especially for the occasion. Black tie was obligatory in the Mexican high society.

Of course, he told me about General Porfirio Diaz, of Limantour, of Justo Sierra and Rincon Gallardo, all of whom he had met.

When important groups of Jews arrived, first to Veracruz and then to the capital, they would settle in Calles de Jesus Maria, Del Carmen, Corregidora, Correo Mayor, and Republica de Cuba. As their economic situation improved, sometime in the thirties, they would move to the new neighborhoods which were just beginning to appear, like Alamos and Hipodromo Condesa. The Jews that came from the Arab countries, those from Aleppo and Damascus, settled in Colonia Roma. They built several synagogues there, one on Calle de Cordoba and another on Calle Queretaro. Many years later, those who had become more successful moved to Polanco.

Much later there were some who settled in the new neighborhoods of Chapultepec Heights, now known as Lomas and Tecamachalco, where my good friend Boris Albin built many homes and would refer to it as "Lomas de Galilea." Later the migration extended to Bosques de las Lomas and Bosques de la Herradura.

When I arrived in Mexico the German immigrants lived principally in Tacubaya and San Pedro de los Pinos. French immigrants lived in Colonia del Valle. The immigrants from Spain and Lebanon lived also in Colonia del Valle, and those who were most successful lived in Polanco.

One of the more relevant figures among the immigrants was Don Luis de Carbajal. He was governor of what is now the state of Nuevo Leon and was sent to his death during the Inquisition. His nephew, Don Luis de Carbajal, "El Mozo", was a mystic and poet, as well as a sort of Rabbi. He later changed his name to Josef Lumbroso and also died at the stake at Plaza de Santo Domingo. Al Kiddush HaShem.

To this day in the south of the city, there is an area known as El Cerro del Judio, which shows some Jewish presence in Mexico.
I learned of an interesting Mexican custom. On Thursday of Corpus, Don Javier Arriaga took his son Javier and me to the Zócalo and then to the Cathedral. At the Zócalo there was an unexpected spectacle: hundreds of children dressed in native garb, with their parents, waiting for the Archbishop. He came out dressed in his priestly garments. Since he was not allowed to leave the cathedral, he gave his blessing from behind the iron gates. Ever since 1917, no priest was allowed in public while wearing religious garb.

In Palestine, things were heating up for the British. The existence and activities of the Palmach, headed by Eliahu Golomb, was a threat. The troops were ready. The Irgun Zvai Leumi, headed by Menachem Begin, blew up two floors of the King David Hotel in Jerusalem. Among its victims was Count Folke Bernadotte, an observer from the United Nations, as well as thirty two officials from the "Occupying Forces", which is how Begin referred to them.

One act, even more brazen, was carried out by the Irgun at the fortress of Acco, on the northern coast of Israel. On May 4, 1947, Dov Cohen, along with a group of fighters wearing British uniforms, penetrated the fortress built by the Crusaders, rebuilt by the Turks and under siege by Bonaparte in 1803. It had been converted into a prison by the British. Once they reached the courtyard they placed dynamite charges and burst open the main entrance. In less than twenty minutes, and after getting hold of the keys to the cells, they liberated fourteen prisoners. Most were from the Irgun but there were some from the Haganah.

The act was a reprisal for hanging four members of the Stern: Dov Gruner, Yechiel Drezner, Mordechai Alkahi and Eliezer Kashani, who had all carried out the bombing at the King David Hotel.

In April 1948, troops from the Irgun and Lechi attacked Dair Yassin from where the
Palestinians attacked convoys trying to reach Jerusalem. The head of the Palestinians in that area, Abba el Kadir Al Husseini, was killed along with four hundred inhabitants of the town.

The bloody act, which had been totally unnecessary, was condemned by the majority. Many Palestinians fled the country as they feared the Jews and were told by their leaders that they would soon be able to return. On the other hand, the thousands of refugees were not accepted by their neighbors. Thus was born the problem of the Palestinian refugees, manipulated by the Arab governments. If they had accepted them and assimilated them into their societies, instead of keeping them in refugee camps, history would have been much different.

The morning of May 15, the state of Israel was invaded by the well-armed troops from Syria, Jordan, Iraq, and Egypt. The Jordanian army, led by Glubb Pasha, was the best and most feared. The Egyptian troops were headed by Gamal Abdel Nasser, who many years later, along with other officials like Anwar el Sadat, would defeat the corrupt regime of Farouk. Iraq just sent two volunteer brigades.

Initially, the Arab troops were victorious. The Syrians overtook the Masada and Sha'ar HaGolan kibbutzim, and besieged Degania at the shores of the Kineret. The Egyptians had also besieged the Yad Mordechai kibbutz in the Negev, named after Mordechai Anielewicz, fighter from the Warsaw Ghetto.

The Jordanian legion took over the old Jewish section of Jerusalem. The Jewish residents were allowed to leave. The recently organized Israeli army suffered many losses trying to take over the Latrun police station, a strategic point on the road to Jerusalem.

Incidentally, before the creation of the Tzahal or Israeli Defense Forces, the Irgun had been able to purchase arms from Europe, which arrived on a ship purchased in France and renamed "Altalena" which was the literary pseudonym of Vladimir Zabotinsky, founder of the Betar in Odessa. Said ship was in open seas, close to the coast of Eretz Israel, making time before docking in Yaffo. It had instructions to await the proclamation of the State of Israel before docking. The authorities, upon finding it, ordered it to stop. The new government would take its cargo. The Irgun disagreed. Menachem Begin boarded the Altalena confident that the help of the eight hundred volunteers at the beach would solve the problem.

Two rounds of artillery were fired before Begin, the captain, and the crew abandoned the ship and the new Israeli authorities took over the cargo. Finally it could take charge of all the arms needed for the defense of the new State. The ship was then set afire and sunk within view of Tel Aviv.

The Egyptians conquered, after a long battle, the Yad Mordechai kibbutz and then advanced on Ashdod.

The Israeli army slowly began to achieve its first victories. They were able to bomb and sink the Emir Farouk by Gaza and managed to take over the airport in Lod and the city of Ramallah.

They took Galilee and the city of Nazareth, where Jesus Christ was born, as well as the city of Sfarad. The Jews also suffered many losses while trying to occupy Jenin and Kalkylia. Many fell in the defense of Babel Waad on the road to Jerusalem. Yaffo had been captured by the Irgun.

The battle in Latrun cost many lives, on the road to Jerusalem, where a monument to the War of 1948 as erected.

The Stern group was still active, headed by Fridman Yelin. They specialized in stealing arms from the British bases as well as their Jeeps while disguised in a way that even the British could not tell them apart.

In the meantime, the Arabs were purchasing arms. Palestine was ready for the battle.

The Yishuv, under the mandate, had achieved an impressive social, political, and cultural infrastructure. It is a service organization for all the people. Since 1906, they had superior education. In 1908, Bezalel was founded, a fine arts school. In 1912, the Engineering School, Haifa Technion, was founded.

In 1923, with the presence of Lord Balfour, future Nobel Laureate Albert Einstein, and future President of Israel Chaim Weitzman, the Hebrew University of Jerusalem was opened on Mount Scopus.

In 1925, the "Davar" newspaper of the working class was founded, organized by the General Federation of Land Workers of Israel or Histadrut, which had been in operation since 1920. Also the Kupat Holim, a network of hospitals and clinics was created, something like our Seguro Social which serves all the citizens.

In 1928, the theatrical group "Habima,"which had been founded in Moscow in 1917, started to work in Tel Aviv. In 1936, the Philharmonic Orchestra was formed, thanks to the efforts by Bronislav Huberman, originally from Breslau, with world class musicians from all over the world. The inaugural concert was conducted by Arturo Toscanini, who had fled Italy due to Musolini's persecution of those democratic and free thinking elements in his country. This orchestra would perform in the kibbutzim and moshavot, where there were eager audiences.

In 1938, the national newspaper "Yediot Achronot" began, a moderate to left-wing publication. Its founders were German Jews. That year, too, the "Jerusalem Post," founded by "Yekkes" and published worldwide, started to publish in English. It is, along with the "Jerusalem Report," the most valuable source of information that us Jews in the Diaspora have regarding Israel.

The long-awaited day was finally here, May 14, 1948. At midnight, everyone was on out on the street in Tel-Aviv, Jerusalem, and Haifa. The British High Commissioner, Lord Cunningham, had left. The provisional government was meeting at the Tel Aviv Museum, on Rothschild Avenue, since there was no other large enough building.

The proclamation ceremony took place under a giant photograph of Herzl who, like Moses, had glimpsed the Promised Land from afar. Ben Gurion, on that memorable day—the eighth day of the month of Yiar of the year 5708—proclaimed the independence of the state of Israel.

That proclamation, also known as the Law of Return, invited all Jews from the Diaspora to return to their land.

Meanwhile, I was in Chiapas, invited by a classmate, Alberto Oñate. Teodoro Hoppenstedt, Miguel Ramirez (who was known as "strawberry" because of all the marks on his face), and I traveled together. Since we did not have a lot of money, we traveled on a cargo truck, which left from La Merced, the old city market, towards Arriaga, Chiapas. We made a deal with the driver. He asked us to be there at 4 AM. He would charge us only $15 in pesos each, way less than the cost of a regular bus ticket. The trip turned out to be somewhat uncomfortable as he was transporting metal furniture, such as hospital grade cots. It took us two days to get there, achy and uncomfortable, but we made it.

The trip took us through Cuautla, then Izucar de Matamoros, Oaxaca, then Tehuantepec Isthmus. We stopped at the picturesque town of Juchitán, where I saw for the first time the impressive Tehuana women. Tall and graceful, some were very beautiful and dressed in their local costumes. It was a magnificent spectacle.

There for the first time I tasted mezcal, a potent beverage made from agave, but different from tequila.

At a place along the road known as El Cruce, Alberto and his father awaited our arrival. They came with three horses ready to leave for La Piedad, their ranch.

We spent some unforgettable days. We were very well taken care of. The food was delicious. The second day we hunted deer, which we then ate for dinner. Every day they had fresh Panela cheese, fresh warm milk, and handmade tortillas. For me it was a totally new experience to see how they lived in a Chiapanecan rancho.

Chiapas is one of Mexico's states with the largest indigenous population, comprised of Chontales, Tzotziles, Tzeltales, Quiches, and Lacandones. Each tribe has its own traditional attire and they still pray to their ancestral gods. They are suspicious of authorities. They have been subjugated since the time of the Conquest.

Since 1524, when Cortes took his disastrous expedition to Las Hibueras, taking the last Aztec emperor Cuauhtemoc with him, the situation for the indigenous groups has not improved. The ranch owners are mestizos, Spanish, and, since 1860, German immigrants who created wonderful coffee plantations. It is strange that they take care of the archaeological ruins of the area but do not take care of the descendants of the same people who built them.

Other states with large indigenous populations are Yucatan, with its Mayas; Oaxaca, with its Zapotec and Mixtec people; Michoacan, the old Tzintzuntzan, with its Purepechas; Sonora, with its Yaquis; Chihuahua, with its Tarahumaras; and Jalisco, with its Huicholes. At that time there were approximately six million Indigenous people in the Mexican republic who did not speak Spanish. They tried to Hispanicize and modify their customs. Luckily that has slowly been changing.

The majority of the indigenous people were stripped of their lands and forced to evangelize thanks to the Church. The important thing was, in time of the Conquest, to bring converts to the Lord and territories to the Crown.

In school, my classmates were not all aware of the many different groups of indigenous peoples, something that surprised me; it felt like a lack of solidarity.

We also went hunting for rooks, birds that were jet black but with multicolored reflections, sort of like crows but bigger.

During the first three days my bones hurt, first since we had sat on metal bedframes on the truck and then because of the horseback riding, the only way to get around the ranch.

Now with Alberto's father's station wagon, we drove to San Juan Chamula, to Tuxtla Gutierrez, the state capital, and to San Cristobal de las Casas, named after Bartolome de las Casas. He was the "Protector of the Indians" who tried to protect them from the indignities of the conquest and who had suggested the importation of slaves from Africa, arguing that the slaves were stronger and more resilient. I have no doubt that he wanted to help the Indians, I only question his judgement. To fix one inhumane treatment by replacing it with another.

San Cristobal de las Casas was the most beautiful place I saw in Chiapas. We also visited Arriaga and Tapachula. This last one borders Guatemala, separated by the Suchiate river.

When I heard on the radio about the proclamation of the State of Israel and about the subsequent invasion by the Arab countries, I felt that I had to return to the capital and volunteer to go fight in Palestine. I bid my friends goodbye. Señor Oñate took me to Arriaga where I boarded a train back to Mexico City.

The train ride was very interesting, traversing towns like Juchitán and Loma Bonita, with large pineapple plantations. Sayula in Veracruz, Tierra Blanca, Cordoba, and Puebla. In each area, not only did the landscape change, but the look and dress of the passengers as well.

From Estacion Buenavista I went directly to Avenida San Juan de Letran, where the Mexican Jewish Agency was located. At the time, the representative and future consul was Dr. Adolfo Fastlich, Samuel's brother. The man in charge was Dr. Elio Da Silva, an Italian Jew who had immigrated during the war. He was an ardent Zionist.

I went to see Da Silva and told him my purpose. He was not surprised and only asked what my skills were. I told him I could drive. He asked me to write my name and phone number on a notebook, indicating whether my telephone was made by Mexicana or Erickson. End of conversation.

I was quite disillusioned. I had come all the way from Chiapas to fight and all they wanted was for me to write my name down? "So was bloedes," what nonsense!

Obviously the new State needed help from pilots, artillery men, naval captains, people with experience and extensive training. Not young men like me, with good intentions but no training.

The State of Israel was admitted to the United Nations on May 11, 1948. The Jews sent as its first representative in New York the eloquent Abba Eban, a Jew originally from Johannesburg. He was received with a standing ovation. That day all the representatives from the Arab nations left the hall in protest.

An initial cease-fire was negotiated but quickly broken.

For his part, Abba Eban denounced the Syrian, Iraqi, Jordanian, and Egyptian invasion, but without any success. There was only one way—Israel would have to defend itself, otherwise it would lose its recent gains. The Arabs kept threatening to throw all the Jews into the sea.

The Israeli Air Force was comprised of six older motor aircrafts and two twin-engine planes purchased from France. The Navy had three speedboats, also purchased from the French. The arms that the new army had were precarious. The cannons had been taken from the British. They lacked all the essentials. The army mobilized using buses from the kibbutzim and private cars. There was an essential problem: volunteers arrived by the hundreds, speaking fourteen different languages, complicating communication.

The women brought food to the soldiers. The children and older people helped in any way they could. They all knew that combat would mean life or death. No one hesitated to help.

Israel was living through its first massive Aliyah; Jews arrived from all over the world, including, of course, concentration camp survivors. Those interned in Cyprus arrived in Greek boats to Haifa.

Immigrants arrived from Morocco, from Argelia, from Tunis, Syrian refugees who had managed to leave during the short-lived ceasefire, also Jews from Yemen and Ethiopia. It caused a huge problem as there was not enough housing for all of them. Israel built improvised housing called Maabarot. Nevertheless, all were welcome to their new country and were given housing, even if it was only temporary.

We the Jews from around the world were very excited. People went to their local synagogues to thank the Lord, as that day had arrived and we had been witnesses. They were crazy days, historic days, not only for the Jews. All of humanity witnessed the miracle of a people returning to its ancestral land after almost two thousand years of exile.

The tourists who visit Israel wonder why there is such fervor and excitement around Yom Haatzmaut. I was there in 1965, and I was told that it was because not all had been able to celebrate when the State of Israel was born. Men and women had to be on the frontlines defending their nation.

In 1948, the Arab League decreed a total boycott against Israel, which lasted for a very long time.

Israel adopted a secular constitution which separated church and state, guaranteeing its inhabitants freedom of religion and speech. It would be a parliamentary democracy, Western style. At the time, the majority were left wing, from Histadrut. However, there was a strong orthodox religious block, the Agudat-Israel, who advocated for a state governed according to *Halakha* or Jewish Law. They were eventually able to gain concessions, such as the obligatory day of rest on Shabbat, and marriages to be performed by a Rabbi under a Chupah. They also were successful in that the shechita or slaughtering of animals would be under their supervision. As a result, all hotels and restaurants would only carry kosher meat.

Menachem Begin never forgot the Holocaust, the Shoa, the exiled Jews, and the Diaspora, in contrast to other politicians. He was totally opposed to any relations with Germany. Begin, who would many years later become Prime Minister, had a very special talent in interpreting history, very rare in politicians. During his first visit to Great Britain he said to the British Prime Minister: "Speaking of the Jews, when the Celts, Welsh and Scotts were just leaving their huts, we had already created a Parliament—the 'Sanhedrin.'" And he told Anwar Sadat, right by the pyramids: "You had us working on the building of Goshen, your palaces and pyramids," as if that had just happened the week prior.

Thanks to him, during his government, the Yiddish language, the customs and traditions of the Shtetl, were relived. It was especially important to the young people for whom their only language was Hebrew, a reborn language thanks to the Philologist Ben Yehuda. There weren't many reminders of their old home in Europe and elsewhere.

He was a good politician who forged acceptance not only from those of the Ashkenazi Yishuv, but also from other sectors of the population like the "Frenkim" or Jews from other Arab countries, who always supported him.

The founding of the State of Israel came with new responsibilities and many problems to resolve. The Yishuv in Palestine, prior to the massive immigration, was a society of idealists like the pioneers of Chalutzim, like their predecessors the Biyulim, the Joveve Zion who had come to this land beginning in

1882. They wanted an almost Utopian society, like Leo Tolstoy, who wanted a farming society, of collective effort, without parasites.

In the kibbutzim they did not utilize any labor from the Arabs. The labor had to be done by the Chaverim, or members. There was no private property. Later, with the creation of the State and with the massive immigration numbers, things began to change.

Little by little, Israel became a nation like all the other nations; there were Jewish robbers, Jewish killers, prostitution, and other ills like corruption or "Protektsia".

To be a nation along with all the other nations was a source of pride to all Jews. Having our own nation means having a refuge in times of danger, a home should we desire it. It was a totally new situation for us. The Mexican Jewish youth, myself included, felt happy and overjoyed.

Elie Wiesel, Nobel Peace Prize Laureate of Romanian descent, wrote this from Paris:
> "We are bound by tradition to believe that together we have stood at Sinai, that together we have crossed the river Jordan, [entered the land,] and built the Temple. That together we have been driven thence by the Babylonians and the Romans; that together we have roamed the dark byroads of exile; that together we have dreamed of recapturing a glory we have never forgotten – every one of us is the sum of our common history."

Eretz Israel's diplomatic experience was comprised until then by the Schlicht, or envoys from the Jewish Agency, and thus a change was needed. They reached out to the "Yekkes," or Jews of German or Austrian descent, to be the diplomacy pioneers, representing the new State around the world.

Here are some jokes that were said at the time:

A Jew in Palestine, a Sabra, asks a Yekke: "*Atta Mevin?*" or "Do you understand me?" The Yekke replies, "Lo, lo ani lo me Win ani me Berlin." The Yekke had thought he had been asked whether he came from Vienna, to which he replied "No, I come from Berlin."

One of the Chalutzim in the kibbutz hears a strange sound, like a buzzing sound coming from the construction site next door. He goes to investigate and sees fifteen Yekkes who have formed a chain and are handing over bricks. Each one says to the other as he hands him the brick, "Bitteschoen Herr Doktor," and the other would reply; "Dankeschoen Herr Doktor" and so on. That was the source of the buzzing sound.

A third joke alludes to the Anstaendikeit or rectitude of the Yekke. A German Jewish immigrant, who had arrived in 1934 and who had been able to keep his car, is driving on the cobblestone streets of Safed, when a cat crosses the street and is run over by the car. Correct as he is, he stops and parks the car, and goes door to door asking who the cat belongs to. Finally, the distraught owner opens the door. Embarrassed by his crime, he asks the owner how he can repair the damage. The distraught owner replies: "Mais japen kent ir?" "Do you how to catch mice?"

The orthodox Jews, in general, were never more than 10% of the population of the new State. However, their vote in the Knesset has been decisive in its coalition with the other parties, whether it is with the Labor or Likud party. This is where their unparalleled political strength lies.
One of the extreme right groups is formed by the Neturei Karta which, despite living peacefully in Jerusalem, openly denies the state that provides them a home and security. Sure that the Messiah is still coming, they are intolerant and irreverent of others. You can find them in the streets of Jerusalem, dressed as if they were still in a medieval Shtetl. The men wear their black suits and round hats, covered in fur, whether it is summer or winter. The women wear long dresses and when they go out they never have their heads uncovered. A sheitel or wig protects them from the onlookers' stares.

Unfortunately, since the birth of the new State, the government has been fractured by the different sectors, mostly intolerant of each other.

Several years later, after the Seven Day War, a religious rebirth was observed. Especially the Israeli youth, and because of the influence of extremist Jews, such as Rabbi Meir Kahane and Lichtenfeld. They had emigrated from the United States of America. Thousands of them settled in Judea and Samaria, in the West Bank, where they built cities in the Promised Land.

In reality, I never finished my studies. The demands of work forced me to initially drop my morning classes and change to afternoon classes for three years. I soon realized that I could not handle both work and study, so I suspended my studies at the ESIME–Escuela Superior the Ingenieria Mecanica y Electrica–and dedicated all of my time to work.

It is said in Yiddish: "*Di yorn gueyen zij, di reder dreyen zij.*" The years go by and the wheels go round.

Many things have happened since 1948. In 1953, I met a beautiful and intelligent woman, Harriet Neumann, born in Guatemala of German Jewish parents. We fell in love and she became my life companion. A great woman who is the mother to our four children.

Harriet is the daughter of Jorge Neumann Schacher and Hertha Schlesinger Semler. Jorge was born in Kempen, in Upper Silesia, in 1900. His parents Leopold Neumann and Henrietta Schacher had four children. In 1905 they moved to Breslau, now Wrozlav in Poland, which was then the most important city in the area. Breslau had a Jewish community of approximately 30,000 souls. The writer and Jewish thinker Ferdinand Lassalle came from there, as did Walter Laqueur. During the war, in 1916, Jorge immigrated to Guatemala where some other Jews from Kempen had settled.

Hertha, was born in Hamburg, also in 1900. Her parents were Bernhardt Schlesinger and Laura Semler. They had five children. The Schlesingers were owners, in Hamburg, of a clothing store for workers.

Hamburg was the most important port in Germany, a prosperous and liberal city. The Jewish population was approximately 25,000. The Warburg family, the Delbancos, and the Hambros, all famous bankers, came from there.

Composer Johannes Brahms and historian Heinrich Graetz also came from there. In the Altona neighborhood you can find the oldest Sephardic cemetery in Europe, dating from the 17th century. Its tombstones have inscriptions in Ladino and are from the same era as those found in Amsterdam. Last names such as Delmonte, Mercado, Toledano, Shealtiel, and Luria are common. The first Reformed congregation was formed in Hamburg in 1820.

Hertha arrived in Guatemala in 1926, along with her sister Paula who was already married and had lived in Guatemala before. Jorge saw Hertha while she was walking along the Sexta Avenida, and fell in love with her. Without even having met her, he said "She is going to be my wife." They married that same year in the Magen David Synagogue in Guatemala.

Harriet and I had four children, two boys and two girls. Leonardo David (1955), Gaby Deborah (1957), Eva Jaqueline (1961) and Roberto Daniel (1965).

All four are already married and we have, Baruch Hashem, nine grandchildrenand four great-grandchildren. "If God grants life and the necessary means, what is destroyed is restored and the tree will again flower."

Adolf and Yolanka Lanksner lived in Brussels until 1961. In August of 1962, they immigrated to Savyon, close to Petach-Tikva, in Israel. Lech, lecha...

they returned to their ancestral land. For Buci, making aliyah, the ascent to Israel, had always been his dream. Besides, his mercantile business in Belgium was becoming too much. We decided finally to buy a house for them in Israel. Harriet and I chose it. They lived happily in Savyon for ten long years in a healthy environment which surely lengthened their lives.

I would visit them every year during my business trips to Europe. They met three of our children. But, there came a time where they could no longer fend for themselves. I found a retirement home for them, a Beit Avot. For Yolanka, it was an absolute requirement that they spoke Hungarian. In Israel, built by immigrants from one hundred and eighteen nations, one can find even that. Of course it was kosher and they were willing to take them in. The retirement home was located in Netanya at the shores of the Mediterranean.

Buci lived until 1973 and Yolanks lived for six more years. They are buried in Savyon. By the way, Buci was the Gabay or Bedel of their local synagogue. May god keep them in his Gan Eden. I owe them my survival.

I worked with my uncle Ellenbogen until 1956. I then became independent. To be precise, on December 12, 1956, the day of the Virgin of Guadalupe, patron saint of Mexico. I partnered with Javier Arriaga, my "brother" and friend from the Poli, who had worked with me at Ultramar since 1949. I asked him to be my partner and in 1957 we founded Nacional Importadora, NISA. We were representatives and distributors of European-made gifts and decorative items.

We decided to specialize in porcelain, crystal, artistic glass, lamps, oil paintings, bronzes, wall clocks, and mirrors. And by the way, Harriet, my wife, was our first secretary. She typed the dozens of letters that we sent to the European Chambers of Commerce, the origin of our possible vendors.

The young state of Israel grew rapidly. The majority of the concentration camp survivors managed to immigrate to Israel or other countries. With the birth of the new State, serious problems began for the Jewish communities in the Arab countries. Many had to flee their home.

There were massive Jewish migrations from Syria, Lebanon, Morocco, Argelia, and Tunisia. In the 1950's, the Jewish Agency organized Operation Solomon which was able to evacuate, in just 24 hours, 14,000 Ethiopian Jews. They used fourteen large cargo planes, some of which made multiple trips, as they only had one day to complete their mission.

The young state had to withstand several wars. After the fight for Independence in 1948, there was the so-called Sinai Campaign in 1956, which ended in retreat due to pressure by the USA, but which managed to eliminate the constant incursions by the Fedayeen. In 1967, the Seven Day War took place, where Israel was able to annex the Eastern section of Jerusalem and capture Judea and Samaria, as well as the Golan Heights. That was the heyday of Israel.

After two thousand years, the flag with the Star of David flies again over its seven seas. The Jews had returned to the Mediterranean. This sea, which had been the Mare Nostrum to the Romans when the Jews were expelled from Judea, is now a shared waterway to all the lands that surround it.

In 1991, Operation Entebbe took place when hostages from an Air France flight were taken by a group of Palestinians aided by a German terrorist. This rescue operation was conducted by brave commandos from the Israeli Army, among them Jonathan Netanhayu, brother of the current Prime Minister of Israel, who sadly lost his life.

I remember getting the news of the operation while on vacation with the family in Austria. We had visited my friend Claus Riedel in Kufstein. He received us effusively with a kiss on the cheek and a hug, saying that "This could have only been accomplished by 'Die Juden'" –the Jews, he said–"Oder die Deutschen" –the Germans. This he said surely because of the feat of the Austria, Skorzeny, who had rescued Mussolini when he was captured by the partisan Italians in 1943.

In 1973, the Arab countries surprised Israel, attacking in during the holiest of days, on Yom Kippur. That is how that war is known, a war which cost thousands of lives. Israel was victorious defeating the Egyptian Army in its own land.

The wars, regardless of the victories, have brought the Israeli families to desperation. Today they yearn for a real and stable peace.

Of my children, Leonardo was the first to marry. He studied Business Administration at the Tecnologico de Monterrey and then received a Master's Degree from Wharton. He married Susana Tavel Weitzner, whose parents were born in Mexico. Her grandparents emigrated from Lithuania and Grodno. Susana and Leonardo have two daughters: Diana, born in 1982, and Nili, born in 1984. They have four grandchildren.

My daughter Gaby studied Graphic Design at the University of Houston in Texas. She then worked for an advertising agency in Mexico. She worked with me at Iluminacion Tecnica for two years. She was then offered a position in Marketing at Lightolier in New Jersey. She moved to New York and married Michael Fleischmann Medalie, originally from Saint Louis, Missouri. Michael's parents were born in the United States, and his grandparents came from Lithuania. They have two daughters: Hannah, born in 1990, and Laura, born in 1992.

My daughter Eva studied Interior Design at the University of Texas in Austin. She left her studies to marry Jaime Mustri Penhos, whose parents were born in Mexico and whose grandparents immigrated from Aleppo and Damascus. They have triplets who were born in 1984: Isaac, Tessy, and Jorge.

My son Roberto studied Business Administration at the Universidad Iberoamericana in Mexico City. He worked as a General Director at Illuminacion Tecnica and is now a salesperson for Seguros Monterrey. He married Gabriela Perez Arnabar and they have two children: Ari, born in 1999, and Sofia, born in 2006.

Six years after arriving in Mexico, I applied for and received my Naturalization papers. I was the proud owner, finally, of a Mexican passport, my first in my life!

I did not need to ever again travel using my FM2 or my Vish, which up till then had been my only identification.

I learned to love my new country, the land of the eagle and the serpent. Little by little, I learned its history, admired its landscape, learned to love and live with its people. I quickly made it my own.

My Spanish diction has improved, although I have never been able to get rid of my accent. On the other hand, I adopted a new country to which I am grateful for the asylum granted and the opportunity to live, study, work, and, in due time, form a family. One more family in Mexican land. May G-d bless this land. Amen.

EPILOGUE

To my grandchildren: Ani Ma'amin: I believe in the nobility of the human being. I believe in kindness and tolerance and in diversity. Because diversity enriches us. Intolerance impoverishes us. As long as there is a single just person on earth, it is enough for me. Man is born free to choose between good and evil. Sometimes he surprises us and chooses the tortured or wrong path.
Let's examine what happened with the old Yugoslavia: people massacred because of their beliefs. The Bosnians belonged to the same ethnic group as the Serbs, their aggressor. They had even adopted Islam during the Ottoman domination, because of economic reasons and to move ahead with life. Whatever the reason was, no one deserved genocide.
We are witnesses to the eternal problems between the Irish. The frustrated efforts at independence from the Kurds. The endless killings among the African tribes. And looking backwards, nothing justified the Holocaust, the killing of millions of human beings during the Second World War. And in the future, nothing will have justified the hate and extermination between men. Today like yesterday, we must take care of the peace and tolerance; not allowing the bad seeds to destroy kindness, tolerance and diversity among its peoples. We must strive against all extremism, whatever its name and in a timely manner.
The worlds indifference with us allowed the Holocaust to happen. Never be indifferent to the injustices committed against others.
We, the Jews, are the survivors of Hitler and of Stalin, although of different proportions. History will not forget either one. Repressors of minorities, they are examples of intolerance and tyranny. Hitler dreamed of a millennial empire; Stalin yearned for a world governed by a communist system. Neither one cared that the price would be so high, that millions of lives would pay.
Our responsibility- and that of the younger generations- is to fight against tyranny. It does not matter what you call it. It begins by stripping us of our basic civil rights, then our political ones. Once lost, we lose all human dignity and we can even lose our lives.
The human being is weak, it can succumb to the temptation to feel mightier than others. Be straight, be tolerant, be kind...... be Jewish.

We have been during twelve generations. That is our tradition and our heritage; it is our strength, our rock. Do not break the hundreds of links in the golden chain of Judaism... Do it for the generations that preceded us, because of the example that they gave us, in spite of the intolerance and the persecution where they were the victims.
Educate your children as Jews so that they can know who they are. Form a Jewish home; the family is and has always been the most important part of being Jewish. A Jew will be Jewish even if he does not go to the synagogue or if he does not go to a Jewish school. But he ceases to be a Jew without a Jewish home to nourish him and motivate him. A home to provide him with warmth and to cover him with parents who lead by example; who show him the road to be led. We are responsible for the continuity of our people.

The responsibility of keeping our Judaism and our Jewish people rests of each one of us. We have the responsibility to forge ahead with our tradition, through educating our children, teaching them our values so they can do the same with their children.

We are different than other religions in that we do not have a hierarchy or kings. We only have the Torah with its precepts and its life philosophy, which has nourished and sustained us for more than three thousand years. We count on the Talmud for its daily guide.

It is true that there is now a Jewish state in Israel, our inspiration, security and pride. However, we are citizens of other countries where we live and work. We owe our countries respect and all our dedication, our creativity and our effort in exchange for their asylum and protection. In Mexico, we live thank G-d, in our regimen of freedom, of tolerance and opportunities; one of which is to live and grow as Jews.

Veshinantam! You must educate! It is your duty! *Divrei Torah;* as our Torah tells us. Teach your children to me just people, decent, straight and respectful to others. Be tolerant with your fellow beings, so that you can be good human beings and good Jews. You will see that it is not so hard. But you have to do it willingly with dedication and perseverance.

This is my life history, I nourish myself with the history of our people. I am proud to be part of a nation that has been able to maintain and cultivate the precepts of universal justice. I also feel proud of the contributions of our people to science, culture and the preservation of the rights of man.

I have learned this by myself, it is a result of living. In my various lectures that I have given, I include the Torah, the Talmud, the Shulchan Aruch, the history of the Golden Years of Span, the poetry of Chaim Nachman Bialik, the stories of Sholem Aleichem, of Shalom Ash and of the multiple testimonies published about the Holocaust.

Books are always our best friends and readily accessible.
I fully identify with the long history of our people. I copy Ezer Weizmann's words, President of Israel to the German Bundestag in 1995, first time that a Jewish president had addressed both Parliament houses:
"I was a slave in Egypt, I received the Torah in the Sinai, I entered Jerusalem with King David. I fought with the Romans and was expelled from Spain. I rebelled in Warsaw' I lost my father in Auschwitz and my mother in Opole and I finally returned to Israel, the land I was expelled from by the Romans."

In spite of everything that happened, I do not hate the Germans and I say that sincerely. I believe in the human regeneration, it is one of its gifts. The new post war German generations are proof positive of this.

Since 1949, every year Christian German people travel to Israel as volunteers. There they work and live with young Jews.

In Berlin, ancient capital of the Reich and now capital of the reunified Germany, many plaques commemorating the Holocaust can be found, that invite its citizens not to forget.

We will also never forget. We will never forget our loved ones being annihilated by gas, fired upon and burned alive. Six million human beings massacred only for the crime of being Jews. Among them my parents, your great grandparents. Leo and Grete...."*Mir zenen do*"- we are here to always remember and never forget.

I am happy to have written the story and destiny of one more Jewish family, like so many others. I hope that it survives as a testimony of a time in history and of a

generation that will soon disappear. Soon there won't be any more survivors that can share their stories. And the perpetrators will also be gone.
Unfortunately there are those that still deny that the Holocaust took place, as if it were a book of fiction. In my hands is the historic message from Simon Dubnow who perished in Treblinka, and who before being deported said *"Shraibt un farshraibt"*- write and tell what has happened. I only hope- as I hope many others do- to obey the sacred message.

Bibliography and Documentation

Carl Schorske, Fin de Siecle Wien (New York, 1980)
Theodor Herzl, Der Judenstaat (Wien, 1905)
Heinrich Benedikt, Geschichte Der Republik Oesterreich (Wien, 1954)
Eugen Guglia, Geschichte der Stadt Wien (Wien, 1897)
Karl Kraus, Eine Krone Fuer Zion (Wien, 1898)
Pail Hofmann, The Viennese (New York, 1988)
George Berkley, Wien and Its Jews (New York, 1988)
Martin Gilbert, The Holocaust (New York, 1985)
Leni Yahil, The Holocaust (Yad Vashem, Jerusalem, 1987)
Olga Lengyel, Souvenirs de L'au Dela (Paris, 1948)
Jean Francois Steiner, Treblinka (Paris, 1966)
Menachem Begin, The Revolt (Steinmatzky, Jerusalem, 1967)
Juedisches Museum, Hakoah (Wien 1995)
Aliluyeva Svetlana, My Father (New York, 1968)
Walter Laqueur, Stalin (New York, 1990)
Ilya Ehrenburg, La Chute de Paris (Paris, 1945)
Primo Levi, Se questo e un uomo (Milan, 1958)
Elie Wiesel, La Nuite Trilogie (Paris, 1962)
Eli Barnavi Et Al, Historical Atlas of the Jewish People (New York, 1992)
Mark Dvorszetzky, Yerusholayim Dlite (Paris, 1948)
Stanislaw Poznanski, Kampf Tod Andenken (Warzawa, 1963)
Hugh Thomas, The Spanish Civil War (London, 1958)
Martin Gilbert, Atlas de la Shoah (Paris, 1992)
Lucy Dawidowicz, Der Krieg Gegen Die Juden 1933-1945 (Wiesbaden, 1979)

www.ingramcontent.com/pod-product-compliance
Lightning Source LLC
Chambersburg PA
CBHW021938290426
44108CB00012B/889